GREEK WARFARE

GREEK WARFARE

From the Battle of
Marathon to the
Conquests of
Alexander the Great

Lee L. Brice, Editor

 ABC-CLIO

Santa Barbara, California • Denver, Colorado • Oxford, England

Library of Congress Cataloging-in-Publication Data

Greek warfare : from the Battle of Marathon to the conquests of Alexander the Great / Lee L. Brice, Editor.
    p. cm.
  Includes bibliographical references and index.
  ISBN 978-1-61069-069-0 (hbk. : alk. paper) —
ISBN 978-1-61069-070-6 (ebook)   1. Greece—History, Military—
To 146 B.C.   2. Military art and science—Greece—History—To 1500.
3. Military history, Ancient.   I. Brice, Lee L.

  DF89.B75   2012
  355.00938—dc23   2012024992

ISBN: 978-1-61069-069-0
EISBN: 978-1-61069-070-6

16   15   14   13   12   1   2   3   4   5

This book is also available on the World Wide Web as an eBook.
Visit www.abc-clio.com for details.

ABC-CLIO, LLC
130 Cremona Drive, P.O. Box 1911
Santa Barbara, California 93116-1911

This book is printed on acid-free paper ∞

Manufactured in the United States of America

to
Keith W. Armatage and Ruth E. Armatage,
. . . inspirational teachers and friends.

Contents

Documents, 211

Introduction

Standing as we do in the shadow of the 2,500th anniversary of the Battle of Marathon, it seems a good time to consider the continuing interest in classical Greek warfare. More than two millennia ago, in 490 BCE, a Greek army of Athenians and Plataeans stood between a Persian expeditionary force and Athens. The battle's result was not a foregone conclusion; the Greeks could have lost. They won, however, so we celebrate their victory, still. We also study the battle and the military history of the period that followed. Indeed, despite all the interest in Alexander the Great, it is not possible to understand his career without considering the development of warfare after Marathon. Despite all the changes that have occurred in warfare, ancient Greek military history continues to attract attention of all sorts. Considering the variety of reasons for this interest can tell us much about the topic I address in this volume.

One overarching reason for interest in Greek warfare is the vitality of the field. Students often joke with me that ancient history should be easy because it is ancient. Like many people, they think it does not change because it is ancient. Given how much warfare has changed they are convinced that the military history of Greek warfare is stuck in an unchanging past. In a way, they are correct. The reasons for this are not hard to locate. Much of what has been written about Greek warfare in the last two centuries has focused heavily on battle narratives and consideration of famous personalities (Brice and Roberts, 2011). This type of military history has carried the label "drums and trumpets" because of its traditional focus on battle narratives. Much of what we call "drums and trumpets" style work is stuck in old methods and styles, which is why students who think ancient military history does not change are correct to an extent. Despite that, it remains immensely popular with general readers.

As a type of scholarly history "drums and trumpets" is often anti-quated in its methods. As a result, military history is no longer as popular with academic historians as it was before the mid-20th century. This dismissive attitude by other historians has been the trend for much of the last four decades. The opprobrium is largely because scholars in other fields assume military history is still all "drums and trumpets" and remain unaware of methodological advances in the study of warfare. The reality is that military history, including the history of ancient warfare, is changing all the time.

Just as historians in other specializations started drawing on new methods and engaging in more social history, post-colonial history, and cultural history after 1945, so did military historians even if they did so a bit later than everyone else. This led to the emergence of a "War and Society" approach that became increasingly popular. By 1970 historians could refer to a "New" military history that drew heavily on the social sciences and other fields to consider warfare in new ways. Even traditional or "drums and trumpets" history has changed thanks to John Keegan's *Face of Battle* (1976). His soldiers' perspective approach to the sharp end of battle has affected many discussions of battles and campaigns even in ancient history (Brice and Roberts, 2011). More recently other specialized fields of study have opened up military history. Conflict archaeology, crowd psychology, game theory, and forensic anthropology are examples of fields having an enormous impact on the way historians approach ancient warfare. In these ways we have new topics of detailed study like mutiny, battlefield physiology, and gender as well as new ways of looking at traditional topics like logistics, economics, combat motivation, and death. The result is that military history is more popular in the classroom than it used to be (Wheeler, 2011), but more importantly, this new work has made some "drums and trumpets" histories much better. It has also had an impact on ancient history.

The methodological changes are just as true of military historians of ancient Greek warfare as of modern warfare. In addition to changes in the field of military history, there have been similar developments in ancient history and classical studies that have changed the way we look at Greek warfare. Archaeologists, for example, uncover new artifacts, sites, and sources such as new inscriptions that illustrate features of Athenian cavalry. Specialists in various fields using new laboratory sciences reveal previously unavailable data including the ways in which particular weapon-use can appear in the skeletal remains of users and victims. Historians employ new ways of looking at old and new evidence to reveal lost information, examine neglected topics, or elaborate new interpretations. As a result, the field of ancient history, including military history, is a far cry from my students' misconceptions of it as static; it is an exciting and dynamic field of study that advances constantly and attracts continued interest. While some readers are drawn by activity in the field, others are drawn by the appeal of the content.

A traditional reason for the continuing fascination with ancient military history is the inspirational quality found in famous leaders and battles of the past. Alexander III of Macedon served this function ever since his death, as his epithet "the Great" demonstrates. Alexander inspired Romans like Pompey, Caesar, and Caracalla. Other Greek generals have provided inspiration to modern readers, even if less so than Alexander, but so have some battles. As can be seen in their titles Richard Billows's book *Marathon, How a Battle Changed Western Civilization* (2010) and Paul Cartledge's *Thermopylae: The Battle that Changed the World* (2006) some ancient battles have a reputation for inspiration. The Western Tradition still often presents Marathon and Alexander's Persian campaign as triumphs of "civilization over barbarians" or "West over East," while Thermopylae is the first in a tradition of glorious defeats. Tim Rood's book *American Anabasis* (2011) has shown that Xenophon's *Anabasis* has inspired numerous modern readers. Inspiration has provided a strong attraction for many readers, but education has also played an important role for interest in ancient warfare.

Traditional military history focused on battles and leaders has customarily had a strong educational element—training leadership skills through biographies of famous commanders and how they won or lost. Even portions of careers and leaders' command decisions have been subject to discussion and analysis when entire biographies have been unavailable or unsuitable. Some leaders' biographies have been studied in search of a distinct recipe for success or failure in warfare that authors could isolate, as if there was one particular set of skills and experience that, if learned, would lead to consistent success in warfare. Ancient Greek warfare has provided a number of leaders who have been the subject of such analysis. Alexander is the most obvious example, but we cannot ignore Miltiades, Cimon, Agis, Agesilaus, Epameinondas, and Philip II, among so many others. Regardless of their success in locating the elusive recipe, authors such as Victor Hanson (2009 and 2010) and Barry Strauss (2012) continue to present the lives and actions of important ancient leaders for the leadership and historical lessons we may draw from their careers.

Readers have found battles and campaigns popular topics for military education too. Modern works devoted to battles were popularized in the 19th century. These works have lost none of their popularity since and have expanded to include books, articles, and videos devoted to campaigns, operational histories, and wars. While many of these works entertain, they also have the goal of teaching military skills including tactics, strategy, and operational arts. Methods of combat and warfare have changed, but the human aspect of land combat has actually changed little. Airplanes may be able to demolish a patch of ground, but as Alexander demonstrated in 328–327 BCE in Bactria, infantry must hold territory to win the conflict (Holt, 2005). Also, men in combat in ancient and modern armies still react to combat stress in many similar ways (Brice, 2012; Tritle, 2000). Ancient Greek battles such as First Mantinea, Leuctra, and Hydaspes have long been the subject of military education within and outside the military since there is much that students and enthusiasts can learn about leadership and military skills from these engagements. There is, of course, much more to learn from ancient warfare than traditional military skills.

Warfare is also an important topic for readers because it was a fact of life in ancient Greece. While it is popular to look at democratic Athens as a highpoint of Classical civilization with its art, architecture, literature, and philosophy, it is important to remember that Athens' wealth, which was unusual in the Greek world, made those achievements possible. Most Greeks did not participate in or enjoy the benefits of Classical Athens, indeed many Greeks' closest tie to Athens was through warfare.

Ancient warfare was a feature of life common to all of ancient Greece, across all regions, tribes, cities, and levels of society. Every person's life would have been affected by warfare, not just as an officer, soldier, or camp follower, but also as victim, relative of a victim, taxpayer, or even resident participating in military and related institutions. Because of the potential sacrifice, warfare was the most important civic activity anyone could engage in at any level. Participating in the military was often at least an expectation if not a requirement for every member of the community who could afford to purchase weapons (Sabine et al., 2007). There were institutions in most cities designed to prepare veterans and would-be soldiers for fighting. In poorer communities where hunting was a part of life these skills often translated into warfare as light-armed infantry. Warfare also provided some men with economic opportunities as mercenaries in Greece or abroad. Since warfare was so common in Greece it remains one of the few ubiquitous cultural ties available for historians and interested readers wishing to understand features of ancient culture and society shared by all Greeks. This truism is another reason Greek warfare remains important and interesting to a diverse audience.

The last reasons ancient Greek warfare remains popular are the enduring entertainment quality of its stories and the recognition that it remains relevant. Alexander the Great's life is a stunning story of achievement against immense odds coupled with the tragedy of his early death. Regardless of the historical knowledge we glean from the sources about him, it is also an entertaining story. Little wonder it has inspired so many novels, works of art, television episodes, and films. His war in Persia is difficult to understand without knowing the stories of the Persian Wars; the immensity of his achievement is difficult to appreciate without knowledge of the ways in which Greek warfare changed over time. The stories of Miltiades at Marathon, Leonidas at Thermopylae, and Themistocles at Salamis have entertained readers since the ancient world. Alcibiades' youth and adventures during the Peloponnesian War similarly entertained contemporaries and continue to delight readers of many ages. As noted previously, Xenophon's story of the Ten Thousand marching back from Mesopotamia has been and remains popular entertainment with soldiers and veterans of many different backgrounds. The struggles of these commanders and soldiers against great odds and human flaws make their stories timeless. The ways in which later authors write their history in styles similar to the military histories of Herodotus and Thucydides have contributed to giving these stories from Greece continued life.

This continued interest resonates in the modern relevance of aspects of Greek warfare. In the cases of Miltiades, Themistocles, and Alcibiades their stories are also inextricably linked with the success of the Athenian democracy. As Victor Hanson (2009, 2010), Michael Meckler (2006), and others have demonstrated, modern democracies have enjoyed drawing connections between themselves and Athens. Marathon is simply one example among many Athenian victories that Western democracies have used in creating their own sense of identity. The reported militarism of Sparta has also found explicit connection with various modern military institutions (Rawson, 1991). The way in which Philip and Alexander reformed the Macedonian army and rendered other forms of warfare obsolete was a Revolution in Military Affairs (Brice, 2011), a popular concept in strategic studies as leaders seek the means to triumph more quickly over opposition. Also, as noted previously, we can learn about modern soldiers' responses to combat stress and ways of responding to it by examining ancient warfare (Tritle, 2000). Despite all the changes in war, aspects of Greek warfare remain relevant and attract interest. Given all these attractions, there should be no surprise that ancient Greek warfare remains an important and popular topic.

The present volume is testament that ancient history does change, sometimes dramatically. The timeline may not change much, but other aspects of this book I have selected with recent work in mind. There are some reference entries that would not have appeared in the past and the contents of all the entries reflect modern work on Greek warfare. The selection of primary documents has been made to illustrate specific aspects of Greek warfare especially in terms of how warfare changed over time. Tables are one feature of this volume where I have striven for a level of honesty with readers. Ancient authors were not capable of or even interested in recording numbers that we can trust and put in tables. Therefore, I have provided tables readers can trust and use as starting points for more investigation into warfare. The bibliography also reflects recent work. Even the selection of terms in the glossary has been heavily influenced by changes in the ways historians approach ancient warfare.

In writing the entries I have tried to adhere to some standardization in treating terms and names drawn from an ancient language. In transliterating Greek words and names I have stuck to traditional anglicized practice such as substituting C for the Greek letter Kappa in all cases. Reflecting the difference between the modern rank of general and the various types of commanding officers in the ancient world I have consistently preferred using the word "commander" for chief military officers. The array of information and the updated nature of it make this volume a useful reference tool for readers with diverse interests.

In closing, I need to acknowledge various debts. I am indebted to my editor Maxine Tucker and her director, Pat Carlin, of ABC-CLIO. They have assisted me in locating various items and bringing everything together, but most importantly their faith in the project and enduring patience helped keep the project on target. I am indebted to my students in several years worth of Greek history and military history classes. They were not afraid to ask tough questions, hold my feet to the fire, and respond to the topic with enthusiasm. I am grateful to the many teachers who attended the Dupage Valley Social Studies Conference year after year who have heard some of this material in advance and whose observations improved the final project. I am deeply grateful to Dr. Georgia Tsouvala of Illinois State University who has reviewed parts of the manuscript and made various suggestions. Her encouragement and support made the project feasible.

Any factual errors that remain are entirely my own responsibility. Lastly, I am most indebted to two of my teachers, Keith W. and Ruth E. Armatage, who started me on the path of wisdom and nurtured a strong enthusiasm for history and teaching. This volume is dedicated to them both with affection.

Lee L. Brice
Summer, 2012

A

Aegospotami, Battle of

Athens' defeat in the Battle of Aegospotami in 405 BCE led directly to their loss in the Peloponnesian War. In the naval battle, Sparta destroyed most of the Athenian fleet and set up an effective blockade to stop Athens' grain shipments.

In the summer of 405, Lysander, the de facto Spartan commander (nominally, he was second in command), brought the Peloponnesian fleet into the Hellespont (Dardanelles Strait) and captured the city of Lampsacus, an Athenian ally, on the Asian side of the straits. The immediate Peloponnesian strategy was to capture Athenian allies and, if possible, lure the Athenian fleet into a battle and destroy it. The larger strategy, of which this was the first step, was probably to cut off Athens' food supply by blocking grain shipments from the Black Sea regions. The Athenian fleet of 180 triremes, led by Philocles, Conon, and Adeimantus, took up position on the European shore of the strait at Aegospotami, a beach on the European side, either directly across from Lampsacus or about three nautical miles to the north where there is a narrow spot. Daily, they sought to engage the Peloponnesians in a naval battle. The Athenians would sail out, but despite having his men aboard and fitted for combat, Lysander would not oblige them. When he repeatedly refused to engage, the Athenians found themselves in a predicament because of the lack of provisions at Aegospotami. Alcibiades, who had a tower to the north, visited the Athenian camp and recommended moving the fleet 10 nautical miles to Sestos, where supplies were available, but his advice was ignored. The Athenian generals were afraid to let Lysander out of their sight.

The Battle of Aegospotami occurred when in 405 BCE the Spartan commander Lysander caught the Athenian ships at Aegospotami beached and unprepared to fight. The foreground is a beach that may be where the battle occurred. In the distance is the Asian side of the Hellespont. (Lee L. Brice)

According to the ancient Greek historian Xenophon, the Athenians tried for five successive days to engage Lysander in battle; each day, Lysander stayed in the harbor but sent ships to follow and spy on the Athenians. On the fifth day, after the Athenians had returned to Aegospotami and were foraging away from the beach and their ships for food, Lysander, on a signal from his spy ships, attacked suddenly and caught the Athenians off guard. He captured almost all their ships on the beach except for nine triremes: the state trireme, the *Paralus*, and eight triremes under Conon, who sailed to Cyprus.

The Athenian defeat was complete. The Peloponnesian allies voted to execute the 3,000–4,000 sailors taken prisoner. Philocles was executed, but Adeimantus was allowed to go free. The *Paralus* sailed for Athens and brought the bad news. Suspicions in Athens that one or more of the Athenian generals had betrayed the fleet are understandable but probably unfounded. Lysander was able to sail north and cut off much of Athens' grain supply and capture some more allies. When he later captured those men who had escaped the battle, he sent them back to Athens where they further strained the limited food resources.

In any case, the Athenians had no means to build a new fleet. Besieged by land and sea, the Athenians finally came to terms in the spring of 404 with the idea of ending the war, a direct result of the Battle of Aegospotami.

George E. Pesely and Lee L. Brice

See also: Alcibiades; Lysander; Peloponnesian War, Overview; Trireme; Xenophon

References

Hale, John. *Lords of the Sea: The Epic Story of the Athenian Navy and the Birth of Democracy*. New York: Viking Press, 2009.

Lazenby, J. F. *The Peloponnesian War: A Military Study*. New York: Routledge, 2004.

Tritle, Lawrence A. *A New History of the Peloponnesian War*. Malden, MA: Wiley-Blackwell, 2010.

Agesilaus II

A king of Sparta from 399 to 360 BCE, Agesilaus II successfully defended Sparta during the Corinthian War from 395 to 387; however, he reigned primarily during a period of decline in Sparta's power. Historians debate whether he managed to sustain Sparta as a potent force during a difficult period or contributed to Sparta's waning military might.

Born ca. 444 into the Eurypontid family, Agesilaus was the second son of King Archidamus II. Agesilaus was reportedly small in stature with one leg shorter than the other. Despite this feature, he was raised, educated, and trained in the usual Spartan manner—learning modest living, obedience to the law, and military duty.

Agis II, Agesilaus' older brother, ruled from 426 until 400, but a succession crisis emerged when he died. Agis had rejected his son as illegitimate because of a reputed affair between his wife and Alcibiades. Most Spartans favored Agesilaus, and he was championed by Lysander, the victor of Aegospotami, thus Agesilaus became king.

Soon after, he received news that Persia was assembling a large navy and becoming a threat to Sparta's maritime supremacy. Encouraged by Lysander, Agesilaus commanded an expedition into Asia Minor. His campaigns there, like those of his predecessors, achieved little meaningful result and he was called home again by war in Greece.

The Corinthian War started in 395 when disaffected leaders in Thebes, Corinth, and Athens agitated for war against Sparta and found Persia to be an interested financial backer. Led by Agesilaus, Sparta eventually won battles against each city. With those successes, Greek armies would not

Dascylium was the capital of the Persian satrapy of Hellespontine Phrygia in Anatolia, where Agesilaus was active. (John W. I. Lee)

oppose the Spartans for the next two decades. Meanwhile, Sparta and Persia negotiated in 387 the King's Peace, an agreement stating that all Greek city-states in the mainland were to be independent and autonomous with peace enforced by Sparta and guaranteed by Persia. Greeks in Asia were again to be subsumed by Persia, which was an admission of Agesilaus' failure in Asia. During the King's Peace, Agesilaus tended to take a hard line against Sparta's enemies, especially Thebes.

Peace lasted until 379, when Thebes revolted and expelled a Spartan garrison. Agesilaus twice led Sparta in battle against Thebes and looted the city, but he could not regain control. Another Spartan force led by Cleombrotus, Agesilaus' younger colleague, invaded Boeotia in 371. The smaller Theban army under Epameinondas and Pelopidas prevailed. With its forces depleted, Sparta had begun relying on mercenaries. Agesilaus, now more than 70 years old, was given full power to strengthen the army. The Boeotians attacked Sparta directly in 370, but rather than meet them in the field as the Spartans wanted, Agesilaus closed ranks within Sparta. The Thebans soon departed.

Two years later, Thebans liberated the people of Messenia who had performed labor for Sparta as helots and gave them the fertile land on which Sparta was dependent. That action led to the economic collapse of Sparta. In 367, unable to gain support from Persia, Agesilaus joined forces against it, but the Spartan–Athenian coalition was defeated. Agesilaus began an alliance with Egypt against Persia, but after winning an initial victory he fell ill and died in Cyrene in 360, and his body was taken back to Sparta. He was succeeded by his son, Archidamus II.

Roger Matuz

See also: Conon of Athens; Corinthian War; Epameinondas; King's Peace; Leuctra, Battle of; Lysander; Pelopidas; Sparta

References

Buckler, John. *Aegean Greece in the Fourth Century BC*. Leiden: Brill, 2003.

Hamilton, Charles D. *Agesilaus and the Failure of Spartan Hegemony*. Ithaca, NY: Cornell University Press, 1991.

Rhodes, P. J. *A History of the Classical Greek World, 478–323 BC*, 2nd edition. Malden, MA: Wiley-Blackwell, 2010.

Strassler, Robert B., ed. *The Landmark Xenophon's Hellenika*. New York: Pantheon Books, 2009.

Agis III

A king of Sparta from 348 to 330 BCE, Agis III became king in a time of weakness. He attempted to revive Sparta's fortunes by resisting Macedon. His actions resulted in the first serious Greek insurgency during Alexander's reign, but it failed on all levels.

Born into the Eurypontid line, Agis became king in 348 during continued weakness. After the Battle of Chaeronea, when Sparta refused to join the League of Corinth, it lost its border territories. Agis was determined to resist Philip, but he was initially impotent.

After the Battle of Issus, Persian officers stationed in the Aegean, wishing to cause trouble for Alexander by stirring up Greek resistance, provided Agis with funds and ships. His insurgency began on Crete where he successfully took control of the island for Persia and recruited mercenaries there. He then moved into the Peloponnese and defeated the local Macedonian commander, Corrhagus. Afterward Agis gained allies—including Elis as well as Arcadian and Achaean cities—and laid siege to Megalopolis.

Antipater raised a Corinthian League force and crushed Agis' force in 330. In the ensuing battle, Agis died and his insurgency collapsed.

Although his insurgency was a potential threat, its defeat demonstrated the effectiveness of the league and Antipater.

Lee L. Brice

See also: Alexander the Great; Antipater; Corinth, League of; Philip II of Macedon

References

Buckler, John. *Aegean Greece in the Fourth Century BC*. Leiden: Brill, 2003.

Heckel, Waldemar and Lawrence A. Tritle, eds. *Alexander the Great: A New History*. Malden, MA: Wiley-Blackwell, 2009.

Alcibiades

An Athenian commander (*strategos*) during the Peloponnesian War between Athens and Sparta, Alcibiades was a courageous and intelligent soldier but also a self-centered politician. He is remembered as one of the most notorious leaders in ancient Greek history.

Alcibiades was born ca. 450 BCE in Athens. His father, a commander in the Athenian military, died when Alcibiades was a young boy, so he became a ward of his relative Pericles who was then the foremost leader in Athens. A student of the philosopher Socrates, Alcibiades' ambition, aristocratic lineage, great wealth, and remarkable good looks encouraged his popularity and marked him for leadership. In many ways, his youth was typical of wealthy Athenian elites in this period except that his association with Pericles gave him opportunities that few other youths enjoyed. He participated as an infantryman in the siege of Potidaea in 432 and fought on horseback at the Battle of Delium in 424. According to Athenian tradition, in the former battle, his friend Socrates saved his life, and in the latter conflict, Alcibiades returned the favor by protecting Socrates during the Athenian retreat.

After the death of Pericles in 429, Alcibiades cultivated his political ambitions and became an important speaker in the Athenian assembly (*Ecclesia*). During the Peace of Nicias, which ended the first phase of the Peloponnesian War in 421, he advocated an aggressive policy toward Sparta. Elected one of the 10 commanders, he played a central part in the infamous attack on the small island state of Melos and the resulting massacre of all its men. He then encouraged Athenian allies in the Peloponnese to create an anti-Spartan alliance. This alliance considerably increased tensions with Sparta but did not result in the collapse of peace. The coalition came to grief at the Battle of Mantinea in 418 despite direct Athenian aid. Since he had supported it, the loss hurt Alcibiades' reputation, but only temporarily, as the superb performance of his chariot teams in the Olympian Games of 416 bolstered his reputation in Athens.

In 415, Alcibiades argued successfully for Athens to undertake a military expedition to Sicily. He was elected one of its three commanders. However, implication of him in the scandalous and sacrilegious activities the night before the expedition departed—when stone busts of Hermes were defaced throughout Athens—led to his recall for trial just as the fleet reached Sicily. Fearing prosecution in Athens, Alcibiades avoided arrest and defected to the Spartans. Once there, he advised them on how to blunt the Athenian assault on Sicily and penetrate Athenian home defenses. By those actions he severely weakened Athens.

Alcibiades served with the Spartan fleet in 413–411 until he defected to Persia because of Spartan suspicion. While in Asia Minor, Alcibiades encouraged an oligarchic revolution at Athens, but after the coup in 411, he cast his lot with the democratic Athenian government in exile on Samos, which elected him admiral. He sailed back to Athens and played a key role in ending the oligarchic coup. He continued to serve the navy, and his brilliant naval victory against the Spartans at the Battle of Cyzicus allowed him to return to Athens ca. 408 and accept an extraordinary naval command. He was generally successful until 406, when the defeat of his fleet in a minor battle during his absence led his political enemies to demand his final exile from Athens. He then settled in the Dardanelles not far from the site of Aegospotami.

Despite that rejection, in 405, Alcibiades visited the Athenian fleet on the Hellespont to warn them of their precarious position, but his advice was not trusted. The Spartans subsequently destroyed the Athenian fleet in the Battle of Aegospotami, the final battle of the Peloponnesian War. Shortly thereafter, Alcibiades died in an ambush in Phrygia, ca. 404. Sources report different reasons for his death, stating that he was killed either by the Spartans or by a family in revenge for his seduction of one of their women.

James T. Chambers

See also: Aegospotami, Battle of; Mantinea, Battles of; Nicias; Peloponnesian War, Overview; Pericles; Sicily, Athenian Expedition against

References

Ellis, Walter M. *Alcibiades*. New York: Routledge, 1989.

Forde, Steven. *The Ambition to Rule: Alcibiades and the Politics of Imperialism in Thucydides*. Ithaca, NY: Cornell University Press, 1989.

Lazenby, J. F. *The Peloponnesian War: A Military Study*. New York: Routledge, 2004.

Rhodes, P. J. *Alcibiades*. Barnsley: Pen and Sword Military, 2011.

Strassler, Robert B., ed. *The Landmark Thucydides: A Comprehensive Guide to the Peloponnesian War*. New York: Free Press, 1998.

Alexander the Great

King of Macedon and ruler of Persia, Alexander III's conquest of the Persian Empire, his military ability as one of history's truly great captains, his vision of a unified people, and his role in spreading Greek culture that changed the Mediterranean world and ushered in the Hellenistic period all warrant the appellation of "Great."

Alexander was born in Pella in Macedonia in 356 BCE to Philip II, king of Macedon, and Olympias of Epirus. Bright and charismatic, Alexander was fortunate to have the philosopher Aristotle as his teacher after 342. Although Alexander had a tumultuous relationship with his father, much of his later success is attributable to his father's training and generals. Philip created the superb Macedonian phalanx that his son used to conquer the known world. Philip also secured control of Greece, an essential prelude to an invasion of the Persian Empire. This is in no way meant to diminish Alexander's accomplishments, which were nothing short of amazing. Alexander proved himself as a military commander, having charge of the Macedonian left-wing cavalry in Philip's victory over the allied forces in the Battle of Chaeronea in August 338. In 337, Alexander fled with Olympias to Epirus following a violent quarrel between her and Philip, but they both returned to Pella some months later.

Philip was preparing to invade Persia when he was assassinated in July 336. Suspicions reportedly swirled around Alexander and Olympias, but the succession was not contested, and Alexander became king. Before he could carry out his father's plan of invading Persia, Alexander first shored up his power base in northern Greece. In 335, he won a series of victories

Alexander the Great's conquest of Persia, excursion into India, military skill, and role in changing Greek culture and the Mediterranean world in a multitude of ways all justify his fame. Late Hellenistic marble bust, Archaeological Museum of Pella, Greece. (Jupiterimages)

in Paeonia, Thessaly, and Illyria, and he brutally suppressed a revolt in Thebes, after which he razed the city.

In 334, Alexander invaded the Persian Empire, the world's then largest empire. He did so as leader (*hegemon*) of the League of Corinth, the confederation Philip had created after his victory at the Battle of Chaeronea in 338, directing a Hellenic campaign of revenge for the sacking of Athens in 480 and 479. He left Antipater behind as regent of Macedonia with orders to keep the peace. Departing with an army of Macedonian and Greek soldiers drawn from the league, Alexander crossed the Hellespont (Dardanelles) into Asia Minor, with the aim of first liberating the small Greek city-states of Asia Minor. His army was small for the task ahead of it: approximately 30,000 infantry and 5,000 cavalry. What moved his men was Alexander's leadership. He brought victories repeatedly despite the odds, but also shared the soldiers' hardships and was often in the thick of the fighting.

The Persian satraps (governors) of Asia Minor assembled a much larger force to fight Alexander and waited for him on the east bank of the Granicus River. In May 334, Alexander personally led his cavalry across the river into the Persian line, and the Macedonians achieved a stunning victory. This dramatic triumph established Alexander as a bold commander and inspired fanatical devotion to him among his men. Thereafter, he sent spoils to Greece and continued his campaign south along the Ionian coast, freeing Greek cities as he went.

Having freed the Ionian cities from Persian control, Alexander worked his way across Anatolia through Caria and then north to Gordium and south to Cilicia, the whole time moving steadily toward the Levantine coast. He won successive battles and sieges in central Anatolia, and in September the swift-moving Alexander surprised the Persian defenders of the Cilician Gates (near Bolkar Daglari) and seized that vital pass without a fight. Alexander then moved against the main Persian army under Darius III. That engagement, the decisive Battle of Issus (November 333), again proved Alexander's reputation. Darius escaped, but Alexander captured his family and all his baggage. He treated Darius' mother well and later married one of his daughters. Alexander refused an offer from Darius of 10,000 talents in gold (300 tons) and the captured territory in return for his family.

Alexander then pushed south. In one of the great siege operations in all history, he took the island city of Tyre and then captured Gaza at the end of 332. All Phoenicia passed under his control, an essential prelude to a new invasion of Persia as far as his lines of communication back to Greece were concerned. He then occupied Egypt and made a special trip into the desert to consult the oracle of Ammon at Siwa in 331, where he was greeted by the chief priest as the son of Ammon (Zeus, to the Greeks). It is not clear whether Alexander believed in his own divinity at this point though he did seek recognition of it later.

Learning that Darius had put together a huge new army, Alexander departed Egypt and marched north into southern Mesopotamia in the spring of 331. He crossed the Tigris River that September, and in October 331 at the Battle of Gaugamela, with nearly 50,000 men, he again defeated Darius III's numerically superior force. Alexander's victory effectively ended Achaemenid rule of the Persian Empire as he claimed it for himself.

Later in 331, Alexander peacefully took Babylon and then Susa. Cities rallied to him, knowing of his leniency and toleration of their gods if they surrendered and of his terrible punishments if they resisted. In December, in a lightning strike, Alexander secured the Persian Gates and then occupied the Persian capital of Persepolis, which he sacked and burned before departing the following year. Having burned Persepolis, he declared the Hellenic league campaign of revenge over and enlisted the Greek soldiers as mercenaries. When Darius was killed in 330 by members of his own entourage, Alexander became the actual king.

Alexander shocked Macedonians over the next few years by gradually adopting Persian dress and ceremonies and by advancing Persians to high posts. He insisted that his generals take Persian wives. Aristotle had told him to treat the Persians as slaves. Alexander was determined to rule successfully, and he needed the support of the Persian nobility to achieve that.

Alexander now ruled the greatest empire of antiquity, but he needed to secure the entire empire. He campaigned along the southern shores of the Caspian Sea. Suppressing a plot from among his senior officers, he ordered the execution of both Philotas and his father Parmenion in December 330. In 329, Alexander invaded Bactria and Sogdiana. Wherever he went he founded new cities, many of them named for him. He then campaigned along the Oxus River before besieging and capturing the reputedly impregnable fortresses of the Sogdian Rock and the Chiorenes Rock in 327. He then married Roxanne, daughter of the lord of the Sogdian Rock, reportedly to secure an heir, but also certainly for diplomatic reasons. That same year, Alexander crushed a plot against him from among the corps of pages, executing its leader.

Leaving 10,000 men behind in Bactria, Alexander then invaded India by the Khyber Pass, crossed the Indus River in April 326, and defeated King Porus in the Battle of the Hydaspes in May. The following July, after extended marching in the monsoon rains, Alexander's army expressed frustration with continued marching east. Although the incident was not a mutiny, it was a sign of the increasing military unrest among his soldiers, primarily due to the extended and difficult campaigning. Alexander then led his army south along the Indus, subduing more territories and making peace treaties along the way.

Near the mouth of the Indus he split his army into several parts, sending part of it northwest with the popular commander Craterus and part of it along the sea with his commander Nearchus. In a difficult and nearly disastrous march across the Gedrosian Desert during September–November 325, Alexander returned to Persepolis in January 324. He marched to Susa where he held an enormous wedding ceremony for his men and officers to take Persian wives, probably intended to link Persian and Macedonian nobility. Thereafter, he continued on to Babylon and then, while camped at Opis, crushed a mutiny that erupted when he announced he would send most of the Macedonian veterans home and enlist Persians to fight in Macedonian style. In the spring of 323, he arrived in Babylon, evidently intent on making it his capital. In June 323, after a night of heavy banqueting, Alexander took ill for several days before his death on June 11, 323. Reportedly, when asked on his deathbed to whom he would leave the empire, he said "to the strongest." In any case, his generals were soon fighting to see who would control the empire, which was ultimately divided among the survivors.

The Empire of Alexander the Great

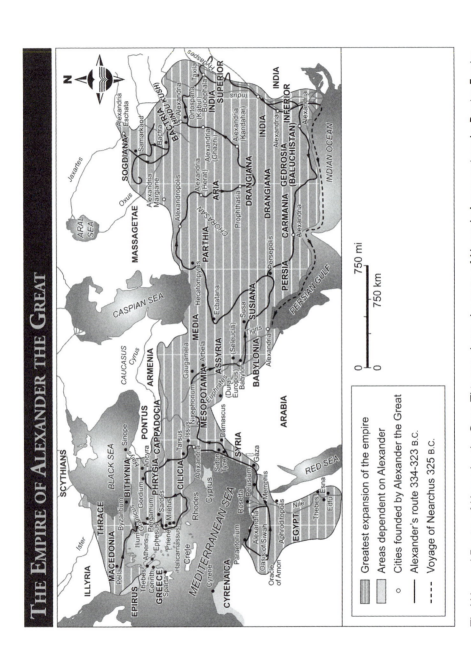

The Wars and Empire of Alexander the Great. This map shows the route of Alexander's war against the Persian Empire from 336-323 BCE. It also demonstrates how much territory he conquered in becoming king of Macedon and Persia.

Alexander was a general of unmatched leadership who excelled in every type of combat, including sieges and irregular warfare. He was also a master of logistics and possessed a keen administrative sense. He was never defeated in battle. It was not just that Alexander conquered much of the known world, for his reign also ushered in a new era in which Greek culture spread to new areas. The rulers who followed him adopted similar court practices and continued his Hellenizing policy.

Spencer C. Tucker

See also: Agis III; Antipater; Chaeronea, Battle of; Corinth, League of; Darius III; Gaugamela, Battle of; Gaza, Siege of; Granicus River, Battle of; Hydaspes, Battle of the; Issus, Battle of; Mutiny; Phalanx, Macedonian; Philip II of Macedon; Thebes; Tyre, Siege of; Wars of Alexander the Great, Overview

References

Bosworth, A. Brian. *Alexander and the East: The Tragedy of Triumph.* Oxford: Oxford University Press, 2001.

Bosworth, A. Brian. *Conquest and Empire: The Reign of Alexander the Great.* Cambridge: Cambridge University Press, 1988.

Fox, Robin Lane, ed. *Brill's Companion to Ancient Macedon.* Leiden: Brill, 2011.

Hammond, Nicholas G. L. *Alexander the Great: King, Commander, and Statesman.* London: Duckworth, 1981.

Heckel, Waldemar and Lawrence A. Tritle, eds. *Alexander the Great: A New History.* Malden, MA: Wiley-Blackwell, 2009.

Roisman, Joseph and Ian Worthington, eds. *A Companion to Ancient Macedonia.* Malden, MA: Wiley-Blackwell, 2010.

Romm, James, ed. *The Landmark Arrian: The Campaigns of Alexander.* New York: Pantheon, 2010.

Amphipolis

Amphipolis was one of the most important Greek colonies in Thrace during the Classical and Hellenistic periods. Founded by Athens during 437–436 BCE on an important trade route from Thrace to Macedonia, the city was economically valuable and militarily well located. Various powers came to fight over the city including Athens, Sparta, and Macedonia.

Modern view of the Strymon River and the flood plain where Cleon of Athens battled with Brasidas of Sparta in 422 BCE for control of Amphipolis. (Lee L. Brice)

Amphipolis was founded by Athens on an indigenous Thracian site located on a sharp bend in the Strymon River so that the river surrounded the city on three sides. It was only three miles from the coast of the Aegean Sea, so the Strymon allowed easy access to the sea or to inland locations. In terms of natural resources, gold and silver mines at Mount Pangaeus were located within several miles of the city. Timber suitable for building ships could be obtained nearby, and shipbuilding facilities were located on the river at Amphipolis. Founded just before the Peloponnesian War, Athens considered Amphipolis the jewel of its empire.

When the Peloponnesian War went badly for Sparta, one of its commanders, Brasidas, marched a small force across Greece to attack Amphipolis in 424. He captured it, but in the ensuing struggle he and the Athenian leader, Cleon, died. Under the terms of the Peace of Nicias in 421, Amphipolis should have been returned to Athens, but the population refused. The city became independent and remained so during much of the early fourth century even though Athens retained strong commercial ties with it and sought to regain it.

In 357, after some diplomatic exchanges with Athens Philip II of Macedon captured the city, thus earning the strong enmity of Athens. He made it a regional administrative center in the Macedonian Empire. During the reign of Alexander the Great, Amphipolis became his primary mint. It continued as an important Macedonian city during the Hellenistic era.

Tim Watts

See also: Brasidas; Cleon; Macedon; Peloponnesian War, Overview; Philip II of Macedon

References

Buckler, John. *Aegean Greece in the Fourth Century BC*. Leiden: Brill, 2003.

Lazenby, J. F. *The Peloponnesian War: A Military Study*. New York: Routledge, 2004.

Strassler, Robert B., ed. *The Landmark Thucydides: A Comprehensive Guide to the Peloponnesian War*. New York: Free Press, 1998.

Worthington, Ian. *Philip II of Macedonia*. New Haven, CT: Yale University Press, 2008.

Anabasis

The *Anabasis* is an account by Xenophon of the campaign during which 10,000 Greek mercenaries caught in Mesopotamia in 401 BCE had to fight their way back to the Greek world. The text has been a significant source for military historians, but the campaign demonstrated for some observers that Persia was internally weak.

The march of the "Ten Thousand" (also known as the Cyreans) began in early 401 when Cyrus, younger brother of the Achaemenid Persian king, Artaxerxes II, revolted and gathered a force of more than 10,000 Greek mercenaries in addition to troops raised in Anatolia. The force set out from Sardis in February with the goal of Babylon. They marched to Mesopotamia where they met Artaxerxes' force at Cunaxa.

The Battle of Cunaxa in August 401 showed that well-led Greek hoplites were still able to beat Achaemenid armies. Clearchus, the Spartan mercenary commander, refused to place hoplites in the center of Cyrus' line out of concern that they would be encircled if the Anatolian troops gave way. Finally arranged on the right of Cyrus' line with a river to guard their flank, the hoplites routed the Persian forces in front of them. In the confusion of battle, however, Cyrus was killed. Artaxerxes could claim a decisive strategic victory.

In the aftermath, the Greek mercenaries declined to surrender, but also failed to find a new candidate to lead the rebellion. Outnumbered and far from the Aegean the officers accepted an invitation to dinner and negotiations with Tissaphernes, the lead satrap. There the officers were arrested and killed on Artaxerxes' orders. The mercenaries then elected new officers, one of whom was Xenophon, a mercenary from Athens.

The mercenaries then marched north out of Mesopotamia and through Armenia, occasionally fighting and defeating harassing Persian forces.

The army, along with its camp followers, held together and created its own internal organization and society. Not until January 400 did the mercenaries reach the Greek city Trapezus on the Black Sea. They then took ship and traveled west along the coast raiding as they went until they reached Byzantium. Afterward, most of them settled on the Thracian side of the Bosphorus where they hired their services to Seuthes, a local Thracian king. The following year they joined Thibron's Spartan expedition in Ionia.

The importance of the march of the Ten Thousand is undeniable. The successful march out of Mesopotamia suggested to some fourth-century Greeks that Persia was vulnerable. Thanks to Xenophon's *Anabasis*, the retreat, in which the army has long been recognized as operating similarly to a Greek *polis*, has been a valuable source for aspects of warfare and society. The tale has also inspired numerous modern authors.

Lee L. Brice

See also: Mercenaries; Persian Empire; Wars of Alexander the Great, Causes of; Xenophon

References

Anderson, J. K. *Military Theory and Practice in the Age of Xenophon.* Berkeley, CA: University of California Press, 1970.

Briant, Pierre. *From Cyrus to Alexander: A History of the Persian Empire.* Winona Lake, IN: Indiana University Press, 2005.

Lee, John W. I. *A Greek Army on the March: Soldiers and Survival in Xenophon's Anabasis.* Cambridge: Cambridge University Press, 2007.

Antipater

A Macedonian noble and high-ranking commander, Antipater was a confidant to King Philip II of Macedon. On the king's death in 336 BCE, Antipater helped ease the succession of Philip's son, Alexander the Great, and was put in charge of Macedon during the king's absence. At the time of Alexander's death in 323, Antipater was about to be replaced by Alexander, but he became a short-lived successor instead.

Antipater was born in Macedonia ca. 397. He served as a cavalryman and diplomat under King Perdiccas III and became a high-ranking officer and advisor to the next king, Philip II. In this role he participated in Philip's campaigns of conquest in northern and central Greece. When Philip II was murdered in 336 Antipater and another general, Parmenion, ensured that Philip's son, 19-year-old Alexander, succeeded him by having the army proclaim Alexander as king. The following year, Alexander appointed Antipater regent of Macedonia in his absence and commander of the Corinthian League forces that would not go with him to Asia. Antipater supported Alexander's conquests by sending out trained recruits as requested and maintaining stability in Greece. This latter task required him to fight two significant threats before 323.

Antipater defended Macedonian interests when threatened by the Persian Navy until the defeat of that navy in 332. He also had to counter the threat of Agis III's revolt in central Greece in 331. He defeated both threats in turn and maintained stability. Meanwhile, in Macedonia, Antipater had a volatile relationship with Alexander's mother, Queen Olympias, who claimed misconduct on the part of Antipater. Alexander did not take action until 324, when he returned to Babylon after his campaigns further east. He ordered Antipater to meet him in Babylon. Antipater was to be replaced by Craterus, a popular infantry commander; however, due to increasing tension in Greece Antipater did not travel to Babylon. He sent his son, Cassander, instead—a move that apparently angered Alexander. Antipater was disgraced, but that was soon overshadowed when Alexander died in 323 and a succession crisis emerged.

Antipater had three daughters, Phila, Euridice, and Nicaea, all of whom would marry powerful leaders. Antipater's son, Cassander, would become a major figure in the wars of Alexander's successors, which were fought after 323.

Roger Matuz

See also: Agis III; Alexander the Great; Macedon; Philip II of Macedon; Wars of Alexander the Great, Overview

References

Baynam, E. J. "Antipater, Manager of Kings." In *Ventures in Greek History*, ed. I. Worthington, 331–56. Oxford: Clarendon Press, 1994.

Heckel, Waldemar. *The Marshals of Alexander's Empire*. New York: Routledge, 1992.

Heckel, Waldemar and Lawrence A. Tritle, eds. *Alexander the Great: A New History*. Malden, MA: Wiley-Blackwell, 2009.

Artemisium, Battles of

The Battles of Artemisium comprised three important naval battles during the Persian Wars. Although the naval engagements off Cape Artemisium in August 480 BCE did not halt the Persian invasion of Greece, they set the stage for the eventual Greek victory at Salamis by weakening the Persian naval force and familiarizing the Greeks with Persian tactics.

Xerxes I invaded Greece with an infantry force of perhaps 200,000 men, hundreds of supply ships, and a naval force of up to 1,200 triremes. In its size lay the weakness of the Persian force as it required regular sea-borne delivery of supplies, which could not be guaranteed without naval protection. Themistocles of Athens saw that a crippling attack on the Persian fleet would cause the whole Persian campaign to collapse. While the Hellenic Alliance land force attempted to hold the strategic pass of Thermopylae, Themistocles and the Spartan admiral Eurybiades took the Greek fleet—271 triremes, most of them Athenian, and nine smaller ships—to nearby Cape Artemisium on the northern tip of the island of Euboea. From that position they could block the Persian fleet's access to Thermopylae and still preserve the option of escaping should events warrant it.

The Persians won first when an advance squadron of their faster triremes captured two Greek scout ships, but shortly thereafter a violent storm struck the Persian fleet at anchor off the coast of Magnesia and destroyed 400 triremes. As the survivors made their way to harbor at Aphetai opposite Artemisium, 15 storm-battered vessels stumbled into a Greek squadron and were captured.

The odds improved further when the Persians sent 200 triremes down the east coast of Euboea to block the Greeks' best avenue of escape; that entire squadron was wrecked on the rugged coast of Euboea. As a result of those developments, the fleet at Artemisium faced a Persian force reduced to about 585 triremes.

In the first battle, the Greeks adopted a defensive circular formation with rams pointing outward and then suddenly attacked in all directions and captured 30 Persian triremes. In the second engagement, aided by the arrival of 53 additional Athenian triremes, the Greeks refused battle until just before dark and then suddenly struck to sink several Persian ships. The third engagement was a draw, and the Greeks sank a number of Persian ships but suffered considerable damage themselves. At that moment, they learned of Thermopylae's fall and withdrew south to the island of Salamis near Athens.

The encounters at Artemisium were important to the defense at Thermopylae and weakened the Persian fleet with minimal losses to the Greek side. They revealed much about Persian naval capabilities, and bought time for the Athenians to complete the evacuation of their city-state and prepare for a second fight at Salamis.

James T. Chambers

See also: Greco-Persian Wars, Overview; Hellenic Alliance; Salamis, Battle of; Themistocles; Thermopylae, Battle of; Trireme; Xerxes I

References

Burn, A. R. *Persia and the Greeks: The Defence of the West*. Stanford, CA: Stanford University Press, 1984.

Hale, John. *Lords of the Sea: The Epic Story of the Athenian Navy and the Birth of Democracy*. New York: Viking Press, 2009.

Morrison, J. S., J. F. Coates, and N. B. Rankov. *The Athenian Trireme*, 2nd edition. Cambridge: Cambridge University Press, 2000.

Artillery

According to Diodorus Siculus, specialists working for Dionysius I ca. 399 BCE invented the first form of artillery. This weapon, based on an enlarged composite bow, was called the belly-bow (*gastraphetes*) and was similar in design to a large crossbow. The long composite bow arms required an extra mechanism to pull the string into position thus storing potential energy through tension in the bow arms. It fired a single large arrow at a much greater range than normal bows. As builders and users mastered techniques for building and firing these weapons, larger weapons appeared with platforms and more complicated loading mechanisms. Dionysius I used these weapons to great effect against Carthaginian forces when he laid siege to Motya in 396, and Onomarchus employed them in battle against Philip II in Thessaly ca. 353.

Efforts to improve torsion weapons led specialists working for Philip II of Macedon to invent torsion catapults by 340. These weapons differed by using springs made of rope coils to store the energy that propelled the throwing arms. The loading, firing, and platform mechanisms for these catapults came from the earlier forms of artillery. Because the amount of stored energy could be much greater these weapons had greater range (300 yards or more) and could fire rocks or larger bolts. The length of the springs determined the range and size of the projectile so that a variety of sizes evolved. Torsion catapults were mostly used in sieges for attack and defense. Philip used torsion catapults in several sieges and Alexander employed them during his campaigns in Asia.

The impact of catapults in fourth-century warfare remains a matter of debate because there is little evidence that they changed the course of most sieges. Whether this pattern was due to the fact that they were seldom used or because of limits in our sources remains unclear. That they eventually became a valued tool is indicated by their appearance in Hellenistic military manuals and the regular use of catapult-based features in Hellenistic city walls.

Lee L. Brice

See also: Alexander the Great; Dionysius I; Philip II of Macedon; Tyre, Siege of

References

Keyser, Paul T. "Use of Artillery by Philip II and Alexander the Great." *Ancient World* 25 (1994): 27–59.

Marsden, Eric W. *Greek and Roman Artillery: Historical Development*. Oxford: Clarendon Press, 1969.

Athens

Located in central Greece and occupied since the Neolithic Age, Athens became an early center of democracy in the late sixth century BCE. It possessed a strong, well-watered acropolis, was surrounded by the large Attic countryside, and had superb harbors at Phalerum and Piraeus. Athens also benefited from large deposits of silver in the area of Laurion, which would make it possible to build its fleet in the years before the Persian Wars.

Despite its geographic advantages, Athens was merely another successful city-state during the ninth to the sixth centuries—neither the wealthiest, nor the largest, nor the most powerful. Solon's political and economic reforms ca. 594 nudged it toward later preeminence and by the

The Acropolis of Athens as viewed from the Hill of Philopappus (also known as the Hill of the Muses). Its position on a high limestone outcrop provided defense and housed civic and religious buildings. Persian armies burned it in 480 and 479. Pericles rebuilt the temples with Delian League funds. The burning also provided justification for Philip's and then Alexander's campaign against Persia in the fourth century. (Pictorial Library of Bible Lands)

mid-sixth century Athens was a leading economic center. After a period of tyranny under Peisistratus and his sons, Cleisthenes reformed the political organization of the state ca. 508 so that what emerged was essentially democracy. The democracy continued to develop with Ephialtes' and then Pericles' reforms, but before that could occur Athens became involved in the Persian Wars.

Athens quickly rose in power, sending aid to the Ionian Revolt in 499. When Darius I responded in 490 Athens defeated the Persians at the Battle of Marathon. Then in 483 they began building up the fleet of triremes with funds raised from an enormous silver strike at the Laurion mines. Athens played an integral role in the Hellenic Alliance against Persian invasion during 480–479. Athens took advantage of discontent in the alliance to form the Delian League and continued fighting Persia until 450. During this period Athens used the income from the league to build and maintain a large fleet that commanded the Aegean making it possible for the city to safely import food and project Athenian power. Under the leadership of Pericles, Athens' league evolved into an Athenian empire that dominated the Aegean. This growth brought it into conflict with members of the Peloponnesian League, finally resulting in the Peloponnesian War beginning in 431. Despite having numerous advantages Athens eventually lost the war in 404.

In the competing hegemonies of the early fourth century Athens recovered some of its political and economic power and even formed a new naval alliance, but it was not able to achieve preeminence again. After Philip became king of Macedon, Athens vigorously opposed Macedon's northern expansion and rise to hegemony in central Greece. At the battle of Chaeronea in 338 an alliance led by Thebes and Athens fell to Philip's army. In the aftermath he created the League of Corinth, thus ending the political independence of Athens for much of the rest of its existence.

During Alexander's campaigns Athens continued to be an unenthusiastic ally. There was even an anti-Macedon movement centered there. After Alexander's death the insurgency blossomed into the Lamian War during 323–321, which Athens and its allies lost. Afterward, for the rest of its history Athens would remain under the direct or indirect control of various powers, a lesser but not insignificant city.

Ken Tuite

See also: Chaeronea, Battle of; Corinth, League of; Delian League; Greco-Persian Wars, Consequences; Greco-Persian Wars, Overview; Hellenic Alliance; Peloponnesian War, Causes; Peloponnesian War, Overview; Pericles; Plataea, Battle of; Salamis, Battle of; Trireme

References

Buckler, John. *Aegean Greece in the Fourth Century BC*. Leiden: Brill, 2003.

Kinzl, Konrad, ed. *A Companion to the Classical Greek World*. Malden, MA: Wiley-Blackwell, 2006.

Munn, Mark. *The School of History: Athens in the Age of Socrates*. Berkeley, CA: University of California Press, 2000.

Osborne, Robin. *Greece in the Making, 1200–479 BC*, 2nd edition. Routledge: New York, 2006.

B

Bactria

Situated at the crossroads of Central Asia, Bactria was an important region in the ancient world for more than 1,200 years. Founded as a satrapy by the Persians, but brought to even greater heights by the Greeks, Bactria was a catalyst for cross-cultural exchange in the diverse and well-traveled region.

Bactria's borders lay between the Hindu Kush mountain range and the Oxus River in parts of modern-day Afghanistan, Tajikistan, and Uzbekistan. An extremely fertile land, Bactria has also been known as Bactriana and Zariaspa. Prior to the sixth century BCE, Bactria was probably populated by Persians, and it may have been one of the places where Zoroaster, the founder of Zoroastrianism, preached his new faith. During the sixth century, Bactria was incorporated into the Persian Empire.

Alexander the Great reached the area in 329 and spent three years trying to pacify it and the neighboring satrapy of Sogdiana. During this campaign Alexander faced his most serious insurgency, led by Spitamenes. Only after a difficult campaign and a diplomatic marriage to Roxane had Alexander sufficiently pacified the region to leave more than 10,000 men behind before he moved into India. Thus began a long period of Greek influence over the diverse populations of Central Asia. After Alexander's death and the early Diadochic Wars, Bactria became a province of the kingdom of Seleucus I.

Nancy Stockdale

See also: Alexander the Great; Cavalry; Mercenaries; Wars of Alexander the Great, Overview

References

Holt, Frank L. *Thundering Zeus: The Making of Hellenistic Bactria*. Berkeley: University of California Press, 1999.

Holt, Frank L. *Into the Land of Bones: Alexander the Great in Afghanistan*. Berkeley, CA: University of California Press, 2005.

Sidky, H. *The Greek Kingdom of Bactria: From Alexander to Eurcratides the Great*. Philadelphia, PA: University Press of America, 2000.

Brasidas

Brasidas has the reputation, thanks to the Greek historian Thucydides, of being the most effective Spartan commander during the first decade of the Peloponnesian War. His bold campaign in northern Greece in 424 BCE regained the military advantage for Sparta and led to the Peace of Nicias in 421.

Surviving sources tell few specifics about Brasidas' life before the beginning of the Peloponnesian War. His father was named Tellis and his mother was Argileonis. His family was among the "Equals," citizens of Sparta, and so he began intensive military training at an early age. Brasidas was a successful officer, active in engagements at Methone, Piraeus, and Pylos before the surrender of Spartan forces at Sphacteria in 425. As a result, Brasidas was assigned the mission of regaining the initiative for Sparta. Raising a small army of freed helots and mercenaries in early 424, he engaged in a series of brilliant campaigns intended to force Athens to end the war or at least sign a peace treaty.

Brasidas began by thwarting an Athenian assault on Megara. He then marched north, successfully maneuvering through hostile territory, and negotiated favorable terms with King Perdiccas II of Macedonia. After helping Perdiccas, Brasidas rapidly secured the allegiance of several Greek cities including Acanthus and Stageira, before launching an attack on the city of Amphipolis, the most significant of Athens' northern allies. Thucydides, who had been assigned to defend the city, did not arrive in time to defend the city, and Brasidas was able to persuade the people of Amphipolis to surrender in exchange for generous terms. His victory was a setback for the Athenians, who were using revenue from silver mines near Amphipolis to finance the war.

Brasidas then successfully detached additional cities from the Athenian empire, putting further pressure on Athens. When in 423 he supported revolts against Athenian rule in the cities of Scione and Mende, Athens responded with a large force led by Cleon. After some initial successes Cleon marched on Amphipolis, but during their retreat outside the city Brasidas attacked inflicting heavy casualties, including the death of Cleon. However, Brasidas was fatally wounded in the fighting. His soldiers carried him to Amphipolis where, after his death, he was honored as a new founder of the city. Following the Battle of Amphipolis, the leaders of Sparta and Athens agreed to the Peace of Nicias in 421, which halted hostilities for six years.

Ryan Hackney

See also: Amphipolis; Cleon; Peloponnesian War, Overview; Sparta; Thucydides

References

Kagan, Donald. *The Peloponnesian War*. New York: Penguin, 2003.

Lazenby, J. F. *The Peloponnesian War: A Military Study*. New York: Routledge, 2004.

Strassler, Robert B., ed. *The Landmark Thucydides: A Comprehensive Guide to the Peloponnesian War*. New York: Free Press, 1998.

Tritle, Lawrence A. *A New History of the Peloponnesian War*. Malden, MA: Wiley-Blackwell, 2010.

Tritle, Lawrence A. and Brian Campbell, eds. *The Oxford Handbook of Classical Military History*. Oxford: Oxford University Press, 2012.

C

Cavalry, Greek

In general, during the period 490–350 BCE cavalry seems to have been of mixed effectiveness in Greek warfare. The reasons for this record can be found in the expense of horses, the topography, the dominance of hoplites, and the bias of the sources. Discussions of Greek cavalry must rely heavily on Athenian sources. When employed in tasks for which they were suited such as scouting, pursuit, and flank attack cavalry could make a difference, but most Greek city-states lacked an effective cavalry force.

Sources provide few examples of Greek cavalry activity during the Persian Wars and it seems not to have come into effective regular use until the mid-fifth century. Even then a few regions including Athens, Phocis, Thebes, Thessaly, Macedonia, Southern Italy, and Sicily seem to have effectively employed cavalry. Each of these regions had terrain suitable for horses and a tradition of horse breeding. Sparta, for example, had a poor reputation for cavalry so they relied on Thebes, Locris, and Phocis to provide cavalry for the Peloponnesian League. Athens, however, employed its own cavalry effectively during the Peloponnesian War and the early fourth century just as Thebes would during its period of hegemony in the fourth century.

Greek cavalry could be armed with a variety of weapons including javelins for missile combat and a spear or sword (or both) for close quarters. Horse archers were uncommon and lances were not employed before the Macedonians began using cavalry *sarissas*. This period predated the use of saddle, stirrups, and horseshoes. Despite these limitations on equipment there were a variety of tasks, both independent and in support of infantry, in which cavalry engaged. The tasks for which cavalry was most

This idealistic relief of a fifth-century BCE Athenian cavalryman shows that he carried a spear (now lost) and did not use a saddle. This is a modern copy of the funerary monument for Dexileos in the Athenian cemetery at Kerameikos. (Lee L. Brice)

commonly used were scouting and raiding as well as pursuit, harassment of enemy detachments and flank protection/attack, all of which could be employed defensively or offensively.

Because of their expense, cavalry forces were never large, but examples of cavalry action demonstrate their potential. Athens employed its cavalry effectively in central Greece during much of the Peloponnesian War. While it could not keep the Spartans from invading Attica repeatedly, the cavalry shadowed Spartan movements and harassed detachments and foragers. During the 415 expedition against Sicily the Athenians failed to bring cavalry as they expected to obtain mounts in Sicily, but the Syracusan cavalry was important initially against the Athenians and in the pursuit and capture of the fleeing Athenian force at the end.

In the fourth century, Greek cavalry remained important and saw some new employment. The Spartan campaigns in Ionia relied heavily on allied and Spartan cavalry. Their weakness in these units contributed to their overall lack of success. Epameinondas drew on Thebes' traditional cavalry strength as he forged the Theban hegemony. He was flexible in his use of it, occasionally stationing cavalry on his flanks, but also setting it in front of infantry at Leuctra and Mantinea to drive away enemy cavalry and shield his infantry movements. Cavalry too continued to play a role in the fortunes of the Thessalian cities, especially the tyrants of Pherae.

Philip II of Macedon was responsible for the greatest change in Greek cavalry warfare. Macedon had, like Thessaly, a long reputation for superior cavalry. The riders, drawn mainly from the elite, were called the "king's companions" (*hetairoi*). Philip adopted the wedge formation and the *sarissa* before 338 and may have enlarged the cavalry. The *sarissa* was a lance of 14–16 feet made of strong wood. Because they lacked stirrups and saddles, riders carried their lance low on the right against opponents. Philip and then Alexander still used cavalry in many of the traditional ways, but the *sarissa* also opened up a new tactic. The great length of the shaft coupled with the wedge formation gave the cavalry an opportunity to exploit gaps in opponents' infantry line such as occurred at the battles of Chaeronea and Gaugamela. Alexander the Great relied heavily on his "companion cavalry," which he rode with, and it became the preeminent unit of his army during the campaigns in Persia. Afterward, cavalry retained its primacy for only a few years as infantry tended to dominate Hellenistic warfare.

Lee L. Brice

See also: Alexander the Great; Athens; Epameinondas; Peloponnesian War, Overview; Philip II of Macedon; Sicily, Athenian Expedition Against; Sparta; Thebes; Wars of Alexander the Great, Overview

References

Rhodes, P. J. *A History of the Classical Greek World, 478–323 BC*, 2nd edition. Malden, MA: Wiley-Blackwell, 2010.

Sekunda, Nick V. "The Macedonian Army." In *A Companion to Ancient Macedonia*, eds. Joseph Roisman and Ian Worthington, 446–71. Malden, MA: Wiley-Blackwell, 2010.

Spence, I. G. *The Cavalry of Classical Greece: A Social and Military History with Particular Reference to Athens*. Oxford: Oxford University Press, 1995.

Cavalry, Persian

The Persian Empire in the period 490–331 BCE maintained a deserved reputation for superior cavalry in the Eastern Mediterranean. Employed similarly to Greek cavalry, the Persians enjoyed advantages in numbers and organization, but fell short against the Macedonian *sarissa* and Alexander's tactical flexibility. The Persian cavalry's reputation is hardly surprising since effective and numerous cavalry contributed to the emergence of Achaemenid Persia, but the importance of their cavalry has recently become a topic of debate.

Whereas the Neo-Assyrians had experimented with cavalry in which two horses were harnessed together, the Persian Empire was the first to exploit fully the advantages of cavalry. Whereas only a few Greek regions had territory suitable for horses, much of the Achaemenid Empire was suited to horse breeding and enjoyed an independent cavalry tradition. The Achaemenid administration organized the cavalry into regional units based on tens. The size of the empire meant that the cavalry force raised and thus organized could be enormous, even if not quite as large as our more fanciful Greek traditions insist.

Persian cavalry could be armed with a variety of weapons. A Persian document from ca. 432 reports the arms of a cavalryman as including an iron corselet, a helmet with neck and face protectors, two spears for throwing or thrusting, and 130 arrows with a bow. Such an array of defensive armor ensured the rider's effectiveness in combat while the arms provided sufficient flexibility for different circumstances. The use of horse archers gave the Persians an added offensive capability that Greek cavalry could not match. This entire period predated the use of saddle, stirrups, and horseshoes. By the early fourth century the Greek author Xenophon reports that the Persians were using armor on their horses and it is probable that by the time of Alexander's campaign Achaemenid cavalry included mostly light units with less armor and some heavy or cataphract cavalry that relied on heavy armor for men and horses along with their thrusting spears.

There were various tasks, both independent and in support of infantry, in which cavalry engaged. The tasks for which cavalry was most commonly used were scouting and raiding as well as pursuit, harassment of enemy detachments, and flank protection/attack, all of which could be employed defensively or offensively. What made the Persian forces so effective in these tasks in comparison to their typical Greek counterparts was their numbers.

A look at its record in warfare against the Greeks shows that until it came against Alexander the Great, the Achaemenid cavalry was repeatedly effective. Greek sources provide a skewed impression of Persian cavalry effectiveness during the Persian Wars, but it was present. It was at

Marathon in 490 even if most of the horses had been embarked on ship by the time of the Greek attack, and at Plataea, Mardonius' cavalry attack pressed the Greeks hard. In the fourth century, Persian cavalry harassed the Ten Thousand as they marched away from Cunaxa and later won a number of victories against Greek forces in Asia Minor including the Spartan campaigns in Ionia. Against the Macedonian "Companions" armed with the long *sarissa* and employing the wedge in Alexander's tactics the Persians were unable to hold the field in battle and failed to provide much of a threat to foraging parties who were often accompanied by cavalry.

After the fall of the Achaemenid dynasty and Alexander's return to Babylon he began to incorporate Persian cavalry into his army, a trend that continued in the Seleucid Army during the Hellenistic age.

Lee L. Brice

See also: Alexander the Great; Athens; Gaugamela, Battle of; Granicus River, Battle of; Greco-Persian Wars, Overview; Marathon, Battle of; Mardonius; Persian Empire; Plataea, Battle of; Sparta; Wars of Alexander the Great, Overview

References

Briant, Pierre. *From Cyrus to Alexander: A History of the Persian Empire.* Winona Lake, IN: Indiana University Press, 2005.

Spence, I. G. *The Cavalry of Classical Greece: A Social and Military History with Particular Reference to Athens.* Oxford: Oxford University Press, 1995.

Tuplin, Christopher. "All the King's Horse: In Search of Achaemenid Persian Cavalry." In *New Perspectives on Ancient Warfare*, eds. Garrett Fagan and Matthew Trundle, 101–82. Leiden: Brill, 2010.

Chaeronea, Battle of

Philip II of Macedon met Athens, Thebes, and their allies in battle at Chaeronea in 338 BCE. The Athenians and their allies were trying to halt Philip's advance into central Greek affairs. The result of the battle fundamentally altered Classical Greece as the period of independent city-states ended.

During the 20 years after he became king of Macedon, Philip II had slowly spread his influence well beyond his kingdom to include Thrace, Paeonia, Epirus, Chalcidice, and Thessaly. He controlled some of these

The plain at Chaeronea on which Philip II defeated Athens and Thebes in 338 BCE was well suited to Philip's tactics. Alexander led the cavalry on the Macedonian left against the Thebans near the point where this image was taken. Looking west down the battle line toward the town of Chaeronea. (Lee L. Brice)

regions directly and held immense influence—hegemony—over those he did not directly rule. Although his army contributed much to his success, his diplomatic skill and timing were equally important. Athens and Thebes had watched, and had at times worked against him, only to find themselves often outmaneuvered.

The Fourth Sacred War put Philip in the position of military leader (*hegemon*) of the Delphic Amphictiony. He was directed in late 339 to chastise the city of Amphissa for not meeting its obligations to Delphi. After some diplomatic maneuvering on all sides, Thebes and Athens united to oppose Philip militarily. The resulting campaign, which Philip won handily, led to an engagement on the plain at Chaeronea in late summer 338. Philip and his Amphictionic allies including Thessaly, Phocis, and the Aetolians took the field against Athens and Thebes with support from Achaea, Corinth, Megara, Phocis, and some islands.

Accounts of the battle are limited in detail, but there are some facts we know. The Athenians and Thebans with their allies arrived first and set their line across the plain with Athens on the left flank anchored in the hills and protected by light infantry units. The Theban Sacred Band of elite warriors was stationed on the right flank with the Cephisus River protecting their flank from cavalry. The Macedonians arrived and took a similar position opposite. Philip commanded the battle line but stationed himself with the Macedonian phalanx as usual while his 18-year-old son, Alexander, was on his left flank in command of the cavalry. Exactly how the battle progressed is uncertain, but Philip won by maneuvering the allied line into disorder thus revealing gaps into which Alexander led the Macedonian cavalry. The Thebans were destroyed in the charge. Philip was victorious, becoming the recognized master of all Greece.

After the battle Philip set garrisons in key cities including Ambracia, Corinth, and Thebes in order to control military movement. He then established the League of Corinth to provide him the means to maintain his hegemony in Greece. The league named him its leader (*hegemon*) and its military commander (*strategos*) in the war of revenge against Persia. He thus ended the political independence of the Greek cities. Although we know little of how the battle unfolded, its results made it one of the most important battles of the Greek world.

Lee L. Brice

See also: Alexander the Great; Athens; Corinth, League of; Philip II of Macedon; Sacred Wars; Thebes

References

Hammond, Nicholas G. L. *Philip of Macedon*. London: Duckworth, 1994.

Sekunda, Nick V. "The Macedonian Army." In *A Companion to Ancient Macedonia*, eds. Joseph Roisman and Ian Worthington, 446–71. Malden, MA: Wiley-Blackwell, 2010.

Worthington, Ian. *Philip II of Macedonia*. New Haven, CT: Yale University Press, 2008.

Cimon

During the early fifth century BCE when the Delian League was established, Cimon was the most important Athenian military commander in the generation after the Persian Wars. A political opponent of Themistocles and Pericles, he is generally associated with the policy of attacking Persia and maintaining friendship with Sparta.

Born ca. 510, Cimon was the son of Miltiades the Younger, hero of the Battle of Marathon, and a member of one of the wealthiest families in Athens. In 478 he helped Aristides transfer leadership of the Greek forces from Sparta to Athens to form what would become the Delian League. Cimon became its principal commander down to 462.

Cimon's first known command was in about 476, when he captured the Persian stronghold of Eion at the mouth of the Strymon River. He was active throughout the period down to 463 during which he enlarged the Delian League and won a number of victories against Persia. The most important of these occurred in about 466 when his forces won dual land and naval victories on the same day at the Eurymedon River in southern Asia Minor.

In 462 Cimon led an Athenian army to assist Sparta in putting down a rebellion of Messenian helots. When Sparta insulted Athens by dismissing the force Cimon lost popularity and was ostracized (exiled for 10 years). After his return, he negotiated a five-year truce with Sparta and then led an expedition against Persian-held cities on the island Cyprus in 451 or 450.

While besieging the city of Citium ca. 450, Cimon fell ill and died, and the expedition returned home unsuccessful. Soon afterward, Athens signed the so-called Peace of Callias with Persia to end hostilities.

George E. Pesey

See also: Delian League; Eurymedon River, Battle of; Greco-Persian Wars, Overview; Hellenic Alliance; Pericles; Trireme

References

Meiggs, Russell. *The Athenian Empire*. Oxford: Clarendon Press, 1972.

Rhodes, P. J. *A History of the Classical Greek World, 478–323 BC*, 2nd edition. Malden, MA: Wiley-Blackwell, 2010.

Cleon

Cleon, an Athenian leader during the Peloponnesian War played an important role in the capture of Spartan soldiers at Sphacteria in 425 BCE. He was an ardent supporter of the war, but his death in 422 made peace possible.

The son of Cleaenetus, Cleon was born ca. 470 into a wealthy family that had not traditionally held political power. Little is known about him before he rose to prominence after Pericles' death in 429. Although rivals dismissed him as a demagogue, Cleon achieved influence through his rhetorical skills in the assembly where he pursued aggressive policies against all Athens' enemies.

He first became prominent in 427. When Mytilene (on the island of Lesbos) revolted against Athenian rule, Cleon proposed that the city be destroyed, all its men killed, and the remaining people sold into slavery. The act failed on a revote, but at Cleon's urging 1,000 leaders of the revolt were put to death and the city walls destroyed.

In 425, an Athenian naval force led by Nicias surrounded a Spartan force on the island of Sphacteria, which faced Pylos in the western Peloponnesus. When Nicias resigned under pressure Cleon took command. He led a force to the island and aggressively attacked the trapped Spartans. The unprecedented surrender of 120 Spartan soldiers and about 170 allied troops boosted Cleon's standing in the Athens and led Sparta to ask for peace.

Cleon rejected their terms on the grounds that Athens should press its advantage. Perhaps in response, in 424 the Spartan general Brasidas embarked on an aggressive campaign in northern Greece. His force took many northern cities allied with Athens, including the wealthy city of Amphipolis. In 422, Cleon led an army to take back Amphipolis and stop Brasidas. After recapturing several former allies Cleon led his large army against Amphipolis, but during his retreat Brasidas attacked and defeated the Athenian force. Cleon died during the battle and Brasidas was mortally wounded.

Cleon had repeatedly rejected Spartan requests for peace negotiations, but with his death both sides negotiated the Peace of Nicias.

Ryan Hackney

See also: Amphipolis; Brasidas; Nicias; Peloponnesian War, Overview; Sphacteria

References

Kagan, Donald. *The Peloponnesian War*. New York: Penguin, 2003.

Strassler, Robert B., ed. *The Landmark Thucydides: A Comprehensive Guide to the Peloponnesian War*. New York: Free Press, 1998.

Tritle, Lawrence A. *A New History of the Peloponnesian War*. Malden, MA: Wiley-Blackwell, 2010.

Tritle, Lawrence A. and Brian Campbell, eds. *The Oxford Handbook of Classical Military History*. Oxford: Oxford University Press, 2012.

Conon of Athens

Conon of Athens was one of the top Athenian naval commanders during the final years of the Peloponnesian War. After Athens was defeated in that conflict, he commanded a Persian fleet and was largely responsible for ending Spartan naval hegemony and enabling Athens to return to the sea as a naval power.

Conon was born into a prominent Athenian family about the middle of the fifth century BCE. When he was a young man, the Peloponnesian War erupted in 431 between Athens and Sparta. Conon is first mentioned in the historical record as commander of a force at Naupactus, the Athenian naval base in the Corinthian Gulf, in 414.

By 407, Conon had achieved the rank of admiral. Early in 406, Conon replaced Alcibiades as commander of the 70 Athenian ships at the island of Samos. Soon thereafter, the Spartan admiral, Callicratidas, threatened Conon's small fleet at Mytilene. The Athenians scrambled to assemble another fleet and won a decisive victory at the Battle of Arginusae in August 406.

The following year, the Spartan commander Lysander crushed the Athenian fleet at the Battle of Aegospotami. Conon was the only Athenian commander to escape from Aegospotami, but fearing to return to Athens, he took refuge with Evagoras, the pro-Athenian king of Salamis in Cyprus. Meanwhile, the devastating Athenian defeat at Aegospotami led Athens to surrender in 404, bringing the Peloponnesian War to an end.

Conon resurfaced ca. 400 when war broke out between the Persian Empire and Sparta. From 397, he was admiral of the Persian naval forces under the command of the satrap Pharnabazus. In the summer of 394, Conon defeated a Peloponnesian fleet led by the Spartan commander Peisander near Cnidus. Conon's victory at the Battle of Cnidus ended Spartan naval supremacy in the Aegean Sea. In the aftermath, he and Pharnabazus removed Spartan governors and pro-Spartan regimes from many Greek cities of Asia Minor and the Aegean Islands.

In 393, Conon visited Athens, bringing funds for rebuilding the fortifications of the Athenian port of Piraeus and the Long Walls between Piraeus and Athens. About 392, the Spartans brought him in disrepute to Tiribazus, satrap at Sardis, who arrested him, but he escaped and died ca. 390 of natural causes on Cyprus. His son Timotheus also had a distinguished military career.

George E. Pesely

See also: Aegospotami, Battle of; Athens; Lysander; Mercenaries; Peloponnesian War, Consequences of; Peloponnesian War, Overview

References

Buckler, John. *Aegean Greece in the Fourth Century BC.* Leiden: Brill, 2003.

Hale, John. *Lords of the Sea: The Epic Story of the Athenian Navy and the Birth of Democracy.* New York: Viking Press, 2009.

Kinzl, Konrad, ed. *A Companion to the Classical Greek World.* Malden, MA: Wiley-Blackwell, 2006.

Munn, Mark. *The School of History: Athens in the Age of Socrates.* Berkeley, CA: University of California Press, 2000.

Pritchett, W. Kendrick. *The Greek State at War*, vol. 2. Berkeley, CA: University of California Press, 1975.

Strassler, Robert B., ed. *The Landmark Xenophon's Hellenika.* New York: Pantheon Books, 2009.

Corinth

Corinth is located on a narrow isthmus connecting central and southern Greece between the Saronic Gulf and the Gulf of Corinth. The city is distinct from Acrocorinth, a large and easily fortified mountain that dominates the region. Its position on the crossroads for north–south land traffic and east–west sea traffic and its proximity to the formidable defenses of Acrocorinth made Corinth economically and strategically important throughout its history.

Corinth was settled as early as the Neolithic Age. In the period after 1000, it became a major trading center with ties to the eastern and western Mediterranean. Those commercial contacts made Corinth one of the wealthiest Greek cities. The population grew and the city could not expand its territory, so beginning in the eighth century BCE Corinth drew on its maritime tradition and played a significant role in Greek colonization, founding numerous cities including Corcyra, Ambracia, Potidaea, and Syracuse. After a successful period of tyranny from the mid-seventh to the mid-sixth centuries under Cypselus and then his son Periander, an oligarchy ruled Corinth during much of the Archaic and Classical periods.

Corinthian fortunes waned as Athens' commercial importance grew, but it remained significant and a member of the Peloponnesian League.

Acrocorinth, the high defensible hill next to Corinth, contributed to the strategic importance of the wealthy, mercantile city. There was a fortification, a temple, and a spring on top. When Philip of Macedon created the League of Corinth he installed a garrison on Acrocorinth. The eighth-century Temple of Apollo is in the foreground. (John W. I. Lee)

In 483 along with other Spartan allies it joined the Hellenic Alliance opposing Persia and supplied men and troops at each of the major battles in Greece. When there was falling out between the league and Sparta in 477 it withdrew. In the later fifth century, Corinth advocated most for war with Athens in the lead-up to 431 and then played a major role in a number of key naval engagements during the Peloponnesian War. In particular, it was the Corinthians at Erineus who started using bow-to-bow ramming tactics against the superior Athenian ships. Then in 414 they sent reinforcements including numerous ships to Syracuse during the Sicilian expedition where they helped defeat Athens. When in 404 victorious Sparta refused to destroy Athens as its allies demanded, Corinth became less supportive of Sparta.

The Corinthian War, which erupted in 395 against Spartan hegemony, greatly damaged Corinth since much of it occurred in its territory and relegated the city to a minor role in Greece during the remainder of the early fourth century. In the years before and immediately after Leuctra Corinth continued to provide support to Sparta even if the Peloponnesian League was no longer a reality, but throughout the Theban hegemony Corinth was militarily impotent in the face of Boeotian invasions and internal meddling.

Corinth was more active in the mid-fourth century in Sicily, sending Timoleon and some mercenaries in 345 to support Syracuse. When this campaign initially went well it sent more support and prospered from the booty sent back. The campaign of Timoleon seems to have initiated a brief period of Corinthian imperial activity when it was active in Sicily and all its former colonies minted a similar coinage. Corinth sent men to join the Theban–Athenian alliance against Philip II of Macedon at Chaeronea. After his victory at Chaeronea in 338 he installed a garrison on Acrocorinth and made the city home of the League of Corinth. After Alexander became king of Macedonia in 336, Corinth was one of the first cities he visited. He ensured the continued existence of the league and asserted his role in it and the forthcoming campaign against Persia. After Alexander's death Corinth continued to figure prominently in the ongoing wars of the successors.

Kenneth Tuite

See also: Athens; Corinth, League of; Corinthian War; Hellenic Alliance; Leuctra, Battle of; Peloponnesian League; Peloponnesian War, Causes of; Peloponnesian War, Overview; Philip II of Macedon; Thebes; Timoleon

References

Osborne, Robin. *Greece in the Making, 1200–479 BC*, 2nd edition. Routledge: New York, 2006.

Rhodes, P. J. *A History of the Classical Greek World, 478–323 BC*, 2nd edition. Malden, MA: Wiley-Blackwell, 2010.

Salmon, J. B. *Wealthy Corinth*. Oxford: Clarendon Press, 1984.

Corinth, League of

The League of Corinth is the modern name for the Hellenic League created in late 338 BCE by Philip II of Macedon after the Battle of Chaeronea. Although formed with the official goal of creating and safeguarding a common peace, the league allowed Philip and then Alexander to control most of Greece. The league became the formal basis for Alexander's campaign against the Persian Empire.

After winning the Battle of Chaeronea, Philip moved to exert control over the Greek cities. Initially he had reorganized territory and installed

ANCIENT GREECE

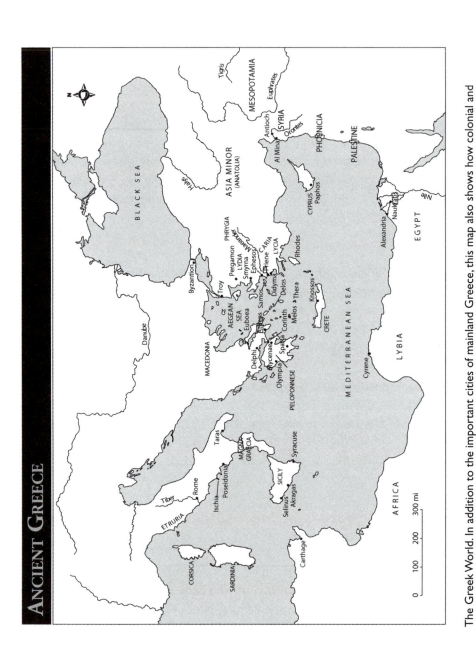

The Greek World. In addition to the important cities of mainland Greece, this map also shows how colonial and commercial expansion resulted in Greek culture spreading throughout the Mediterranean.

garrisons, but perhaps realizing that these were not enough, he called a meeting of the Greeks in 337 at Corinth. At that meeting, they created a new league including all the Greek cities except Sparta, which had refused.

The ambassador from each city took oath to honor the Common Peace and created a league assembly (*synedrion*) of city representatives responsible for deliberations and decisions, and a military leader (*hegemon*). Additional terms included guarantee of cities' autonomy, forbade changes in members' constitutions, required combined action against any member violating the agreement, and called for each member state to contribute militarily. The assembly would determine all league decisions. Philip presented at this time his planned Panhellenic war on Persia. The league approved his plan and voted him general in charge (*strategon*).

After Philip died in 336, the assembly confirmed Alexander as *hegemon* of the league and general against Persia. Afterward, while Alexander dealt with troubles in the north Thebes withdrew from the league. As a result, the league assembly called on Alexander to punish Thebes, which he did by sacking and razing it to the ground. When Alexander invaded Persia league members supplied military support. During his campaign Alexander continued to act officially on behalf of the league and use it to exert control in Greece. After the Battle of Granicus he sent spoils to Athens in the name of the league and later used the league to punish Greek cities that revolted. When Alexander burned Persepolis in 330 he declared the league's war against Persia complete. The league disbanded soon after Alexander's death.

Lee L. Brice

See also: Alexander the Great; Athens; Chaeronea, Battle of; Corinth; Granicus River, Battle of; Philip II of Macedon; Thebes; Wars of Alexander the Great, Causes of

References

Buckler, John. *Aegean Greece in the Fourth Century BC*. Leiden: Brill, 2003.

Heckel, Waldemar and Lawrence A. Tritle, eds. *Alexander the Great: A New History*. Malden, MA: Wiley-Blackwell, 2009.

Tritle, Lawrence A. and Brian Campbell, eds. *The Oxford Handbook of Classical Military History*. Oxford: Oxford University Press, 2012.

Worthington, Ian. *Philip II of Macedonia*. New Haven, CT: Yale University Press, 2008.

Corinthian War

The Corinthian War, 395–387 BCE, was so named because much of it occurred in Corinthian territory. Resulting from tensions between Sparta and
former members of the Peloponnesian League it set the tone for much of
the intercity warfare during the early fourth century.

After the victory in the Peloponnesian War, Sparta ignored its allies'
demands by not destroying Athens and at the same time Lysander moved
to turn the Delian League into a Spartan empire. Corinth and Thebes rejected Spartan hegemony and openly refused to participate in Peloponnesian League activities. In 395 Thebes maneuvered Locris into conflict
with Phocis, which was still an ally of Sparta. The Spartan response, led
by Lysander, triggered what became the Corinthian War. Former Peloponnesian League members Thebes, Corinth, and Locris were joined by Athens, Argos, and cities in Euboea and Thessaly against Sparta.

The anti-Spartan alliance won an initial victory at Haliartus in which
Lysander died, and it won a naval victory under Conon at Cnidus in 394.
This win secured Persian support and forced the Spartan king, Agesilaus
II, to return to Greece from his campaign against Persian forces in Ionia.
The allies won victories over Spartan forces, but were unable to capitalize
on their achievements. Sparta maneuvered in Asia Minor and was eventually able in 387 to secure the King's Peace imposed in Greece in return for
giving up Ionia to Persia. This common peace resulted in the end of the
war by forcing Thebes to give up control of Boeotia and forcing Corinth
and Argos to dismantle their union. Sparta secured victory in this first war
for hegemony in Greece, but it exposed for all Sparta's military weakness.

Lee L. Brice

See also: Agesilaus II; Athens; Corinth; Iphicrates; King's Peace; Lysander; Peloponnesian League; Peloponnesian War, Consequences of; Sparta;
Thebes

References

Buckler, John. *Aegean Greece in the Fourth Century BC*. Leiden: Brill, 2003.

Rhodes, P. J. *A History of the Classical Greek World, 478–323 BC*, 2nd edition.
Malden, MA: Wiley-Blackwell, 2010.

Strassler, Robert B., ed. *The Landmark Xenophon's Hellenika*. New York: Pantheon Books, 2009.

D

Darius I

Third king in the Achaemenid dynasty, Darius I ruled the Persian Empire from 522 BCE to his death in 486. During his reign, he improved the way the empire was governed, stimulated the empire's economy and trade, and built the magnificent capital of Persepolis. He also expanded the size of the empire to its greatest extent, adding northwest India, Thrace, and Macedonia to the regions already under Persian rule. Darius is best known for his role in the Persian Wars.

Darius was born ca. 550. He became an officer in the Persian Army and was known and respected as an exceptional fighter and leader. Darius was in command of the Persian Army's elite corps during King Cambyses II's invasion of Egypt in 525. After Cambyses died in 522 on his way back to Persia to depose a usurper, Darius led his troops back to Persia, killed the impostor, and declared himself king.

Darius strengthened, regularized, and centralized institutions for rule and economic growth. He also ordered construction of his own ceremonial and treasury city, Persepolis. Even as he was improving the empire from within, Darius also expanded the empire's boundaries. He expanded east to the Upper Indus River and west into Thrace and Macedonia. After the revolt of the Ionian Greeks in 500 was crushed during 499–493, he moved against the Greek mainland, perhaps intending to expand westward.

His expeditionary force sailed across the Aegean in 490 against the Greek cities that had supported the Ionian Revolt. They conquered the island of Naxos and the city of Eretria on Euboea. The captured inhabitants were deported into the Persian Empire. Guided by Hippias, the former tyrant of Athens, the Persian forces landed in the plain of Marathon where his father Peisistratus had supporters. Athens sent out an army and after a period of standoff Athens, with support from only Plataea, defeated the Persians. The Persians sailed to Athens' harbor, but then sailed home unsuccessful.

Darius made preparations for another invasion of Greece but did not get the chance to carry out his plans since he died of natural causes in 486. The Achaemenid dynasty continued after Darius with his descendants ruling for several generations, but the Persian Empire had reached its greatest extent under Darius' reign. At his death, it covered nearly 2 million square miles and had a population of around 10 million people.

Kevin Marsh

See also: Athens; Greco-Persian Wars, Causes of; Greco-Persian Wars, Overview; Ionian Revolt; Marathon, Battle of; Persian Empire

References

Briant, Pierre. *From Cyrus to Alexander: A History of the Persian Empire*. Winona Lake, IN: Indiana University Press, 2005.

Cawkwell, George. *The Greek Wars: The Failure of Persi* a. Oxford: Oxford University Press, 2005.

Strassler, Robert B., ed. *The Landmark Herodotus: The Histories*. New York: Anchor Books, 2009.

Darius III

Darius III, the last Achaemenid king of Persia, ruled from 336 to 330 BCE. He lost to Alexander the Great. Although he may have been a competent king, his failure to hold the field against the Macedonians ensured the loss of his empire and a negative historical tradition.

Born under the name Codommanus/Artassata from a branch of the royal family, Darius became king after Bagoas assassinated Artaxerxes III (in 338) and then Arses. Darius took up the reign and eliminated Bagoas. Despite hostility in both the ancient tradition and modern evaluations, his reign started normally enough with no suggestion of dissent, disorganization, or decay.

When Darius took power the Persian Empire was undoubtedly aware of the threat presented by Macedonia where Philip II had been openly preparing to invade. Artaxerxes III had defeated Philip's army under Parmenio.

Darius III, the last Achaemenid king of Persia, ruled from 336 to 330 BC and is primarily famous for losing the Persian Empire to Alexander the Great. (iStockPhoto.com)

In 336 Alexander continued the preparations for war. Darius pursued a consistent strategy against Alexander, but despite his best efforts he failed repeatedly against a superior commander. If the ancient sources are accepted Darius twice tried to settle the war by giving Alexander part of the empire, but without success.

By 330 his strategy was in tatters following Alexander's victory at Gaugamela, capture of Babylon, and burning of Persepolis. As Darius fled northeast from Ecbatana a group of his officers, led by Bessus, assassinated him. Found by the Macedonian advance guard, Alexander buried Darius with honors as a means of confirming his own legitimacy. The loss to Alexander completely overshadowed historians' evaluation of Darius III until recently.

Lee L. Brice

See also: Alexander the Great; Gaugamela, Battle of; Issus, Battle of; Macedon; Persian Empire; Philip II of Macedon; Wars of Alexander the Great, Overview

References

Briant, Pierre. *From Cyrus to Alexander: A History of the Persian Empire*. Winona Lake, IN: Indiana University Press, 2005.

Heckel, Waldemar and Lawrence A. Tritle, eds. *Alexander the Great: A New History*. Malden, MA: Wiley-Blackwell, 2009.

Romm, James, ed. *The Landmark Arrian: The Campaigns of Alexander*. New York: Pantheon, 2010.

Delian League

The Delian League is the modern name for the union of Greek city-states established under Athenian leadership in 478 BCE to replace the Hellenic Alliance and continue to fight the Persians. What began as an anti-Persian alliance including most of the Greek cities in and around the Aegean Sea became in truth the Athenian Empire. Its strength and growth was what finally led Sparta to declare the Peloponnesian War in 431. The new league remained active until 404 when Athens lost the Peloponnesian War and had to disband the alliance.

During 478, the Hellenic Alliance was under the leadership of Pausanias of Sparta. Accusation that he abused his authority provided the pretext for the alliance to request Athens to take over leadership. The allies chose the centrally located sacred island of Delos as their headquarters and treasury site. In addition to Athens, initial members included most of the Aegean islands, the Greek cities of Asia Minor, the Propontis (Marmara), and the Hellespont.

They agreed that each member of the league had an equal vote, and each took a permanent oath of loyalty. As leader Athens provided the commander of league forces, and the treasurers who assessed dues annually in the form of either tribute or ships. Athens, Samos, Chios, and Lesbos provided most of the ships while the rest paid tribute. The wealth was intended to pay the costs of building, equipping, and manning ships for the navy.

After defeating Persian forces in Thrace and driving them eastward out of the Chersonese, Greek cities along the eastern and northern Aegean coasts joined the league. Then the commander, Cimon, concentrated his efforts in southwest and southern Asia Minor leading to the major land and sea victory at the Eurymedon River in 466. Membership in the league rose toward 200 cities. Within 12 years, the Persian Navy was driven out of the Aegean Sea, and most Persian forces had been expelled from Greek lands.

Not all members were pleased with the league's success, however. Probably in 467 the island of Naxos tried to quit and the following year Thasos tried breaking away. Naxos was forced to remain a member and the league put Thasos under siege until 462 when it surrendered. The island of Aegina was forced to join the league in 458 and after Athens gained control over Boeotia in 457 a number of inland cities became members. What had started as an anti-Persian alliance was showing open signs of Athenian imperialism.

Campaigning against Persia did not end despite Cimon's ostracism from Athens and the unrest among some members. After 460 league forces were active in the Eastern Mediterranean, primarily in Egypt supporting a local revolt. This effort ended badly in 454 when the expedition was destroyed. The defeat in Egypt provided Pericles the pretext for relocating the Delian treasury to the Athenian Acropolis. After Cimon returned to Athens he again became leader of the league forces and moved against Persian interests in Cyprus. Although the engagement was a draw, Cimon died and Athens agreed to the so-called Peace of Callias thus ending the Persian War and the reason for the league's existence.

Although the war was over the league did not dissolve; instead, it openly became the Athenian Empire. Since Athens was no longer concerned with Persia, it could focus on keeping the allies in line and even expanding. Athens ca. 450 began imposing military settlements called *cleruchies* on unsteady allies and cities forced to join the league. Athens also began to refer to some former allies in terms of control thus making their dominance more obvious. Soon after 450, Pericles began using league funds to rebuild the Athenian Acropolis.

Boeotia broke away ca. 447 followed by revolts in nearby Megara and Euboea. Sparta's invasion in 446 led Athens to sign the Thirty Years' Peace the same year. Now that Athens no longer had to worry about the Peloponnesians, they turned their attention to the restive allies. More *cleruchies* were installed in allied cities, democracy may have been forced on some subject cities, and Athenian courts handled cases against allies. Athens also enforced trade restrictions in the league and required members to use Attic weights, standards, and coinage. Samos tried to break away, but was eventually defeated and forced to pay a large fine. Despite these incidents the league was generally peaceful and loyal.

The growth in the Delian League's strength and dominance in the 430s was, according to Thucydides, what ultimately scared Sparta into declaring war in 431. In the years just prior to the war, the league had intervened in Epidamnus, laid siege to Potidaea, and enforced trade restrictions against Megara, all of which brought Athens into conflict with members of the Peloponnesian League. The Delian League continued to exist, mostly stable, during the early war despite increasing tribute assessments. In 416 they forcibly added Melos to the league.

After the Sicilian Expedition failed in 413, several members including Chios, Thasos, and Euboea revolted, but Athens was able to control the spread of dissent and even conquered some of these insurgent members.

The Peloponnesians won the war in 404 with Persian financial support. Among the terms of the surrender was the dissolution of the Delian League.

Lee L. Brice

See also: Athens; Cimon; Eurymedon River, Battle of; Greco-Persian Wars, Consequences of; Greco-Persian Wars, Overview; Hellenic Alliance; Mycale, Battle of; Peloponnesian League; Peloponnesian War, Causes of; Pericles; Sicily, Athenian Expedition Against; Thucydides

References

Harrison, Thomas. "The Greek World, 478–432." In *A Companion to the Classical Greek World*, ed. Konrad Kinzl, 509–25. Malden, MA: Wiley-Blackwell, 2006.

Kagan, Donald. *The Peloponnesian War*. New York: Penguin, 2003.

Rhodes, P. J. *A History of the Classical Greek World, 478–323 BC*, 2nd edition. Malden, MA: Wiley-Blackwell, 2010.

Strassler, Robert B., ed. *The Landmark Thucydides: A Comprehensive Guide to the Peloponnesian War*. New York: Free Press, 1998.

Delium, Battle of

The Battle of Delium occurred in 424 BCE during the first phase of the Peloponnesian War when a Boeotian force challenged an Athenian force near the town of Delium. Thucydides' detailed account of the battle provides us with a great deal of useful information on hoplite tactics. The battle is important because the Athenians suffered such heavy casualties that they were inclined to sue for peace. More significantly, it was the first battle in which we know the Thebans lined up in a dense formation 25 ranks deep, a tactic used later by Epameinondas.

In the winter of 424, the Athenians launched a campaign to capture several Boeotian cities and build a fort at Delium in Boeotian territory. According to Thucydides, the campaign was supposed to be a combined effort by Demosthenes from the coast and Hippocrates invading overland and both meeting at Delium. Demosthenes had to turn back, but Hippocrates, unaware of his difficulties, made it to Delium with his army where he built the fort in the sanctuary of Apollo. The Boeotians responded by sending an army of their own under Pagondas of Thebes to challenge Hippocrates. Because it took time to assemble their forces, they failed to stop the fortification, but took the field to attack Hippocrates' force on its way back to Attica.

The two armies met on a slope outside of Delium where the Thebans held the higher ground. Hippocrates' army of Athenians and their allies had 7,000 hoplites and some cavalry, but no light infantry as these had been sent on ahead toward Attica since most lacked arms. The Athenians took position on the right and left sides of their battle line and their allies took the center. The larger Boeotian force from Thebes and its allies included 7,000 hoplites, 10,000 light infantry, 1,000 cavalry, and 500 *peltasts*. The Thebans took the right side of the battle line and assembled themselves 25 ranks deep while the rest of the force lined up probably in more normal formations of 6–8 ranks. Pagondas placed cavalry and light troops on his flanks for protection. Although Thucydides provides prebattle speeches for both generals, these are rhetorical compositions intended to fit the situation and his own interpretation of motivations.

The Thebans moved downhill and the Athenians closed with them at a run. The Athenians on the right of the battle line savaged the Boeotians they encountered and the Thebans at the opposite end of the battlefield slowly made progress against their opponents. Pagondas seized the opportunity to send some cavalry from his right flank to his left behind the slope to surprise the Athenians. When the cavalry appeared over the hill, the Athenians on the right panicked and fled just as the dense Theban formation broke the opposition in front of them. The Athenians fled in all directions with the Boeotians in vigorous pursuit. The Boeotians killed Hippocrates and 1,000 hoplites in addition to numerous camp followers and others who had been returning to Athens. Several days later the Boeotians, with assistance from Corinthian hoplites, captured and dismantled the Athenian fortification at Delium. This Athenian defeat occurred the same winter as Brasidas' campaign against Amphipolis and contributed to the climate for peace the following year.

Lee L. Brice

See also: Athens; Brasidas; Peloponnesian War, Overview; Phalanx, Hoplite; Sparta; Thebes

References

Kagan, Donald. *The Peloponnesian War*. New York: Penguin, 2003.

Lazenby, J. F. *The Peloponnesian War: A Military Study*. New York: Routledge, 2004.

Strassler, Robert B., ed. *The Landmark Thucydides: A Comprehensive Guide to the Peloponnesian War*. New York: Free Press, 1998.

Tritle, Lawrence A. *A New History of the Peloponnesian War*. Malden, MA: Wiley-Blackwell, 2010.

Tritle, Lawrence A. and Brian Campbell, ed. *The Oxford Handbook of Classical Military History*. Oxford: Oxford University Press, 2012.

Dionysius I

Born around 430 BCE, Dionysius rose to prominence in fighting against Carthage in 409. In 406 the people of Syracuse elected him general, but assisted by Greek mercenaries, he seized power as Dionysius I and became a tyrant. He became infamous for his ruthlessness, brutality, and desire to increase his own wealth and power, but in the process he played a key role in changing Greek warfare in the fourth century.

Dionysius first subdued other Greek city-states in eastern Sicily and then waged a protracted struggle with Carthage for control of Sicily. At first he relied on large numbers of Greek mercenaries, but around 399 he began a comprehensive program to develop new weapons, including siege engines and warships. Assembling highly paid engineers and craftsmen, he in effect established the world's first true ordnance research and development group. In 397 these efforts paid off when he fielded a number of new specialized siege engines in an attack on the Carthaginian outpost, Motya, where he won a great victory in 396. The weapons employed included massive rolling siege towers and the earliest recorded artillery pieces—mechanical tension-powered catapults. In this way Dionysius introduced Eastern siege techniques to Greek warfare and added some new techniques of his own.

In 396, however, a Carthaginian counteroffensive by Himilcar retook the outposts and even led to the siege of Syracuse itself. An outbreak of plague among the Carthaginians enabled Dionysius to defeat them in 395 and conclude a treaty. In 390 Dionysius invaded Southern Italy and, allied with the Lucanians, defeated the Italiote League in 389. Dionysius' capture of Rhegium in 387 gave him control of Southern Italy.

Dionysius was also occasionally active in Greece where he maintained good relations with Sparta. Throughout his reign he hired many Greek mercenaries. Sparta and Corinth assisted him in defeating Himilcar's siege in 395. He traveled to Greece in 388 on a Delphic embassy and returned in

387 to help Sparta impose the King's Peace. Dionysius sent forces again during 369–368 to fight against Thebes, as a result of which he received Athenian citizenship.

In 383 Dionysius renewed the war with Carthage, invading its stronghold of western Sicily. At first successful, he later suffered a major defeat at Cronium in 378 and was forced to conclude a peace treaty that included a large indemnity and the cession of substantial territory. His final effort against Carthage during 368–367 ended in his death in 367. A bold commander and military innovator, Dionysius' protracted wars weakened the Greek position in Sicily, but his innovations in siege tactics made it to Greece, thus changing the nature of warfare.

Spencer C. Tucker and Lee L. Brice

See also: Artillery; King's Peace; Mercenaries; Sicily

References

Caven, Brian. *Dionysius I: Warlord of Sicily*. New Haven, CT: Yale University Press, 1990.

Sanders, Lionel J. *Dionysius I of Syracuse and Greek Tyranny*. London: Croom Helm, 1987.

E

Epameinondas

Theban general in the fourth century BCE, Epameinondas, with his friend Pelopidas, experimented with new hoplite tactics. His efforts led to the Theban hegemony of Greece during 371–362, the end of Spartan dominance, and influenced the reforms of Philip II of Macedon.

Born in Thebes ca. 418, we know little with certainty about his early life. In 385 he reportedly participated in the siege of Mantinea where he saved the life of Pelopidas. He seems to have played a limited role in the 379 eviction of the Spartan garrison at Thebes.

His career becomes better known from 371 onward. Epameinondas represented Thebes at a congress in Sparta but refused to surrender Boeotian cities controlled by Thebes, preventing a general peace settlement. Then in July 371 he held overall command of Boeotian forces against those of Sparta and its allies in the Battle of Leuctra, winning a brilliant victory through the use of innovative tactics. This battle was a stunning upset of Sparta and established the predominance of Thebes as a land power. In 370 Epameinondas invaded Laconia (first time it ever occurred) and freed the Messenians from Spartan dominance. In 369 he invaded the Peloponnesus again, further diminishing Spartan hegemony there. About this time he was apparently tried on some charge relating to his command, but was acquitted.

In 368 Epameinondas served as a common soldier in Thessaly. Reinstated to his command at Thebes the following year, he returned to Thessaly with an army and liberated Pelopidas from the tyrant Alexander of Pherae. In 367 he again invaded the Peloponnesus and won over the Achaeans as allies. Epameinondas moved in 362 against a broad anti-Thebes alliance

After the battle at Leuctra the Thebans set up a monument on the battlefield, commemorating the victory by their general Epameinondas. This monument remains important as one of our best sources for the size of a Greek hoplite shield, depicted on top of the monument. (Lee L. Brice)

that included Sparta and Athens, meeting in battle at Mantinea. Employing all his innovations it was nearly a stunning victory, but Epameinondas died of his wounds, transforming it into a draw at best. In the aftermath of his death Theban hegemony quickly waned.

The two military innovations for which Epameinondas was most famous were the oblique advance and the massed left wing. He used the oblique advance by "refusing" the left of his line while advancing the right. He also employed an unusually dense formation on his left side, up to 40 ranks deep, whereas 6 or 8 ranks deep was customary. The combination of these tactics, which he employed in several battles, led to victory. Epameinondas was a brilliant tactician; his innovations greatly influenced Greek warfare.

Spencer C. Tucker and Lee L. Brice

See also: Athens; King's Peace; Leuctra, Battle of; Mantinea, Battles of; Pelopidas; Phalanx; Sparta; Thebes

References

Anderson, J. K. *Military Theory and Practice in the Age of Xenophon.* Berkeley, CA: University of California Press, 1970.

Buckler, John. *The Theban Hegemony.* Cambridge, MA: Harvard University Press, 1980.

Laforse, Bruce. "The Greek World 371–336." In *A Companion to the Classical Greek World*, ed. Konrad Kinzl, 544–59. Malden, MA: Wiley-Blackwell, 2006.

Strassler, Robert B., ed. *The Landmark Xenophon's Hellenika.* New York: Pantheon Books, 2009.

Eurymedon River, Battle of

The Battle of Eurymedon River, which occurred in 467 BCE and involved land and naval forces, was the last significant victory of the Delian League against Persia during the Persian Wars. The battle initiated a decade of quiet between the league and Persia.

In 466 Xerxes finally moved against the Delian League. He had his officers assemble a fleet at Eurymedon River in southern Asia Minor. Cimon led a large Delian League fleet of about 250 ships into the Eastern Mediterranean to forestall this effort. He adjusted construction of his triremes to permit carrying soldiers aboard.

When the two fleets met just off the river's mouth the Delian League ships won the initial impact so decisively that the Persian ships pulled for the shore and became entangled. In the general confusion Cimon captured a large portion of the enemy fleet, as many as 200 ships. The local Persian army started to march toward the river delta where Cimon was busy capturing ships and towing them away. Cimon beached a large portion of his fleet and immediately disembarked his soldiers and many rowers in support of them. The soldiers formed in a line of battle and charged the Persians. After some fighting the Persians fled. The Greeks pursued and captured the Persian camp and baggage train with much booty. Cimon then took the league fleet back out to sea and crushed the remaining Phoenician component of the Persian fleet.

In addition to the captured ships and booty, the victory was so complete that the Delian League completely dominated the Eastern Mediterranean for more than a decade. As a result of this dominance some members of the league may have begun to wonder why they continued paying dues, but for the time being the league basked in its enormous victory.

Lee L. Brice

See also: Cimon; Delian League; Greco-Persian Wars, Overview

References

Burn, A. R. *Persia and the Greeks: The Defence of the West.* Stanford, CA: Stanford University Press, 1984.

Cawkwell, George. *The Greek Wars: The Failure of Persia.* Oxford: Oxford University Press, 2005.

Hale, John. *Lords of the Sea: The Epic Story of the Athenian Navy and the Birth of Democracy.* New York: Viking Press, 2009.

G

Gaugamela, Battle of

In October of 331 BCE, Alexander the Great met the Persian king, Darius III, in battle for the last time. In the two years since they had last met at Issus, Darius had raised an enormous force while Alexander had captured the Phoenician coast down to Egypt. Although no one present could have predicted the consequences, this battle determined the fate of the Persian Empire and Alexander's campaign.

Following his conquest of Tyre and capture of Egypt in 332 Alexander rested his men over the winter. In the spring of 331, he marched back toward the Phoenician coast to pick up the route to Mesopotamia and the heart of the Persian Empire. Darius' cavalry shadowed and harassed Alexander's army, but did not block its crossing of the Euphrates. Numbers are notoriously difficult to pin down for ancient warfare, but based on modern estimates Alexander had a maximum of about 47,000 men: 31,000 heavy infantry (phalangites) and 9,000 light infantry (*peltasts*) along with 7,000 cavalry.

Since his defeat at Issus in 333, Darius III had assembled a new army. Although ancient sources credit Darius with a force as large as 1,000,000 men, this is an exaggeration for maintaining such a force would have been logistically unlikely. Modern estimates put the Persian Army at no more than 100,000 including numerous cavalry. By whatever measurement, Alexander's army was greatly outnumbered.

Darius arrived at the plain of Gaugamela first and prepared the ground for his chariots while he awaited Alexander. Darius had selected the location so that he could make effective use of his superior numbers. When Alexander arrived, his second-in-command, Parmenio, urged a night attack

57

to offset the numerical disadvantage, but Alexander refused and had his men rest. As it turned out, Darius had feared a night assault and had kept his troops awake all night.

Alexander, who fought with his Companion cavalry, commanded the right flank of his army, while Parmenio had charge of the left flank. Macedonian and Greek cavalry protected the two flanks. Alexander arranged the army in oblique formation, refusing his left and moving the army laterally to the right across the Persian front. His plan seems to have been to draw the Persians to the flanks, opening a weak point in the center of the Persian line. Everything depended on his own flanks holding until Alexander could detect this weakness and strike a decisive blow.

Darius positioned himself in the center of the Persian line with his best infantry. Bessus commanded the cavalry on the Persian left wing with chariots in front, while Mazaeus commanded the right flank of other cavalry. With their vast superior numbers of cavalry and much longer line, it appeared that the Persians must flank Alexander's army.

Darius ordered Bessus to release cavalry to ride around the Macedonian right wing and arrest Alexander's movement. Bessus committed some 11,000 cavalry to the effort, but they were halted by the numerically far inferior force of Macedonian cavalry and Greek mercenary infantry. Clearly Alexander's cavalry was far better disciplined and more closely knit than Persia's local detachments, which had never trained together.

Darius ordered the 100 chariots positioned in front of his left wing to attack Alexander's elite force of Companion cavalry on the Macedonian right. Alexander's infantry screen of javelin throwers, archers, and light infantrymen somewhat blunted the Persian chariot charge before it reached the Companions. The Companions then wheeled aside, allowing the remaining chariots to pass through unopposed when they came up against the lances of the infantry. The gap then closed, and the Persian charioteers were annihilated in the Macedonian rear.

Darius then ordered a general advance. Mazaeus, who commanded the Persian right wing, advanced against the Macedonian left led by Parmenio. Mazaeus also sent cavalry in an attempt to get around the Macedonian line. At the same time, Bessus sought to push men around the Macedonian right wing to envelop it. These efforts by Bessus and Mazaeus elongated the Persian line as Alexander had hoped, weakening its center. Mazaeus' job was especially difficult as his men had to travel a greater distance to engage Alexander's refused left wing.

Alexander watched for weakness in the Persian line, bringing up his reserves. Once he detected it, he led his Companion cavalry and light infantry in a great wedge-shaped formation into the breach. Twice the Macedonians burst through gaps in the Persian line and drove close to where Darius' chariot stood. Both Persian flanks were now threatened by the great gap that the Macedonians had torn in the center of the line.

The possibility of encirclement led Bessus to retreat, his forces suffering heavy casualties at the hands of the pursuing Macedonians. Darius, now himself in danger of being cut off, panicked and fled. With the Persians in wild retreat, the Macedonians vigorously pressed their advance, scattering the vast Persian host.

Alexander's left wing, heavily engaged with Mazaeus' men, could not keep pace with the rest of the Macedonian advance. Alexander's attempt to encircle Mazaeus failed, however, because his own cavalry drove the Persians back too quickly. The victory was nonetheless sweeping. The Macedonians reported their casualties in the battle at some 500 killed and up to 3,000 wounded while setting Persian losses at close to 50%.

Spencer C. Tucker

See also: Alexander the Great; Cavalry; Darius III; Issus, Battle of; *Peltasts*; Persian Empire; Phalanx, Macedonian; Tyre; Wars of Alexander the Great, Overview

References

Bosworth, A. B. *Conquest and Empire: The Reign of Alexander the Great.* Cambridge: Cambridge University Press, 1988.

Devine, A. M. "The Battle of Gaugamela: A Tactical and Source Critical Study." *Ancient World* 13 (1986): 87–116.

Heckel, Waldemar and Lawrence A. Tritle, eds. *Alexander the Great: A New History.* Malden, MA: Wiley-Blackwell, 2009.

Marsden, E. W. *The Campaign of Gaugamela.* Liverpool: Liverpool University Press, 1964.

Romm, James, ed. *The Landmark Arrian: The Campaigns of Alexander.* New York: Pantheon, 2010.

Gaza, Siege of

With Tyre captured in 332, the Macedonian Army set out on foot in July or August for Egypt. Some 160 miles from Tyre, the army encountered the fortress city of Gaza, situated on a rocky hill on the sole route between

Egypt and Syria. The city's governor, Batis, rejected calls for surrender. Siege operations were quite difficult, as the siege engines sank in the sand. On occasion the defenders sallied to destroy the Macedonian siege equipment. On one such foray Alexander was badly wounded in the shoulder by an arrow.

In two months the Macedonians built an earthen rampart topped by a wooden platform encircling Gaza, a mammoth undertaking. A breach was finally made in the walls, and Macedonian troops entered the city. The Macedonians had also carried out mining operations, and another group went in by a tunnel.

After heavy fighting, the city fell. Reportedly the Macedonians slew 10,000 defenders, and the women and children were all sold as slaves. Batis was among the captured. Alexander ordered him lashed by his ankles behind a chariot and dragged around the city walls until he was dead.

Although it was fortunate for Alexander that during these operations Darius III did not move against the Macedonian lines of communication, the successful sieges of both Tyre and Gaza thoroughly demonstrated Alexander's mastery of this type of warfare and greatly added to his mystique of invincibility.

Spencer C. Tucker

See also: Alexander the Great; Darius III; Issus, Battle of; Wars of Alexander the Great, Overview

References

Bosworth, A. B. *Conquest and Empire: The Reign of Alexander the Great.* Cambridge: Cambridge University Press, 1988.

Heckel, Waldemar and Lawrence A. Tritle, eds. *Alexander the Great: A New History.* Malden, MA: Wiley-Blackwell, 2009.

Romane, Patrick. "Alexander's Siege of Gaza, 332 BC." *Ancient World* 18 (1988): 21–30.

Granicus River, Battle of

The Battle at the Granicus River in 334 BCE was the first battle between Alexander's army and the forces of Persia. The satrapal force arrayed against Alexander was small in comparison to what Darius III could gather; its

Contemporary image of the Granicus River in Turkey, site of the first major battle between Alexander the Great and the Persian Empire in 334 BCE. (John W.I. Lee)

job was to stop Alexander's campaign. The battle was important for its propaganda value and because in this battle he used tactics he would use to great effect in later battles, but most of all because Alexander succeeded.

In 334 Alexander landed in Asia at Abydos and after a quick trip to Troy he moved on the Granicus River to engage the Persian satraps who met him there. Despite the inflated numbers in our sources, historians accept that the Persian force included about 10,000 cavalry and 4,000–5,000 Greek mercenaries. The site they chose was favorable for defense since Alexander's men would have to maneuver down one bank of the river under fire, cross the river despite the mud, current, and enemy fire, and ascend the opposite bank where the Persians awaited them. The Persian cavalry was arrayed on the bank with the Greek mercenaries in reserve behind them on higher ground. This disposition was not because they were uncertain of the mercenaries' loyalties, but because it was a standard Persian tactic in situations like this one.

Alexander's army outnumbered the Persians with 5,100 cavalry, 12,000 infantry and 1,000 light infantry. He arrayed his army for battle with the Macedonian phalanx and *hypaspists* in the center flanked by the Companion cavalry on the right and the allied cavalry on the left. The various accounts of the battle are highly stylized and focused on Alexander but it is possible to discern certain aspects of the action. Alexander started by setting his right flank cavalry in action. Once these had drawn the Persians into exposing a gap in their line Alexander charged forward on the right while Parmenio pushed across the river on the Macedonian left flank. As the cavalry charged into the Persian line the phalanx worked its way across the river and with its added force routed the cavalry in front.

The Greek mercenaries sought surrender, but Alexander chose to punish them as an example for violating the decrees of the League of Corinth forbidding any Greeks to oppose the campaign. The Macedonians had to fight the mercenaries, who stood their ground until only about 2,000 remained. The survivors went to Macedonia to labor in the mines. Alexander buried the Macedonian dead with great honor and sent spoils back to Athens where the shields were hung on the Parthenon with a dedicatory inscription. He was well aware of the propaganda value of such actions. The victory freed him from immediate military threat and made it possible for him to win open support among the Greek cities along the coast.

Lee L. Brice

See also: Alexander the Great; Cavalry; Darius III; Persian Empire; Phalanx, Macedonian; Wars of Alexander the Great, Overview

References

Devine, A. M. "Demythologizing the Battle of the Granicus." *Phoenix* 40 (1986): 265–78.

Heckel, Waldemar. *The Conquests of Alexander the Great*. Cambridge: Cambridge University Press, 2008.

Heckel, Waldemar and Lawrence A. Tritle, eds. *Alexander the Great: A New History*. Malden, MA: Wiley-Blackwell, 2009.

Romm, James, ed. *The Landmark Arrian: The Campaigns of Alexander*. New York: Pantheon, 2010.

Greco-Persian Wars, Causes of

Unlike some wars that have many causes some of which are difficult to identify, the Persian Wars that lasted during 492–451/449 BCE can be traced back to one cause, both pretext and actual—the Ionian Revolt in 499 BCE. It started out as a war of revenge and became a war of conquest.

In 499 the Ionian Greeks revolted against Achaemenid Persian rule. The precise cause of the revolt remains a point of contention among historians and is actually not important to understanding the later war in Greece. The rebellion's leadership sought support in mainland Greece, but only the cities of Athens and Eretria sent support. The rebels burned Sardis, but achieved little else. Darius slowly ground down the opposition until the revolt ended in 493.

The Persian side is worth considering. Persian leadership saw any response against Athens and Eretria as justified because they involved themselves in Darius' affairs when they assisted the Ionian Greek rebels. When Sparta joined them by not submitting (on behalf of the Peloponnesian League) to the demand of "earth and water" they also caught the king's eye. Whether Darius' overall goal in 492 and Xerxes' goal in 480 extended beyond chastising Athens and Eretria cannot now be known with certainty, although the size of their efforts suggests that the campaign was going to involve more than punishing two cities.

Darius I launched a land invasion of Greece in 492 from the north with the putative goal of chastising Athens and Eretria. The main reason this force did not accomplish its goal was the storm that wrecked the fleet off Mount Athos. Since Persia was not distracted by serious internal problems at the time it is no surprise he sent the invasion force in 490. When the Marathon campaign ended in Persian defeat, Darius I, and later Xerxes I, could have ignored Greece because of its insignificance. It was a conflict Persians could ignore, but no one should be surprised that Darius wanted revenge and that Xerxes followed up on his father's plans.

The campaigns of 492 and 490 may have been the result of the king's desire to punish the Greeks, but the campaigns of 480 and 479 provide good evidence that for Xerxes at least the cause or goal of the war was probably conquest of Greece. Regardless of its actual size, the scale of the Persian invasion force suggests that he intended to conquer and occupy Greece. When Xerxes chose to leave his army in Greece under Mardonius' command following the Battle of Salamis it was clear to everyone that the war would continue, and it further suggests that Xerxes intended to make Greece a satrapy.

The cause for the continuing war after the battles of Plataea and Mycale was the decision of some Greeks—initially the Hellenic Alliance and then the Delian League—to continue fighting Persia and freeing Greek territories that would then become members of the league. Once Cimon won at Eurymedon in 467 the war only continued because Athens benefited more from continuing the conflict than it expected to from peace.

Regardless of the causes for the war continuing, the origin of the Persian Wars can be isolated to Darius' desire for revenge on Greece following the Ionian Revolt.

Lee L. Brice

See also: Darius I; Delian League; Eurymedon River, Battle of; Greco-Persian Wars, Consequences of; Greco-Persian Wars, Overview; Hellenic Alliance; Herodotus; Ionian Revolt; Mardonius; Peloponnesian League; Persian Empire; Xerxes I

References

Burn, A. R. *Persia and the Greeks: The Defence of the West.* Stanford, CA: Stanford University Press, 1984.

Cawkwell, George. *The Greek Wars: The Failure of Persia.* Oxford: Oxford University Press, 2005.

Lazenby, J. F. *The Defense of Greece, 490–479 B.C.* Warminster: Aris and Phillips, 1993.

Sabine, Philip, Hans Van Wees, and Michael Whitby, eds. *The Cambridge History of Greek and Roman Warfare*, vol. 1. Cambridge: Cambridge University Press, 2007.

Strassler, Robert B., ed. *The Landmark Herodotus: The Histories.* New York: Anchor Books, 2009.

Greco-Persian Wars, Consequences of

The Persian Wars ended in 451 BCE when hostilities ceased and may have been sealed with the Peace of Callias in 449 BCE. There were short- and long-term consequences of the peace, but the military impact of the wars was emerging well before the two sides made peace.

The first consequences of the war were the immediate changes in Greece. While the 492 campaign did not have much impact in Greece, during the 490 campaign the cities of Naxos and Eretria were sacked and their inhabitants enslaved. Athens gained great prestige as a result of the victory at Marathon. During the 480–479 campaign the Persians burned Athens twice as well as several other Greek cities. After the Battle of Plataea, the

Table 1 Key Military Events of the Greco-Persian Wars

Event Name	Date	Participants	Key Commanders (if known)	Victor
Ionian Revolt	499–494	Persia vs Ionian Greeks, Athens, and Eretria		Persia
Persian campaign in Thrace and Macedon	492	Persia	Mardonius	
Darius sends fleet against Eeretria. Eretria captured	490	Persia vs Eretria	Datis and Artaphrenes	Persia
Battle of Marathon	Aug/Sept 490	Persia vs Athens & Plataea	Miltiades, Datis and Artaphrenes	Athens
Battle of Thermopylae	Aug. 480	Persia vs Hellenic Alliance	Leonidas, Mardonius	Persia
Battle of Artemisium	Aug. 480	Persia vs Hellenic Alliance	Themistocles and Eurybiades, Ariabignes/Ariamenes	Hellenes
Battle of Salamis	Sept. 480	Persia vs Hellenic Alliance	Eurybiades and Themistocles, Ariabignes/Ariamenes	Hellenes
Battle of Plataea	June 479	Persia vs Hellenic Alliance	Pausanias, Mardonius	Hellenes
Battle of Mycale	June 479	Persia vs Hellenic Alliance	Leotychidas and Xanthippus, Tigranes	Hellenes
Campaign on Cyprus	478	Hellenic Alliance vs Persia	Pausanius,	Hellenes
Capture of Byzantium	478	Hellenic Alliance vs Persia	Pausanius,	Hellenes
Battle of Eurymedon River	469	Delian League vs Persia	Cimon, Ariomandes	Hellenes
Campaign in Egypt	460–455	Delian League vs Persia	Achaemenes and Megabyzus	Persia
Campaign on Cyprus	451	Delian League vs Persia	Cimon	Hellenes

This table lists events with the date, participants, commanders if known, and outcome. Participants are listed in order of which side initiated the event.

Persian force had withdrawn from Greece. Once they had withdrawn the destroyed cities had to be cleaned up and rebuilt thus providing opportunities for economic and artistic growth. This destruction was in addition to the numerous deaths that occurred in battle and raids during these campaigns and throughout the war. The death and displacement resulted in an overall decline in Greek population, but one from which Greece would recover in a couple of generations. Among these immediate impacts the most important one was that Persian forces withdrew from Greece and the Aegean.

Another immediate result of the Persian Wars was that Athens quickly became a military power, especially at sea. After Marathon the Athenians won immense prestige among the Greeks. As a result of the Battle of Salamis Athens emerged with more prestige and the dominant naval power in Greece and the Aegean, a position it would retain until the end of the fifth century. Its military success gave Athens the opportunity to form the Delian League in 478 and take the lead in continuing the Persian Wars.

The creation of the Delian League emerged out of the Persian Wars and had the long-term effect of increasing conflict in the Greek world. Through the league Athens created an empire. While the league certainly began as a defensive alliance it gradually changed into an Athenian Empire, a process that was under way after the battle at Eurymedon and accelerated after the Peace of Callias. Athens benefited from the empire not only in terms of protection, but the wealth gathered enlarged the Athenian fleet and made much reconstruction possible. Through the league Athens expanded its reach installing garrisons (*cleruchies*) in recalcitrant subjects and later even forced some cities to join the league. The threat Sparta perceived in the expansion of the Delian League and Athens' growing power in Greece led to the outbreak of the Peloponnesian War in 431.

The end of hostilities between Persia and Athens permitted leaders on both sides to deal with internal problems to which they had been unable to devote their full attention. Athens had allies that wanted to depart the alliance and conflict in the mainland with Spartan allies. Persia sought to crush the revolt in Egypt and reassert its control over all of Cyprus and several other unstable areas.

The short-term impact on Persia was surprisingly limited. When the 490 and 480–479 campaigns ended in defeat, Greece was insignificant and distant enough that Persian authorities could ignore the immediate results. Darius and Xerxes I both had long, successful reigns, as did Xerxes' successor Artaxerxes I who was king when the war ended. The wars were costly in terms of resources, but given its size the Achaemenid Empire could absorb these losses and expenses without discomfort. Despite the way in which the wars ended the Achaemenid Empire continued for more than a century.

In the long term, Persia took advantage of opportunities to meddle in Greek affairs with the goal of recovering control of Ionia, but not militarily. During the Peloponnesian War the king made a treaty with the Spartans to supply wealth and ships in return for uncontested control of Ionia. Later, during the Corinthian War, the King's Peace, and the Social War, the Persian leaders supported different Greek cities depending on which angle would give them control of Ionia. Although some Greek authors report the Persian activity as more of an attempt to embarrass Athens, this was a rationalization and is inconsistent with the monetary support provided to Athens during the Corinthian War. Playing each city against the others worked well and contributed to the weakening of the primary Greek cities by 355 while also gaining Ionia for Persia with minimal military effort.

In a sense, the fall of Achaemenid Persia can be linked back to the Persian Wars. During the early-mid fourth century conflict for hegemony in Greece the philosopher Isocrates called for Greeks to unite in a Panhellenic war of revenge against Persia. Jason of Pherae was one leader who took up Isocrates' message and used it to strengthen his power in Thessaly. Philip II of Macedon also used Isocrates' proposal to further justify formation of the League of Corinth in 338 and later his election as general for the Panhellenic war against Persia. After his father's death Alexander III made certain he was elected general for the war. Regardless of whether either Philip or Alexander had revenge as the actual goal of their planned invasion of Persia, both used the burning of Athens in 480 to justify their efforts toward war and rally support. When Alexander burned Persepolis in 330 he called it just revenge for the burning of Athens and declared the war of revenge over. In this sense the final result of the Persian Wars was the end of the Achaemenid Empire.

While the victory of the Greeks over the numerically superior Persians in the early fifth century has reverberated in Western culture from the ancient world to the present, it remains important to remember the impact for Greek warfare. Because the wars actually occurred and historians know their consequences there is little benefit in counterfactual speculation of what might have occurred in any instance. The withdrawal of Persia was most important in the short term while the fall of the Achaemenid Empire to Macedonia was the most important long-term consequence of the war.

Lee L. Brice

See also: Darius I; Delian League; Greco-Persian Wars, Causes of; Greco-Persian Wars, Overview; Hellenic Alliance; Herodotus; Peloponnesian War, Causes of; Persian Empire; Plataea, Battle of; Salamis, Battle of; Thermopylae, Battle of; Wars of Alexander the Great, Causes of; Xerxes I

References

Burn, A. R. *Persia and the Greeks: The Defence of the West*. Stanford, CA: Stanford University Press, 1984.

Cawkwell, George. *The Greek Wars: The Failure of Persia*. Oxford: Oxford University Press, 2005.

Lazenby, J. F. *The Defense of Greece, 490–479 BC*. Warminster: Aris and Phillips, 1993.

Sabine, Philip, Hans Van Wees, and Michael Whitby, eds. *The Cambridge History of Greek and Roman Warfare*, vol. 1. Cambridge: Cambridge University Press, 2007.

Strassler, Robert B., ed. *The Landmark Herodotus: The Histories*. New York: Anchor Books, 2009.

Greco-Persian Wars, Overview

The Greco-Persian Wars (492–451/449 BCE), a series of conflicts, were collectively a watershed event in not only Greek but also Western history. The might of the enormous Achaemenid Empire failed to conquer the small region of Greece during two invasions leading to naval war in the Eastern Mediterranean for nearly 30 years. The results of the conflict were enormous for Greece and the entire Eastern Mediterranean world.

Despite their immensity as a conflict, sources for the wars, especially the first couple of decades, are sparse. Herodotus of Halicarnassus wrote a work, *The History*, that has survived and remains our primary historical source for the entire war. Our accounts of the battles in 490, 480, and 479 come entirely from his text. Herodotus' account is problematic for a variety of reasons not least of which is his bias and so the accuracy of some of his details remains an issue of debate among scholars. There are also fragments of several near-contemporary works and plays, including *The Persians* by Aeschylus, that preserve some details. There are also some Greek and Persian inscriptions that provide additional details. Without these sources historians would be entirely reliant on later, secondary, ancient authors some of whose accounts of the wars are more trustworthy than others. Despite these limitations, it is possible to get a general sense of the course of the war.

The Persian Wars began in 492 when Darius I launched a land invasion of Greece from the north. The campaign reasserted Persian control in Thrace and established ties with Macedon, but before it could proceed south the support fleet wrecked in a storm off Chalcidice at Mount Athos. The land force suffered attack in Thrace and then returned to Persia. In 491 Darius sent ambassadors to the Greek city-states demanding "earth and water" as symbols of subjugation. Most cities submitted, but Sparta (speaking for the Peloponnesian League) and Athens killed the ambassadors sent to them.

Darius then sent a force in 490 under Datis and Artaphernes to chastise Eretria and Athens. The force stopped in Naxos, burning the city and enslaving the people it captured before moving on to Euboea where it laid siege to Eretria. After several days the city was betrayed to the Persians who razed it and enslaved the people. Then the force continued to Athenian territory, landing at Marathon. The Athenian Army marched out and faced off for several days while waiting for Spartan assistance. The Athenians charged when the Persians were preparing to depart and won a decisive victory. The Persian ships then sailed to Athens, but seeing opposition when they arrived did not land at the city's port and sailed home. Darius, in response to the failure started preparing for a new, larger campaign but was delayed by a revolt in Egypt and his own death.

In 481 Xerxes I assembled an enormous army and sent ambassadors to demand "earth and water" in advance from the Greeks—except Sparta and Athens—to see which cities would oppose him. The 25 cities that did not submit formed the Hellenic Alliance and decided that the Spartans should command. In 480 Xerxes invaded through Thrace. Herodotus' account makes identifying trustworthy numbers of combatants difficult, but it was a ginormous army, at least 2–3 times the strength of the Hellenic League, and required extensive logistical planning. A fleet sailed along the coast protecting the army from surprise attack and carrying supplies. The Hellenic Alliance initially took up position in the Valley of Tempe, but when they learned the position could be turned they pulled back to the pass at Thermopylae. Under Leonidas' leadership the Greeks were able to delay Xerxes' advance for a few days, and the alliance fleet was able to stop simultaneously the Persian fleet at the Strait of Artemisium. Once the pass was turned Leonidas sent the rest of the alliance force away and remained

PERSIAN EMPIRE, C. 500 BCE

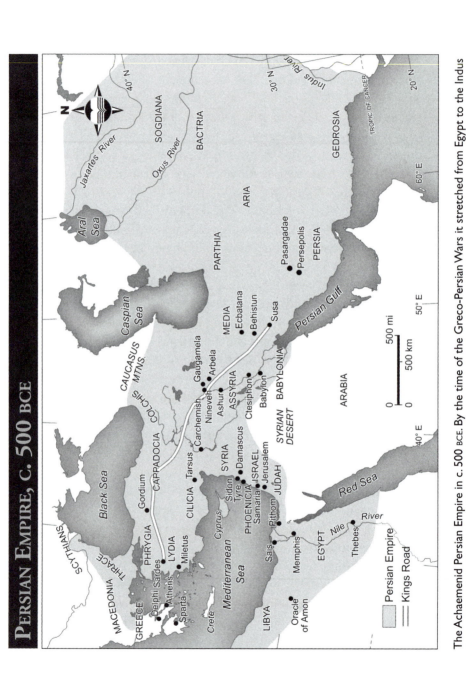

The Achaemenid Persian Empire in c. 500 BCE. By the time of the Greco-Persian Wars it stretched from Egypt to the Indus River and included Northern Greece and Thrace. A network of royal roads made communication easier.

behind with his picked Spartans and men from Thespiae and Thebes to delay Xerxes and give the alliance forces time to get away.

Knowing the Persians were coming Themistocles arranged to evacuate the Athenian people to Salamis. While some of the Peloponnesians argued in favor of holding a line against the Persians at the isthmus near Corinth, Themistocles finally convinced the alliance to fight Persia at sea near Salamis despite being outnumbered. After some maneuvering by both sides, the fleets engaged in the straits of Salamis. Xerxes watched as his fleet, unable to exploit their larger numbers, fell to the Hellenic force. Afterward Xerxes killed some of his officers and returned to Persia, but left his army behind under Mardonius' command. He withdrew northward to Thessaly and Macedonia where he could be certain of logistical support from his allies.

The following year Mardonius moved the Persian army south and recaptured Athens. After sacking it again he withdrew when he learned that King Pausanias of Sparta was approaching with a large Hellenic Alliance force. Mardonius set out to confront the Greek forces at the centrally located city of Plataea in Boeotia, safe in the knowledge that his force was probably nearly double his opponents. In the battle the Greek force became split, but managed to hold their own killing Mardonius and defeating the Persian force after a full day of fighting. The captured spoils were dedicated to the gods at the primary sanctuaries of Olympia and Delphi. At about the same time, according to Herodotus, another Hellenic Alliance force won a large naval and land victory at Mycale in Ionia. The combined victories and continued pressure by the alliance forced the Persians to withdraw from the Greek mainland and pull back to Persia. Some historians treat the Persian Wars as having ended in 479; however, it is important to recall that for the Greeks the war did not end for another 30 years.

The Hellenic Alliance continued pushing against the Persians and securing Greek territory in Ionia and the Aegean, most importantly Sestos in the Hellespont and Byzantium that gave the alliance access to the Black Sea. After some disagreements in 478 between some alliance members over leadership, the Spartans withdrew and took the rest of the Peloponnesian League members with them. The Athenians then founded a new alliance, which historians call the Delian League, in order to continue to fight Persia and free Greek cities in Ionia and the Aegean. The league was successful in keeping the pressure on Persia, especially its fleet, and gaining new members. The conflict continued steady even if at low frequency until in 467 a large league force under the command of Cimon of Athens scored a major sea and land victory at the Eurymedon River. Cimon then

Table 2 Numbers of men and ships during the Greco-Persian Wars

Event	Date	Number	Source
Persian losses in Thrace campaign	492	300 ships, 20,000 men	Herodotus 6.44
Datis' and Artaphrenes' campaign strength	490	600 triremes	Herodotus 6.95
		90,000 men	Simonides F 90 Bergk
		500,000 men	Lysias 2.2 and Plato *Menexenos* 240a
		200,000 men, 10,000 cavalry	Cornelius Nepos *Miltiades* 4.1, 5.6
Athens' strength at Marathon		Unknown	
Persian losses at Marathon		6400 dead and 7 ships captured	Herodotus 6.117
Athenian losses at Marathon		192 dead	Hdt. 6.117
Xerxes' strength for invasion	480	1,700,000 infantry, 80,000 cavalry, 20,000 camel and chariot fighters, 1207 triremes and 3000 small ships	Hdt. 7.60, 184–187
Xerxes' total force at Thermopylae	480	5, 283,220 men	Hdt. 7.187
		800,000 infantry	Ctesias of Cnidus *Archidamus* 100
		700,000 infantry	Isocrates *Panathenaicus* 49
		40–50,000 infantry	Thucydides 6.33.5
		1,000,000+ men	Diodorus Siculus 11.5.2

Event	Date	Number	Source
Hellenic force at Thermopylae	480	400 ships	Hdt. 7.190
		5200 men	Hdt. 7.210
		6400 infantry	Diodorus Siculus 11.4.5–7
Hellenic force at Artemisium		271 triremes	Hdt. 8.1
		280 triremes or 330 triremes	Diodorus Siculus 11.12.4, 13.2
Persian losses at Thermopylae		20,000 men	Hdt 8.24
Persian losses during Artemisium		250 ships	Hdt. 7.194, 8.11,14
Hellenic losses at Thermopylae		3000	Hdt. 8.26
Hellenic naval strength at Salamis		378 triremes and 4 penteconters	Hdt. 8.48
Persian losses at Salamis		unreported	
Hellenic losses at Salamis		unreported	
Persian strength before Plataea	479	300,000 men, incl. cavalry	Hdt. 8.100–101, 113, 9.32
		200,000 men	Diodorus Siculus 11.28.4
		500,000 men	Diodorus Siculus 11.30.1
Greek allies of Persia at Plataea		50,000	Hdt. 9.32
Hellenic strength before Plataea		38,700 holites, 69,500 light troops, and 1800 reinforcements = 110,000 men	Hdt. 9.29–30
		100,000 men	Diodorus Siculus 11.30.1
Persian losses at Plataea		257,000 men dead, 40,000 escaped with Artabazus	Hdt. 9.70

(Continued)

Table 2 Numbers of men and ships during the Greco-Persian Wars (*Continued*)

Event	Date	Number	Source
Greek losses at Plataea		100,000 men dead, up to 400,000 escaped with Artabazus	Diodorus Siculus 11.32.5
		759 men	Hdt. 9.69–70
		10,000+ men	Diodorus Siculus 11.33.1
Persian naval strength at Samos	479	300 ships	Hdt. 8.130
Persian naval strength at Mycale		Less than 300 ships	Hdt. 9.96
Persian army at Mycale		60,000 men	Hdt. 9.96
Hellenic naval strength at Aegina		110 ships	Hdt. 8.131
Hellenic naval strength at Mycale		250 ships	Diodorus Siculus 11.34.2
Hellenic army at Mycale		unreported	
Persian losses at Mycale		40,000 dead, all ships burned	Diodorus Siculus 11.36.6
Hellenic losses at Mycale		unreported	

Numbers of men and ships during the Greco-Persian Wars. This table is intended to provide a sense of how ancient sources reported the size of Persian and Hellenic armies and losses. Accurate numbers would have been extremely difficult for sources to learn and really did not matter to ancient authors as much as the scale the numbers convey.

chased the Persian fleet from the seas around Cyprus, a regular activity of Delian League commanders. After the victory the war entered a long quiet phase.

In the period between 461 and 454 the Delian League campaigned in Egypt in support of the revolt against Persia. Although the campaign initially made progress, by 454 the large force had been destroyed. Engagements in Cyprus in 451 resulted in the death of Cimon and withdrawal of the league force there so that the campaign that year was effectively a draw. Following the defeat in Egypt and the draw in Cyprus, active campaigning between Athens and Persia ended. The existence of a formal peace treaty, the Peace of Callias, has been a subject of considerable debate among historians now as well as in the ancient world. Herodotus and Thucydides do not explicitly mention it although there are suggestions in both their works that support its existence. The peace has traditionally been dated to 449 although there were certainly efforts to negotiate peace as early as 466. The treaty seems only to have ended hostilities although it is possible that it recognized Athenian control of the league. The end of hostilities was encouraged not only by the events in the Mediterranean, but also by fighting in Greece between members of the Delian and Peloponnesian leagues. Persia also had its hands full with internal revolts.

Regardless of whether there was a treaty, hostilities ceased and the Persian Wars ended. Although Persian leaders meddled in Greek affairs later, events that were often seen by Greek authors as having been inspired by the earlier wars, direct hostilities were over. The Persian Empire survived and thrived for more than a century. The conflict continued to reverberate in Greek warfare until the campaign of Alexander the Great.

Lee L. Brice

See also: Athens; Cimon; Darius I; Delian League; Eurymedon River, Battle of; Greco-Persian Wars, Causes of; Greco-Persian Wars, Consequences of; Hellenic Alliance; Ionian Revolt; Marathon, Battle of; Mardonius; Mycale, Battle of; Peloponnesian League; Persian Empire; Plataea, Battle of; Salamis, Battle of; Thermopylae, Battle of; Wars of Alexander the Great, Causes of; Xerxes I

References

Burn, A. R. *Persia and the Greeks: The Defence of the West*. Stanford, CA: Stanford University Press, 1984.

Cawkwell, George. *The Greek Wars: The Failure of Persia.* Oxford: Oxford University Press, 2005.

Lazenby, J. F. *The Defense of Greece, 490–479 BC.* Warminster: Aris and Phillips, 1993.

Sabine, Philip, Hans Van Wees, and Michael Whitby, eds. *The Cambridge History of Greek and Roman Warfare*, vol. 1. Cambridge: Cambridge University Press, 2007.

Strassler, Robert B., ed. *The Landmark Herodotus: The Histories.* New York: Anchor Books, 2009.

H

Hellenic Alliance

The Hellenic Alliance refers to the loose confederation of Greek city-states that joined together in 481 BCE to oppose the imminent Persian invasion by Xerxes. Although not formalized into a league, the alliance made it possible for the Greeks to unite and defeat the Persians during 480–479.

According to Herodotus, our only primary source for these events, after Darius I's failed Marathon campaign of 490 he planned to get revenge with an enormous army. His son Xerxes I followed through on his father's plans and raised an army to invade and subject the Greeks. When the Greek city-states who were inclined to resist learned in 481 about the scale of Xerxes' preparations they sought each other out and formed an alliance. The 31 city-states that joined together and swore oaths included Athens and members of the Peloponnesian League. They did not institutionalize the arrangement so it would perhaps be inappropriate to call it a league, although some historians use that name. The allies met, probably in Corinth, and decided to have Sparta as military leader and seek additional allies as far away as Sicily.

The allies initially tried to help Thessaly by sending an allied force of as many as 10,000 men north to the Valley of Tempe to block the land route into Greece, but when they found out that the position could easily be turned they withdrew and decided to take up position at Thermopylae and Artemisium. When Leonidas realized his position would be turned he sent most of the Greek forces away so they would be available to defend their cities. After a debate in which the Peloponnesians wanted to build a wall across the isthmus, Themistocles successfully argued in favor of a

After the victory at Plataea in 479 BCE the Hellenic Alliance used part of the captured spoils to set up a golden tripod atop a column of three intertwined snakes engraved with the names of the allied cities and their dedication to Apollo. The column was later removed from Delphi to Constantinople (modern Istanbul) by the Roman emperor Constantine. (Lee L. Brice)

naval defense at Athens. The allied Greek naval forces won a huge victory at Salamis. Xerxes returned to Persia, but left his army behind.

After some Persian maneuvering in early 479 the large allied Greek army met and defeated the invaders at Plataea. At about the same time (Herodotus reports it as the same day) another mostly naval allied force won a victory in Asia Minor at Mycale. The alliance kept pressure on the fleeing Persians and within a year they had withdrawn completely from the Greek mainland. In 478 after a disagreement about military leadership the Spartans and their allies in the Peloponnesian League withdrew from the alliance and Athens reconstituted it as the more formal Delian League.

With the spoils from the victory at Plataea the allies dedicated statues at Olympia, Isthmia, and a tripod was dedicated to Apollo that sat atop a triple-serpent column engraved with the names of the 31 allies. The column and tripod were set up in Delphi, but later moved to Constantinople by Constantine. The remains of the snake column with the legible list of cities can still be seen in Istanbul.

Lee L. Brice

See also: Artemisium, Battles of; Athens; Delian League; Greco-Persian Wars, Overview; Herodotus; Marathon, Battle of; Mycale, Battle of; Peloponnesian League; Plataea, Battle of; Salamis, Battle of; Thermopylae, Battle of

References

Cawkwell, George. *The Greek Wars: The Failure of Persia*. Oxford: Oxford University Press, 2005.

Lazenby, J. F. *The Defense of Greece, 490–479 BC*. Warminster: Aris and Phillips, 1993.

Osborne, Robin. *Greece in the Making, 1200–479 BC*, 2nd edition. Routledge: New York, 2006.

Strassler, Robert B., ed. *The Landmark Herodotus: The Histories*. New York: Anchor Books, 2009.

Herodotus

Herodotus of Halicarnassus wrote *The History*, the earliest surviving (and probably the first) Greek narrative history. His work is important for military historians because it includes our fullest history of the Greco-Persian Wars (490–445) and was composed in the latter half of the fifth century BCE, close enough to the events it described to be a primary source.

Born in the early fifth century in Halicarnassus, Herodotus was not from Greece. He was Greek, but Halicarnassus is a coastal city in southwest Asia Minor, in the Persian satrapy of Caria. He went into exile in the mid-fifth century and may have traveled in Asia Minor, the Eastern Mediterranean, Egypt, and perhaps the Achaemenid Empire before settling in Athens. His purpose was to record his research (*histore*) into the origins and events of the Persian Wars. In the process, he reports history along with much that we now call ethnography. In addition to the Persian Wars he includes some information on events in Athens during the latter half of the fifth century.

Herodotus did not participate in the Persian Wars, but he travelled widely, saw much that he reports, and interviewed locals when he could. He wrote about the Persian Wars close enough to the events that he could interview participants and survivors in addition to seeing the sites. This quality of his work makes it critical for understanding the war as well as other events. Herodotus invented what we now call the historical narrative. This means that he provides readers with the earliest form of battlefield narrative.

The primary difficulties inherent in using his work are his biases and certain aspects of his method. As a foreigner composing his book in

Athens, Herodotus was consistently pro-Athenian. The result is that he tends to give Athenians the benefit of the doubt and makes their contemporary enemies, Thebes even more than Sparta, come off badly. The second aspect readers must be cautious about is his use of speeches. Like playwrights, Herodotus composed for his characters speeches that would express views, entertain, illuminate the speaker's character, demonstrate the author's skill, or convey certain observations, or all of these simultaneously. The speeches fit what the author needed a character to say or convey the author's views.

Herodotus' history of the Persian Wars encompassed nine "books." Given that it includes some events from as late as the early 420s, but no later, historians concluded that he must have completed it by 425.

Lee L. Brice

See also: Athens; Greco-Persian Wars, Overview; Ionian Revolt; Persian Empire

References

Roberts, Jennifer T. *Herodotus: A Very Short Introduction*. Oxford: Oxford University Press, 2011.

Strassler, Robert B., ed. *The Landmark Herodotus: The Histories*. New York: Anchor Books, 2009.

Hydaspes, Battle of the

At the Hydaspes (Jhelum) River in 326 BCE, Alexander the Great fought the Indian king Porus so he could continue marching through the Punjab. Although Alexander won and made peace with Porus, historians do not agree on whether this was a great or standard performance by Alexander since the sources for the battle are confusing and contradictory. Regardless, it was the last major pitched battle of Alexander's career.

In 326, after fighting his way across the various regions and tributaries of the upper Indus or Punjab as far as the Hydaspes River, Alexander encountered Porus, the king of the region between the Hydaspes and the Acesines (Chenab) rivers. Porus had refused to acknowledge and submit to Alexander's authority and so arrayed his smaller army on the east bank of the Hydaspes. Alexander, who had an army of up to 20,000 infantry and 5,000 cavalry was in a tough spot despite having a larger force because the river, which was swollen from the spring melt posed a difficulty and every time he tried to maneuver upstream or downstream the Indian cavalry moved with him. Porus seems to have had a smaller force so he stationed his 200 elephants in front of his infantry at the crossing.

Alexander posted a portion of his infantry and cavalry force under Craterus at the bank opposite Porus to pin him down. After some maneuvering over a few weeks to confuse Porus Alexander took a large body of his best infantry and cavalry at night more than 15 miles upstream where an island and a bend in the river would conceal his movements. He crossed the river with part of his force to establish a position and then had Meleagher bring over the rest. Porus responded by dispatching cavalry and chariots, but mud and small numbers hampered the Indians who were outnumbered and defeated.

Porus, realizing that he faced a large army on his side of the river, quickly maneuvered to better position and rearranged his lines, especially his elephants. Alexander then sent part of his cavalry on a long sweep to his left flank while he engaged with infantry and cavalry. The Indian chariots and archers were rendered impotent by the rain and mud. Once the battle began the source accounts are too confused to reassemble a coherent narrative. The combined weight of Alexander's charge, the sweeping force arriving in the rear of Porus' line and Craterus' force crossing the river to attack Porus' line in the rear was more than the Indians could handle. After more fierce combat Alexander's victory was complete and Porus surrendered.

Alexander allowed the Indian king to keep his kingdom and he gave Porus additional territory to control as a satrap east of the Hydaspes. The victory over Porus enabled Alexander to move on across the Punjab now that he had secured an ally on his flank and his rear as he marched and also secured reinforcements. Alexander commemorated his victory with a special issue of large silver coins showing Porus on the back of an elephant fleeing a Macedonian cavalryman.

While some historians have called the victory at the Hydaspes a high point of Alexander's tactical achievement, other historians, more critical of the confusing source tradition, have called it a typical day's work, an ordinary victory. The confusion in the sources means that either position is valid and the final evaluation must remain a point of debate.

Lee L. Brice

See also: Alexander the Great; Persian Empire; Phalanx, Macedonian; Wars of Alexander the Great, Overview

References

Bloedow, Edmund. "Alexander the Great at the Hydaspes River in 326 BC." *Athenaeum* 92.2 (2008): 499–534.

Bosworth, A. B. *Alexander and the East: The Tragedy of Triumph.* Oxford: Oxford University Press, 1996.

Heckel, Waldemar. *The Conquests of Alexander the Great.* Cambridge: Cambridge University Press, 2008.

Romm, James, ed. *The Landmark Arrian: The Campaigns of Alexander.* New York: Pantheon, 2010.

I

Ionian Revolt

In 499 BCE a number of Greek city-states on the coast of Asia Minor re-volted against Persian rule. Although they were initially successful and attracted limited support from the mainland, Darius I, the king of Persia, gathered his forces and gradually won back the territory in a series of campaigns that were mostly complete after the capture and sack of Miletus in 494. The aftermath of the revolt was Darius' campaign against Greece during 492–490.

The Achaemenid Persian kings had acquired political control of the Greeks on the coast of Asia Minor (mostly Ionia) when Cyrus conquered Lydia in the late sixth century. The kings ruled the region with satraps and employed local administrators, called tyrants by the Greeks, in the cities. In 499 after a failed Persian campaign against the Aegean island of Naxos, the Ionian Greeks revolted. Whether the cause of the revolt were the suddenly unbearable tyrants as Herodotus suggests, or economic woes from Persian taxation, as other historians have suggested or simply a de-sire to throw off the Persian yoke remains unknowable. Herodotus, our only source for the Ionian Revolt, blames the whole event on Aristagoras, the tyrant of Miletus, who had overextended himself financially with the local satrap, but this seems insufficient. There is little doubt that it was a much more widespread conspiracy and uprising than Herodotus suggests, as indicated by the rebellious cities issuing their coinage on a common weight standard for the first time.

Other rulers such as the kings in Cyprus and Caria joined the revolu-tion. The rebellion's leadership sought support in mainland Greece, but only the cities of Athens and Eretria sent naval support. Athens sent 20

The Battle of Lade near the islands off Miletus in 494 BCE was the last major naval battle of the Ionian Revolt. The Persian naval force defeated the Ionian Greeks in the waters by Lade Island near Miletos, effectively ending the Ionian Revolt. The islands are now land locked due to silt buildup in the former estuary. (John W. I. Lee)

penteconters while Eretria supplied 5 triremes. The rebels were initially successful in overthrowing the local city tyrants and then the army they raised marched on the local satrapal capital, Sardis, and burned it down. Because the Greeks had captured or destroyed much of his local navy Darius was not able to respond quickly, and that made him look vulnerable. In reality, this revolt was small in comparison to the size of the Achaemenid Empire and even when compared to some of its other revolts such as in Egypt. Darius raised forces and beginning in 497 slowly ground down the opposition, recapturing one region and then another to isolate the Ionians until 494 when he beat the rebel fleet at the Battle of Lade after which he captured and sacked Miletus. The city that had been the richest in the Aegean was destroyed, its population enslaved.

The revolt was completely settled by 493 and control restored by a royal decree that did not impose punitive measures, but offered local administrative compromises where practicable and renegotiated tax amounts from each city. Afterward Darius planned to punish the mainland Greeks who had supported the rebellion, Eretria and Athens. This effort was what led to the Persian Wars that began in 492.

Lee L. Brice

See also: Athens; Darius I; Greco-Persian Wars, Causes of; Herodotus; Persian Empire

References

Burn, A. R. *Persia and the Greeks: The Defence of the West.* Stanford, CA: Stanford University Press, 1984.

Cawkwell, George. *The Greek Wars: The Failure of Persia.* Oxford: Oxford University Press, 2005.

Strassler, Robert B., ed. *The Landmark Herodotus: The Histories.* New York: Anchor Books, 2009.

Iphicrates

An Athenian general (*strategos*) in the fourth century BCE, Iphicrates became famous for effectively using *peltasts* in the Corinthian War. In many ways his career typifies the hegemonic wars of the fourth century with their changing allegiances and reliance on mercenaries.

Iphicrates was an Athenian citizen, the son of a cobbler. The first time he appears in the historical record is for distinguished service at sea, probably in the Battle of Cnidus in 394. He probably served in a variety of military capacities during the early stages of the Corinthian War. According to Xenophon, Iphicrates was commander of a group of mercenaries as early as 392. The mercenary *peltasts* were funded with Persian wealth which allowed Iphicrates to institute a high level of discipline and regularity to the unit of *peltasts*. In 390 he distinguished himself at the battle of Lechaion as commander of *peltasts* when he caught a unit (*mora*, 600 men) of unsupported Spartan hoplites in open country. Taking advantage of his *peltasts'* ability to hit and run against the hoplites he and his men destroyed the Spartan unit. The mercenary *peltast* unit was let go in 389 when the Persian funds stopped and the unit's success was not repeated until the rise of the Macedonian Army under Philip and Alexander.

Athens then sent Iphicrates to the Hellespont with 1,200 *peltasts* and some ships where he ambushed and defeated the Spartan general Anaxibios in 388. After the King's Peace, Iphicrates became a mercenary commander for the kings of Thrace. He saw service in Macedon and Egypt before returning to Athens ca. 373. He was dispatched to Corcyra where he captured nine Syracusan triremes sent to assist Sparta, and then in 370 he was sent to assist Sparta against Epameinondas' invasion, but later Athens officially rebuked him for failing to engage the Thebans. He was then sent to Macedon where he helped secure the kingdom for the Argead mother of the future king Philip II. After failing to recapture Amphipolis for Athens despite several years of effort he served in Thrace again for a while. His last known appearances in the historical record were in service for Athens as a naval commander in the Social War, but his failure led to his trial and acquittal in 353.

Iphicrates' career demonstrates the success that a commander could achieve with highly trained, well-disciplined units and crews regardless of whether they were professionals. Some later ancient authors credited Iphicrates with several military innovations in terms of his *peltasts*, but given his mixed public record and the lack of evidence for such innovations in more contemporary sources it is highly unlikely he actually developed them.

Lee L. Brice

See also: Athens; Corinthian War; Epameinondas; King's Peace; Macedon; *Peltasts*; Sparta; Xenophon

References

Buckler, John. *Aegean Greece in the Fourth Century BC*. Leiden: Brill, 2003.

Pritchett, W. Kendrick. *The Greek State at War*, vol. 2. Berkeley, CA: University of California Press, 1975.

Strassler, Robert B., ed. *The Landmark Xenophon's Hellenika*. New York: Pantheon Books, 2009.

Issus, Battle of

The Battle of Issus was the first battle in which the two kings Alexander III and Darius III led their armies on the field of battle. The battle, which occurred in the fall of 333 BCE, was the result of Darius having brought a large army into Cilicia behind Alexander. Although he planned to crush his opponent, it turned out the other way as Darius fled the field of battle and left Alexander with much spoils and control of Anatolia.

In the summer of 333, Darius decided to take the field personally against Alexander and marched west with the forces then available to him.

Alexander, who had recovered from a serious mid-summer illness in Tarsus mopped up resistance in Cilicia and then pressed south, down the coast toward the Levant. Darius crossed into Cilicia from the east and marched on Issus, thus getting behind Alexander who was a couple of days march down the coast. Once he confirmed the reports that Darius had maneuvered behind him Alexander turned around and marched north to engage the Persian force.

The two armies met at the Pinarus River (Kuru Çay or Payas). Although the exact site of the battle remains a point of debate, it was enclosed on the east by a ridge and on the west by the sea. What matters is that although Darius was behind a river it was neither wide nor deep and the narrow space was not favorable since it would not permit him to fully employ his larger force. No source provides realistic numbers with which to estimate Darius' army size. Alexander marched north with his full army of about 40,000 men.

Arriving from his two-day march and deploying Alexander put his phalanx in the center and posted the Companion cavalry under his command on his right flank, with the *hypaspists* between cavalry and phalanx. On his left he stationed Parmenio with the allied Greek cavalry, joined just before the battle began by the Thessalians. Light troops guarded his flank on the ridge and he kept his allied Greek infantry in reserve. Darius put himself with his bodyguard in the center, flanked by Greek mercenaries on each side with Persian troops on the outside flanks and most of his cavalry on his right flank next to the sea. In an effort to break up the Macedonian formations Darius constructed obstacles on his center-right where the flat ground favored his enemy.

As the battle began the phalanx and *hypaspists* moved across the river and engaged Darius' infantry, permitting the Companion cavalry to charge into the Persian right flank causing the soldiers there to panic and flee. Although this part of the battle went well, Persian obstacles caused difficulty to the left element of the phalanx, and as a gap opened up in the line Darius' Greek mercenaries attacked causing numerous casualties. On the line next to the sea Parmenio had great difficulty holding back the Persian cavalry. The Companion cavalry, however, charged deeper into the Persian position pushing toward the center as the *hypaspists* did the same causing Darius to panic and flee with his bodyguard. Much of the Persian army broke and fled as they learned that the king had departed, leaving Alexander in control of the battlefield and Darius' camp, which was full of stores.

In the aftermath Alexander's army was exhausted from the day's march and battle so as soon as he could he sent Parmenio with the cavalry in pursuit. They captured the war treasury and Darius' family in Damascus. The victory in battle was of great propaganda value and the capture of Darius' family contributed further. Alexander had defeated the Persian king in battle. Although some historians have criticized Alexander's decision to not pursue Darius into Mesopotamia, it made more sense to march into Phoenicia to capture the ports from which a navy could harass his lines of communication as well as take the conflict to Greece.

Lee L. Brice

See also: Alexander the Great; Cavalry; Darius III; Persian Empire; Phalanx, Macedonian; Wars of Alexander the Great, Overview

References

Hammond, Nicholas G. L. "Alexander's Charge at the Battle of Issus in 333 BC." *Historia* 41 (4) (1992): 395–406.

Heckel, Waldemar. *The Conquests of Alexander the Great*. Cambridge: Cambridge University Press, 2008.

Heckel, Waldemar and Lawrence A. Tritle, eds. *Alexander the Great: A New History*. Malden, MA: Wiley-Blackwell, 2009.

Romm, James, ed. *The Landmark Arrian: The Campaigns of Alexander*. New York: Pantheon, 2010.

J

Jason of Pherae

Jason became tyrant of Pherae in Thessaly by 385 BCE. He was an important ally of Thebes at the time of its early hegemony, but became more so for uniting Thessaly under his military leadership and possibly planning a Panhellenic campaign against Persia.

The source tradition about Jason's origins is muddled and lost, but he seems to have been born into a leading family and was probably related (son?) to Lycophron who was tyrant of Pherae during 406–390. It is not known when Jason became tyrant or how. Before Jason became tyrant the city had long been friendly toward Sparta, but Jason broke the ties in favor of Thebes. He became leader (*tagos*) of Thessaly ca. 375/74 when his primary opponent surrendered, although the circumstances in which this occurred are lost.

Under his rule Thessaly continued its involvement in the hegemonic conflicts of the late 370s, but against Spartan interests. He opposed Phocis and had connections with Athens. He made a formal alliance with Thebes after 374, but did not fight at Leuctra in 371. When asked by Thebes to eliminate the remnants of the Spartan army then fleeing home he arranged an armistice. He expanded Thessalian territory to the north ca. 370 and signed a treaty with Amyntas, king of Macedon.

In this same year he strongly advocated Thessalian hegemony and planned to control the Pythian Games at Delphi with the backing of his mercenary army. Some ancient authors credited him with planning a Panhellenic campaign against Persia when he was assassinated in 370. With his death Thessaly became less friendly toward Thebes and then lost much of its preeminence. Although he has often been compared with Philip II of

Macedon, the source tradition is too thin for any treatment of Jason to be more than superficial.

Lee L. Brice

See also: Leuctra, Battle of; Philip II of Macedon; Sparta; Thebes

References

Buckler, John. *Aegean Greece in the Fourth Century BC*. Leiden: Brill, 2003.

Laforse, Bruce. "The Greek World 371–336." In *A Companion to the Classical Greek World*, ed. Konrad Kinzl, 544–59. Malden, MA: Wiley-Blackwell, 2006.

Strassler, Robert B., ed. *The Landmark Xenophon's Hellenika*. New York: Pantheon Books, 2009.

K

King's Peace

The King's Peace was an attempt in 387 BCE by Sparta, with Persian support, to assert its authority by imposing peace among the Greeks in the period of hegemonic conflicts in the early fourth century. This common peace was successful in ending the Corinthian War, but failed to stop the larger competition for power.

The Corinthian War that had begun in 395 with Persian money had by 389 shifted into the Aegean where Athens enjoyed a series of successes against Sparta. The Persian king, Artaxerxes II, concerned about the Athenians withdrew his support from the anti-Spartan alliance and was open to negotiations with Sparta. A series of Spartan naval successes in the Hellespont put them in a sufficiently strong position to negotiate with Artaxerxes for support. Antalcidas, a Spartan naval commander (*navarch*), traveled to Sardis in 388/87 and negotiated the terms so the agreement is also known as the Peace of Antalcidas.

In return for surrendering Cyprus and the Greek city-states of Asia Minor to Persia, Sparta received complete support from Artaxerxes II. The terms of the treaty, recorded by Xenophon, commanded that all Greek city-states (except for three old possessions of Athens) should be entirely independent of each other, the independence would be enforced by Sparta on behalf of Persia, and any city that did not agree would be at war with Persia.

Agesilaus II, king of Sparta, used the King's Peace to assert its authority in Greece, bullying some cities and acting vigorously against some former Peloponnesian League members. They took advantage of an opportunity in Thebes to install a garrison and support a pro-Spartan government there and in other Boeotian cities. Sparta moved against the Chalcidian federation and laid siege to Olynthus until it was dismantled. Sparta was immensely successful.

While the King's Peace did end the Corinthian War, it gave Sparta an opportunity to exercise hegemony in Greece. Spartan behavior toward other cities increased the likelihood that there would be a reaction and in 378 events started to work against them as Thebes ejected the Spartan garrison. A decade later Sparta would be on the receiving end of other city-states' armies.

Lee L. Brice

See also: Agesilaus II; Athens; Corinthian War; Persian Empire; Sparta; Thebes

References

Buckler, John. *Aegean Greece in the Fourth Century BC*. Leiden: Brill, 2003.

Rhodes, P. J. *A History of the Classical Greek World, 478–323 BC*, 2nd edition. Malden, MA: Wiley-Blackwell, 2010.

Strassler, Robert B., ed. *The Landmark Xenophon's Hellenika*. New York: Pantheon Books, 2009.

L

Leuctra, Battle of

In the summer of 371 BCE the Battle of Leuctra was fought between Thebes and its allies against Sparta and its allies. Sparta lost on the field of battle to superior Theban generalship. The result was the end of Spartan hegemony and the emergence of the Theban hegemony. Indeed, it was the end of Sparta as a major power in Greece.

The Spartan king, Agesilaus II, oversaw an effort in 371 to renew the Common Peace that had started in 387 as the King's Peace. During the meeting to formalize the agreement he forcibly excluded Thebes since the Theban leaders wished to swear the oath for all of Boeotia, in contravention of the Common Peace. Then the Spartan king Cleombrotus invaded Boeotian territory with orders to chastise Thebes for not respecting the terms of the Common Peace. After some maneuvering and countermaneuvering the armies of Thebes and Sparta met on the flat plain of Leuctra, a site chosen by the Spartans for its suitability in hoplite warfare.

The Spartan force of around 10,000 hoplites included 1,600 Lacedaimonians of whom only 700 were Spartan citizens. The rest of the army was made up of men from the Peloponnesian League members and mercenaries. There were also around 1,000 cavalry according to Plutarch. Cleombrotus faced serious repercussions (trial) in Sparta if he failed to fight, and Xenophon accused him and the other officers of drinking wine before the battle. When Cleombrotus prepared for the battle he put his Spartans in the place of honor on the right side of the battle line, eight ranks deep. The rest of the force was arrayed outward to his left. He arrayed his cavalry in an unusual position, in front of his lines.

In 371 BCE at the plain of Leuctra the Theban general Epameinondas defeated the Spartan army under its king Cleombrotus. The flat plain was perfect for the hoplite tactics employed by both armies. (Lee L. Brice)

The numbers for the Theban force are even less well attested, but may have included about 10,000 hoplites and around 1,000 cavalry, all of whom were from Thebes and its Boeotian allies. These numbers are generally accepted, but cannot be known with any certainty. The Theban army was under the command of Epameinondas. His friend Pelopidas was in command of the elite 300-member Sacred Band. Epameinondas arrayed the Theban hoplites on his left side, directly across from the Spartans and in a dense formation 25 ranks deep. Traditionally, generals put their best troops on the right side of the line of battle so they could defeat the opposing line and roll up the rest of the enemy before they tried to do the same. In this case Epameinondas clearly intended to overwhelm the Spartans. The rest of the line was eight ranks deep.

The battle began when both lines started toward each other, but then the cavalry started fighting in the space between the two armies. The Spartan cavalry was incompetent and after losing they fell back into their own hoplite ranks causing much confusion. The Thebans who were still marching forward crashed into the tangled Spartan line as it was maneuvering, thus inflicting immense losses. Pelopidas had led his unit directly into the Spartan flank. Cleombrotus and several other officers died. The Spartans began to retreat, but when the Peloponnesians and mercenaries saw the Spartans defeated they fled and any chance of retreat became a rout. Epameinondas' superior tactics and morale won the day.

The Spartan defeat was thunderous in its impact. The Peloponnesian League dissolved later that same year. Epameinondas invaded the Peloponnese several times in the following years and freed the helots. The Theban hegemony emerged at Leuctra.

Lee L. Brice

See also: Agesilaus II; Epameinondas; King's Peace; Pelopidas; Phalanx, Hoplite; Sparta; Thebes; Xenophon

References

Anderson, J. K. *Military Theory and Practice in the Age of Xenophon.* Berkeley, CA: University of California Press, 1970.

Buckler, John. *Aegean Greece in the Fourth Century BC.* Leiden: Brill, 2003.

Kennel, Nigel M. *Spartans: A New History.* Malden, MA: Wiley-Blackwell, 2010.

Strassler, Robert B., ed. *The Landmark Xenophon's Hellenika.* New York: Pantheon Books, 2009.

Long Walls

The Long Walls of Athens, built during 461–456 BCE, connected the port of Piraeus with the city. They provided fortified access to the port in times of conflict so that Athens could securely import food. The walls around Athens and the ports are sometimes confused with the Long Walls, but such conflation is inappropriate.

After the Hellenic Alliance drove the Persians out of Greece in 479, Themistocles led the effort to build strong walls around the city and then the port of Piraeus as well. The city was dependent on imported food. Recognizing that the city would be secure as long as supplies could be brought by sea to Piraeus, they built the wall from Athens to Piraeus, a distance of about four miles. A second wall was built to the south of the first one, between Athens and Phalerum. Later, a third wall was constructed parallel to the northern wall; those two walls formed a secure corridor, about 550 feet wide, to Piraeus. The Long Walls prevented the Spartan Army from cutting off Athens' food supplies during the Peloponnesian War, since it lacked siege engines. The Spartans pulled down sections of the wall in 404, but Conon rebuilt them in 393.

Tim Watts and Lee L. Brice

See also: Athens; Conon of Athens; Greco-Persian Wars, Consequences of; Peloponnesian War, Overview; Pericles; Themistocles

References

Conwell, David H. *Connecting a City to the Sea: The History of the Athenian Long Walls*. Leiden: Brill, 2008.

Munn, Mark. *The School of History: Athens in the Age of Socrates*. Berkeley, CA: University of California Press, 2000.

Lysander

Lysander was a Spartan admiral and general. Little is known of his life before his appointment as Spartan admiral in 407 BCE. His family claimed descent from Hercules, but his family was so poor that he was of inferior social status. His same-sex relationship with the young royal prince Agesilaus greatly assisted his rise to prominence. Appointed admiral following major Spartan naval reverses, Lysander spent most of a year in the Ionian city of Ephesus, winning both the confidence of and financial support from the Persian viceroy in Asia Minor, Prince Cyrus the Younger, for action against Athens. Lysander then assembled a new fleet of triremes and defeated an Athenian detachment at Notium around March 406 when the Athenian admiral Alcibiades had departed with most of the Athenian ships for supplies.

According to custom, Lysander's term as admiral was for one year and was nonrenewable, but after his successor Callicratidas lost his life and half the Spartan fleet in a defeat off the Arginusae Islands, Lysander resumed de facto leadership of the Spartan naval effort in 405 as nominal subordinate of another admiral. New Persian subsidies allowed him to rebuild the Spartan fleet.

Lysander then sailed his ships to the Hellespont to threaten disruption of grain shipments from the Black Sea region in order to provoke a confrontation with the Athenian fleet. Several times refusing battle under less than favorable conditions, Lysander caught the Athenians off guard with their ships drawn up on the shore at Aegospotami and captured practically all of their ships and crews in August 405. Only 9 of 180 Athenian triremes escaped, and the Spartans executed more than 3,000 captured Athenians. This naval victory effectively ended the Peloponnesian War, for it enabled Lysander to then blockade Athens from the sea, starving the city into submission in 404.

Lysander's personal ambition undoubtedly contributed to the harsh Spartan repression of other Greek states following the Peloponnesian War and cost him influence at Sparta, as did his cultivation of a personal following and acceptance of honors, including erection of a statue at Delphi and worship of himself as a god at Samos. He apparently plotted to abolish the hereditary monarchy of Sparta but gave up the plan upon securing Agesilaus as king. Lysander died in 395 during the Corinthian War (395–386 BCE) while leading an infantry attack on the Greek city-state of Haliartus in central Boeotia.

Spencer C. Tucker

See also: Aegospotami, Battle of; Agesilaus II; Alcibiades; Athens; Corinthian War; Peloponnesian War, Consequences of; Peloponnesian War, Overview; Sparta; Trireme

References

Hamilton, Charles D. *Agesilaus and the Failure of Spartan Hegemony.* Ithaca, NY: Cornell University Press, 1991.

Hale, John. *Lords of the Sea: The Epic Story of the Athenian Navy and the Birth of Democracy.* New York: Viking Press, 2009.

Tritle, Lawrence A. *A New History of the Peloponnesian War.* Malden, MA: Wiley-Blackwell, 2010.

Welwei, Karl-Wilhelm. "The Peloponnesian War and Its Aftermath." In *A Companion to the Classical Greek World*, ed. Konrad Kinzl, 526–43. Malden, MA: Wiley-Blackwell, 2006.

M

Macedon

The ancient state that we know as Macedonia in the period 490–323 BCE has been continuously inhabited since the Neolithic period. A region of mountains with a large, well-watered plain that ran to the coast, one could describe Macedon's natural limits roughly as the Haliacmon river to the south, the Strymon or Nestos rivers on the north-north-east, Chalcidice and the Aegean on the east, and the mountains into Paeonia to the west. The core of the later kingdom was Lower Macedonia, on the large plain along the southeastern coast, which included Pieria and Bottiaea. Upper Macedonia was the upland rising into the tall mountains north, west, and south of the plain. These two regions did not always get along politically as these topographical divisions created opportunities for competing claimants to the throne. Its location between the Balkans and Greece meant that Macedonia was cut by north–south routes from Thrace to Central Greece and west–east routes from Illyria to the Aegean coast and south into Central Greece. In addition to being on the transport routes, its natural resources attracted numerous peoples and later states to take an interest in controlling it.

The state that we know as Macedon in the period 490–323 was formed in the seventh century when people from the Pindus mountains moved down into the plain of Lower Macedonia and settled there permanently. This group spoke a dialect of northern Greek with other regional influences. They moved into the plain to take advantage of the resources and opportunities for agriculture. Whether they eradicated the previous inhabitants or merely took over their land and allegiance is a matter of debate. Gradually over the sixth and fifth centuries the kings came to control all of

Lower Macedon and retained strong ties and political control with Upper Macedonia.

The Macedonian kings or leading families all came from the same clan, the Argeads. Herodotus is our best source for early Macedon, but he preserves little besides the names of some earlier kings beginning with Perdiccas I. The earliest king who is historical is Amyntas I, king of Macedon when Darius I was active in northern Greece against the Paeonians in 512. There is little doubt that the Persians dominated Macedonia, regardless of whether it was formerly incorporated into a satrapy. His son, Alexander I, ascended to the throne before Darius I invaded Greece from the north in 492. When that invasion failed in a storm off Mount Athos, a Persian force remained behind in Macedonia and Thrace. At that time he maintained a peaceful relationship with Persian authorities. Given his close proximity to Persian holdings Alexander I submitted earth and water when requested by Darius I and later supplied troops when requested for Xerxes' invasion in 480.

During much of the fifth century the kings of Macedon had to deal with internal and external threats. During the Peloponnesian War Perdiccas II played both sides trying to keep on good terms with Athens and allying with its enemies, including the Spartan general Brasidas, when an opportunity for gain presented itself. The kings who succeeded him worked hard to stay ahead of their enemies both internal and external, with mixed results and little long-term stability as most of them died a violent death. Perdiccas III, for example, became king in 368 after his brother was assassinated, came into his own after killing his regent in 365 and died in battle along with several thousand men fighting the Illyrians in 359. As a result of the death and the Illyrian crisis the army assembly selected Philip II as the new king of Macedon.

Philip immediately moved to stabilize the kingdom. Marshaling all his considerable diplomatic skill he was able to buy time. He created a close relationship between the king and the nobility of Upper Macedonia. He then reformed the Macedonian Army by increasing its size and training and created the *sarissa*-armed phalanx formation. Philip gave out land to men willing to serve in his army, thus increasing loyalty to himself and weakening soldiers' bonds with the local nobility. He also enlarged the cavalry, armed cavalrymen with a long spear, and gave the cavalry a new tactical role in battle. Philip invested in combat engineers and siege technology drawn from numerous sources including Sicily so he could reduce his enemy's strong points. His efforts paid dividends in the improvements in siege technology and artillery. Sources describing in detail how

Philip's army performed in battle are lacking, but the combination was extremely effective. The combination of reforms and diplomacy permitted Philip to enlarge Macedonia and annex Thrace, Paeonia, and Chalcidice to his kingdom. Through diplomatic maneuvering Philip extended the reach of Macedon into Thessaly and then into Central Greece. The victory at Chaeronea in 338 sealed the dominance of Macedon in Greek affairs.

Like so many other Argead kings, Philip's reign ended in assassination. Alexander III succeeded him. After violently demonstrating to Macedon and its enemies that he would brook no dissent Alexander launched his invasion of Persia. While Alexander was away he left Antipater in charge of Macedon. The kingdom was peaceful and supportive, but Antipater had to intervene in Greece twice to put down revolts during Alexander's campaigns. The war with Persia drained Macedonia of some of its citizens, but the wealth sent home enriched the kingdom immensely. After Alexander's death in 323, his brother, Philip III, and son, Alexander IV, ruled jointly over the kingdom, but in reality control of Macedonia was the subject of much competition among his successors. When the dust finally settled the Antigonid dynasty emerged in control of the kingdom. Macedonia would remain important in the Hellenistic world, but not quite on the scale that it had been under Philip and Alexander.

Lee L. Brice

See also: Agis III; Alexander the Great; Antipater; Darius I; Phalanx, Macedonian; Philip II of Macedon; Wars of Alexander the Great, Causes of; Wars of Alexander the Great, Overview; Xerxes I

References

Fox, Robin Lane, ed. *Brill's Companion to Ancient Macedon*. Leiden: Brill, 2011.

Roisman, Joseph and Ian Worthington, eds. *A Companion to Ancient Macedonia*. Malden, MA: Wiley-Blackwell, 2010.

Thomas, Carol G. *Alexander the Great in his World*. Malden, MA: Blackwell Publishing, 2007.

Mantinea, Battles of

Mantinea was a city-state located in the central Peloponnese in a wide valley between the territory of Argos and Sparta, north of Tegea. Because of its location the city's territory was highly contested and became the site of two large hoplite battles in 418 BCE during the Peloponnesian War and in 362 BCE during the Theban Hegemony. The first battle is famous as an example of a traditional hoplite battle while the second demonstrated how warfare had changed in the early fourth century.

Alcibiades of Athens triggered the first battle when he created an anti-Spartan alliance in the Peloponnese. During the Peace of Nicias Alcibiades successfully brought together Argos, Mantinea, and Elis to join Athens in a treaty against Sparta. When Tegea, an active member of the Peloponnesian League, was threatened in 418 the Spartan king, Agis I, took the field with a large army. Agis was under pressure to win a victory or be deposed since he had already lost several allies to the Argives. After some maneuvering by both sides they met in the plain for battle. The Tegeans took the post of honor on the right side of the Spartan battle line. The elite Spartan unit (*sciritae*) took position on the far left with the veterans of Brasidas's campaign, and the rest of the force lined up in between. Agis posted cavalry on each flank. The Argive allies lined up with the Mantineans on their right side with the Argives and allies in the center and the Athenians on the left flank. Thucydides' description of the battle provides a superb account of how hoplite warfare often occurred. The two lines as they march toward one another drift right so that each line risks being outflanked. Agis' attempt to maneuver his left flank failed and it broke, but his right side and

The ancient Greek valley near the city of Manitinea was the site of the largest land battle of the Peloponnesian War in 418 BCE and a second large battle between Thebes and Sparta in 462. (John W.I. Lee)

center won so decisively against the Argives and Athenians that instead of pursuing he was able to turn these men to come to the aid of his left flank. The result was that he won the battle decisively and the Argives signed a peace treaty that ended their alliance with Athens.

The second battle of Mantinea occurred during the period of Theban hegemony, but unlike the earlier engagement it is poorly recorded. After the battle of Leuctra Thebes had invaded the Peloponnese several times to undermine Spartan power by freeing the helots of Messene and creating an Arcadian League in the north under the leadership of Tegea. Sparta and Elis tried to undermine the new league by convincing Mantinea to break away in 362. Athens, expecting Thebes to march, sent an army by ship to aid the Spartans. In response, Epameinondas led a Boeotian allied force into the Peloponnese in support of the Arcadian League. The Spartans tried to have all the forces meet at Mantinea. The Thebans marched directly on Sparta, but Agesilaus II returned just in time to save the city. Epameinondas marched north and caught the Mantineans unprepared, but newly arrived Athenian cavalry stopped the Boeotians and Thessalians from capitalizing on their initiative.

Both sides arrayed for battle in the plain, but most of the Spartan force was still in Sparta with Agesilaus. Epameinondas arrayed his force so that the Thebans lined up in depth of at least 25 ranks on his left with his allies spread out across the line to his right. A large cavalry force screened his maneuvering of these ranks into position and then took up position on the left flank with the *peltasts* and other light-armed infantry. The Mantineans held the right side of their battle line with the Athenians on the left and their allies and some Spartans in the middle. Epameinondas charged into the Mantineans breaking their end of the line completely, but he was mortally wounded in the attack. After he fell the Theban army seems to have lost heart and did not press the rest of the line vigorously or even pursue the fleeing enemy. The Athenians had the better of the engagement on their end of the line. After the fighting subsided both armies set up trophies and sent emissaries for their dead.

The battle effectively ended Theban hegemony in the Peloponnese, but did not give Sparta and its allies any advantage either. The importance of the battle is to be found not in its results, but in the ways in which it highlights the significant changes in warfare.

Lee L. Brice

See also: Athens; Epameinondas; Leuctra, Battle of; Peloponnesian War, Overview; Phalanx, Hoplite; Sparta; Thebes

References

Anderson, J. K. *Military Theory and Practice in the Age of Xenophon*. Berkeley, CA: University of California Press, 1970.

Lazenby, J. F. *The Peloponnesian War: A Military Study*. New York: Routledge, 2004.

Rhodes, P. J. *A History of the Classical Greek World, 478–323 BC*, 2nd edition. Malden, MA: Wiley-Blackwell, 2010.

Strassler, Robert B., ed. *The Landmark Thucydides: A Comprehensive Guide to the Peloponnesian War*. New York: Free Press, 1998.

Strassler, Robert B., ed. *The Landmark Xenophon's Hellenika*. New York: Pantheon Books, 2009.

Marathon, Battle of

Darius I, king of Persia, dispatched a force in 490 BCE to chastise Athens and other Greek cities that had supported Ionian rebels. The battle that followed was important not only for the Greek victory, but because its theme of "free civilization defeating despotic barbarians" has resonated across Western history and culture.

At the battle of Marathon in 490 BCE the Athenians and Plataeans defeated the Persian invasion force. The Athenian dead were buried in this mound on the site to commemorate their sacrifice. The hills occupied by the Athenian army can be seen in the distant background. (Lee L. Brice)

Once he defeated the Ionian Revolt in 494, Darius set out to punish the mainland Greeks who had supported it. After some abortive attempts, in 490 he sent a naval force commanded by his nephew Artaphernes and a Medean commander, Datis. Herodotus, our primary ancient source for the battle, provides typically fantastic numbers for the Persian force, but it probably included around 25,000 infantry and 1,000 cavalry. They took Naxos and Eretria while en route.

The fleet eventually landed in Attica at Marathon, some 26 miles northeast of Athens. The Persians selected this site in part because their guide Hippias, former Athenian tyrant and son of the tyrant Peisistratus, hoped to draw on an area that had supported his father's rise to power. The Persians probably also hoped to draw the Athenian army away from the city's great protective walls. Athens sent an appeal to Sparta. The Spartan leaders agreed to assist, but refused to suspend a religious festival that delayed their march until the phase of the moon changed.

The Athenian army, about 10,000 hoplites, assembled by tribe. Each tribe had its own elected general (*strategos*), one of whom was Miltiades, and they were joined by the city's war magistrate (*polemarchos*), Callimachus. Once assembled, they marched out to Marathon where 1,000 men from Plataea joined them. The Athenians positioned themselves on high ground west of the plain in position to block a Persian advance overland toward Athens. For several days the two armies simply sat in place more than a mile apart. The Athenians were probably waiting for the Spartans.

After four days the Greek generals learned that the Persians were withdrawing to attack the city directly. Miltiades formed the Greek line about a mile long by thinning out the center of the line to perhaps only three or four ranks of men instead of the more typical six to eight ranks. The long line allowed the Greek flanks to be protected by marshes and to extend beyond the Persian line.

The battle began that morning. The Greeks advanced slowly at first until they were 150 or so yards away (within bow range) and began moving quicker. According to Herodotus, they charged the center of the Persian line at a full run. The hoplites broke through the Persian bowmen who were in front. The Persian infantry behind them held in the center defeating the hoplites there, but the Greek flanks defeated the men they encountered and folded in, compressing the Persians in a double envelopment. Authorities differ as to whether this was planned or simply accidental.

The Persian troops fled for their ships. Some sort of Persian rear guard was organized to cover their embarkation, and most of the force escaped. Herodotus claims that the Greeks only lost 192 men killed, including Callimachus, while around 6,400 Persians fell.

Miltiades sent word of the victory to Athens through a runner. Leaving a detachment to guard the Persian prisoners and booty, the remainder of the army marched to Athens. They arrived just as the Persian fleet was debating whether to land. The Persians withdrew home without further incident. The Spartans arrived several days later. They praised the victors, viewed the battlefield, and returned home. The Athenians buried their dead in a mound and recorded the names on inscriptions. They buried the Persian dead in pits.

There is no doubt that the Athenians and Plataeans won an important battle from the Greek perspective, but it was a minor engagement for Persia and it was not decisive since it led to a more damaging invasion 10 years later. While some have wanted to see in the battle the victory of democracy over despotism, it is important to remember that the Greeks may have been highly motivated by the defense of their city-state, but more importantly, they were much better protected with bronze body armor and better disciplined than the Persians.

Spencer C. Tucker

See also: Athens; Darius I; Greco-Persian Wars, Overview; Herodotus; Miltiades the Younger; Phalanx, Hoplite

References

Billows, Richard A. *Marathon: How One Battle Changed Western Civilization.* New York: Overlook Duckworth, 2010.

Cawkwell, George. *The Greek Wars: The Failure of Persia.* Oxford: Oxford University Press, 2005.

Krentz, Peter. *The Battle of Marathon.* New Haven, CT: Yale University Press, 2010.

Strassler, Robert B., ed. *The Landmark Herodotus: The Histories.* New York: Anchor Books, 2009.

Mardonius

Mardonius was the Persian general who was active in Greece during 492–491 and 480–479 BCE. About Mardonius the leader, as is often the case with Herodotus' account, it is difficult to know much with certainty about him.

Mardonius was nephew and son-in-law of Darius I, the Persian king. Darius sent him in 492 to settle affairs first in Ionia and then Thrace. He quieted the rebellion in Ionia by removing tyrannies and permitting democracies and oligarchies. Mardonius then led his army across the Hellespont and occupied Thrace and made Macedonia a subject state. While in Thrace, his supporting fleet was wrecked in a storm resulting in the loss of many troops and supplies. Despite his initial success, the loss of the fleet and his own wounding in battle forced him to withdraw completely.

After Xerxes I succeeded Darius in 486, he gave Mardonius the military command for the invasion of Greece in 480. It is unclear from Herodotus what role he played in commanding the campaign since Xerxes was present too. After the defeat at Salamis, Xerxes appointed Mardonius satrap of Greece. Mardonius withdrew his army to northern Greece where he could count on supplies and support from allies.

In 479 he invaded Attica again and destroyed what remained of Athens before withdrawing toward central Greece. The Hellenic Alliance then united a large Greek army at Plataea and went into battle in September. Mardonius died in the battle and his head was placed on a stake to intimidate the surviving Persian soldiers. After that defeat the remaining Persian force withdrew to northern Greece and then to Asia Minor the following year.

Christina Girod

See also: Darius I; Greco-Persian Wars, Causes of; Greco-Persian Wars, Overview; Hellenic Alliance; Herodotus; Ionian Revolt; Plataea, Battle of; Salamis, Battle of; Thermopylae, Battle of

References

Briant, Pierre. *From Cyrus to Alexander: A History of the Persian Empire.* Winona Lake, IN: Indiana University Press, 2005.

Cawkwell, George. *The Greek Wars: The Failure of Persia.* Oxford: Oxford University Press, 2005.

Strassler, Robert B., ed. *The Landmark Herodotus: The Histories.* New York: Anchor Books, 2009.

Mercenaries

As long as there was war and someone willing to pay for more or specialist fighters, there was a market for opportunities for men who needed to make a living through combat somewhere away from their homeland. Although Greek mercenaries serving elsewhere had a long history, during the late fifth and early fourth centuries BCE mercenaries became increasingly common in Greek warfare.

Sources suggest that there were Greek mercenaries fighting in the ancient Near East and Egypt well before the seventh century. In Greece, mercenaries were uncommon in early hoplite combat, but tyrants such as Pisistratus of Athens employed them to take and maintain control of cities. Their availability as fighters seems to have been more important than any specialist skills they possessed. During the Persian Wars there is no evidence of mercenaries fighting for the Hellenic Alliance, although some may have fought for Persia in the fleet or in the army.

Over the second half of the fifth century, traditional Greek warfare changed as cities sought advantage and flexibility in battle. Men with specialized skills such as archers from Crete, *peltasts* from Arcadia and Thrace, and slingers from Rhodes appear occasionally in combat. Skilled rowers and helmsmen from outside Athenian territory but working for the Delian League should also be considered mercenaries as they sought out opportunities provided by the naval expansion of the league. All types of mercenaries appear in the forces of both sides during the Peloponnesian War, and they were used with varying effectiveness. Although these mercenaries seldom appear in combat before 431, it is unlikely that they would suddenly have been used so effectively by Athens during the war without some attempts to employ them previously.

A combination of factors including poverty, wealth, intercity competition, instability, and changing warfare resulted in mercenaries becoming even more common in the fourth century. The poverty was endemic to some regions of Greece and drove men to seek employment where they could find it. The wealth came primarily from Persia as it funded different Greek cities that were competing with each other for hegemony. In Sicily the instability of Syracuse created a situation in which Dionysus I could use mercenaries to make himself tyrant of the city and then master of much of Sicily and an important figure in Greece too. The rapidly changing nature of warfare was a process that continued from the fifth century.

As already noted, Persia and other powers provided opportunities throughout the period for Greeks who due to poverty or political necessity sought military service elsewhere. The *Anabasis* was about an army of mercenaries fighting in Persia and Conon of Athens, for example, fought for Cyprus and then for Persia for some years after fleeing Aegospotami. Persia was not the only source of such employment. Iphicrates was one of many mercenary leaders who worked for the king of Thrace in the early fourth century. Iphicrates also demonstrated another feature of mercenary service: they were not exclusive—they could sell their services and still fight for their home cities as he did.

Philip II and Alexander III employed mercenaries throughout their campaigns. Philip II employed them as light support troops and other specialists. Not surprisingly, Alexander used them in the same way in his early campaigns. After the burning of Persepolis in 330, Alexander had the Greeks of the Corinthian League sign on to the rest of the campaign as mercenaries. The ways in which various leaders continued to employ mercenaries in the Hellenistic period after Alexander's death owed as much to these Macedonian kings as to the changes in Greek warfare in the Peloponnesian War and the early fourth century.

Lee L. Brice

See also: Alexander the Great; *Anabasis*; Conon of Athens; Dionysius I; Iphicrates; Jason of Pherae; Peloponnesian War, Overview; *Peltasts*; Persian Empire; Philip II of Macedon; Wars of Alexander the Great, Overview

References

Sabine, Philip, Hans Van Wees, and Michael Whitby, eds. *The Cambridge History of Greek and Roman Warfare*, vol. 1. Cambridge: Cambridge University Press, 2007.

Trundle, Matthew. *Greek Mercenaries: From the Late Archaic Period to Alexander*. New York: Routledge, 2004.

van Wees, Hans. *Greek Warfare: Myths and Realities*. London: Duckworth, 2004.

Miltiades the Younger

Miltiades the Younger was an Athenian politician and general who led the Greek forces to victory over the Persian army at Marathon in 490 BCE. That decisive engagement during the Persian Wars saved Athens and thwarted Persian king Darius I's last attempt to conquer mainland Greece.

Miltiades was born into the aristocratic Philaidae family in Athens, around 554. Hippias, the tyrant of Athens, appointed Miltiades in 524 as the next successor to the colony Thracian Chersonesus. Upon his arrival there Miltiades set about strengthening his authority in the region. He was, however, soon forced to submit to the authority of Darius I as he expanded the borders of the Persian Empire. As a subject Miltiades took part in Darius' invasion of Scythia, ca. 513.

Later, when the Ionian Greeks revolted against Persia in 499, Miltiades turned on his Persian overlords and supported the Greek rebels. After the revolt was put down in 493, he was compelled to flee to Athens. Despite a trial and acquittal due to his prominent status and past leadership experience, he was elected to serve as one of the 10 generals (*strategoi*) who commanded the Athenian Army in rotation.

After several abortive attempts, Darius launched a force in 490 against Eretria and Athens in retribution for their support of the Ionian Revolt. The Persian army landed in Attica at the plain of Marathon. Miltiades and the other generals led the Athenian army out to Marathon where they waited for Spartan aid. After several days of waiting they learned that the Persians would withdraw and attack Athens directly. Miltiades, with the support of Callimachus, the war magistrate (*polemarchos*), decided to attack. He formed up the Athenian army and led a charge that broke the enemy's lines and sent the Persians fleeing to their ships.

The surviving Persians embarked on their ships and set sail for Athens. Despite the fact that his forces were exhausted from the battle, Miltiades hurried them back to Athens. The Athenians were successful and the Persian fleet sailed home.

After the Persian withdrawal, Miltiades received command of a fleet tasked with punishing the Aegean Islands that had supported Darius' campaign. To that end, Miltiades led an invasion of the island of Paros in the spring of 489, but his efforts were ultimately unsuccessful. He eventually returned to Athens, having received a wound to his leg during the lengthy engagement, and his political enemies saw to it that he was put on trial for his failure. Although spared from a death sentence upon his conviction because of his past service to Athens, he was fined the extraordinary sum of 50 talents. Unable to pay his debt, Miltiades was imprisoned and died from his gangrenous wound.

Lee L. Brice

See also: Athens; Darius I; Greco-Persian Wars, Overview; Hellenic Alliance; Herodotus; Ionian Revolt; Marathon, Battle of

References

Billows, Richard A. *Marathon: How One Battle Changed Western Civilization.* New York: Overlook Duckworth, 2010.

Krentz, Peter. *The Battle of Marathon*. New Haven, CT: Yale University Press, 2010.

Osborne, Robin. *Greece in the Making, 1200–479 BC*, 2nd edition. New York: Routledge, 2006.

Strassler, Robert B., ed. *The Landmark Herodotus: The Histories*. New York: Anchor Books, 2009.

Mutiny

Mutiny, a term often applied to any incident when soldiers have collectively refused to follow orders, can be applied to some incidents in ancient Greek armies. The so-called mutiny at the Hyphasis in 326 BCE and the Opis mutiny in 324 are the only two events traditionally bearing that name in the years between 479 and 323. While mutiny could undoubtedly be serious, it is important to recognize that mutiny is merely one type of unrest by soldiers; it has a particular definition, and the term cannot, therefore, apply to any rebellion among most ancient Greek armies.

Mutiny is merely one type of "military unrest." Types of military unrest include mutiny, military conspiracy, expression of grievances, indiscipline, and insubordination. Mutiny is defined as collective, violent (actual or threatened) opposition to established, regular military authority. Given that definition, most hoplite armies were insufficiently formal in terms of their discipline and punishments to have had the kind of regular authority one can mutiny against. The Macedonian Army, however, did have formal discipline and penalties for misbehavior. No wonder the only mutinies in Greek warfare occurred in the Macedonian Army. There may have been earlier incidents for which no record remains, but historians have traditionally referred to two incidents during Alexander's campaign as mutiny.

One incident, the so-called mutiny at the Hyphasis, was not actually a mutiny. This incident occurred in 326 after the battle of Hydaspes when Alexander continued marching eastward and reached the Hyphasis (Beas) River. When Alexander announced his intention to continue east the soldiers became quiet as a group and were clearly not open to the plan, even though there was no order to advance and no soldier seems to have actually vocalized discontent. Instead, one of the officers, Coenus, expressed his men's discontent. The result was that Alexander took the omens and finding them unfavorable declared his plan to turn back. The soldiers celebrated loudly and after some appropriate measures marched back to the fleet at the Hydaspes River. Although the incident at the Hyphasis was insubordinate, it was not a mutiny because there was no threat of violence and no orders to oppose. This incident is actually another, less serious type of military unrest called an expression of grievances. These less notorious incidents were often insubordinate, but nonviolent, vocal confrontations or communications in which soldiers typically sought to protest against various grievances, real and illusory, and protect their interests. In this case the soldiers communicated their discontent through their silence and then their officers. The soldiers were successful and during the march down the Indus Alexander restored order.

The Opis mutiny, the only actual mutiny, occurred in 324 when soldiers in Alexander's army mutinied over their discharge and replacement with Persians trained in the Macedonian manner of fighting. The infantry soldiers clamored loudly and even those who were not being discharged refused openly to serve further. In response, Alexander charged the ringleaders and had his bodyguards round them up and execute them. He then harangued the rest of the army and went forward with his plans. In response the Macedonians begged forgiveness and accepted the reforms so that Alexander took them back and restored order.

The fact that Alexander encountered military unrest in his army does not detract from his reputation as a brilliant leader. Every army commander, even in hoplite armies, faced the threat of indiscipline. The resolution of such incidents and restoration of order was what distinguished good commanders. After 323, in the Hellenistic world, military unrest would prove to be a significant problem, but in the hoplite armies of Greece there was insubordination but no incidents that meet the criteria for mutinies.

Lee L. Brice

See also: Alexander the Great; Hydaspes, Battle of the; Phalanx, Macedonian; Philip II of Macedon; Wars of Alexander the Great; Overview

References

Brice, Lee L. "Seleucus and Military Unrest in the Army of Alexander the Great." In *Seleucid Studies Presented to Getzel M. Cohen on the Occasion of his 70th Birthday*, eds. Roland Oetjen and Frank Ryan. Berlin: Steiner Verlag, forthcoming, 2012.

Carney, Elizabeth. "Macedonians and Mutiny: Discipline and Indiscipline in the Army of Philip and Alexander." *Classical Philology* 91 (1) (1996): 19–44.

Mycale, Battle of

The Battle of Mycale was one of two battles that occurred between the Persian Empire and the Greek city-states in 479 BCE ending the second Persian invasion. While the Greek naval victory at Mycale was smaller than the Battle of Plataea, the battle was significant in that the resulting destruction of the Persian Navy led to the subsequent liberation of the Ionian Greek cities of Asia Minor.

The Battle of Mycale took place near Mount Mycale on the western coast of Asia Minor, across from the Greek island of Samos. According to Herodotus, it occurred on the same day as the Battle of Plataea. While Persian and Greek forces were maneuvering on the Greek mainland in the spring of 479, the Greeks of Asia Minor attempted another revolt. The Persians put down this rebellion, so the Greeks of Samos sent a delegation to Sparta for assistance. The Hellenic Alliance sent a fleet of more than

The Hellenic Alliance defeated a large Persian naval and land force at Mycale in Ionia in 479 BCE, close to the date of the battle of Plataea. The victory ensured Hellenic dominance in the Aegean for several years as the Greeks pushed the Persians out of Greece. View of the coast and hill where the victory occurred, seen from the ancient site of Panionion. (Lee L. Brice)

100 ships, manned primarily by Spartans and Athenians, under the Spartan commander Leotychides.

When Artayntes, the Persian general on Samos, learned of this invasion force, he ordered his troops to disarm the people of Samos and leave the island for a more defensible position on the nearby coast of the Mycale peninsula. When the Greeks arrived on Samos and found it undefended, Leotychides ordered an assault on the Persian camp on the mainland. The Persians, meanwhile, beached their ships, drew up their battle lines and, not entirely trusting their Ionian Greek allies, ordered the Milesians to secure the roads to the interior.

The Greeks landed on the mainland and immediately launched an attack, with the Spartans on the right of their line and the Athenians on the left. The Persians retreated to a fort, but the Greeks took this position as well. The Milesian rearguard, meanwhile, had turned against the Persians, leaving them without a safe means of withdrawal. The Greeks destroyed the remaining Persian army and captured their beached ships.

As a result of this capture of a Persian fleet the Hellenic Alliance secured the liberation of the Aegean at around the same period as they had secured victory on land. The Ionian Greeks were more secure from Persian interference. Coupled with the victory at Plataea, the Persians had to withdraw from the Greek mainland and the remaining Aegean islands over the next year.

Ryan Hackney

See also: Greco-Persian Wars, Overview; Hellenic Alliance; Herodotus; Plataea, Battle of

References

Burn, A. R. *Persia and the Greeks: The Defence of the West*. Stanford, CA: Stanford University Press, 1984.

Cawkwell, George. *The Greek Wars: The Failure of Persia*. Oxford: Oxford University Press, 2005.

Hale, John. *Lords of the Sea: The Epic Story of the Athenian Navy and the Birth of Democracy*. New York: Viking Press, 2009.

N

Nicias

Nicias was an Athenian general and statesman during the Peloponnesian War fought between Athens and Sparta beginning in 431 BCE. Although he achieved numerous victories during the war and brokered the Peace of Nicias, which temporarily halted hostilities, Nicias' inability to anticipate the will of the Athenian democracy impaired his effectiveness as a leader, and his excessive religiosity contributed to the greatest Athenian loss of the war and his own death.

Born ca. 470 to a family outside the aristocracy, his association with Pericles and his great wealth made him an important figure in Athens. His acts of public largesse enhanced his civic image and demonstrated a deep and genuine piety.

Nicias was one of the most active Athenian commanders of the first phase of the Peloponnesian War, and over the years 427–422, he achieved victories at Minoa, Cythera, Corinth, and Mende. Because he never adopted a rabidly anti-Spartan stance, in 421 he was able to broker the Peace of Nicias, which ended fighting between Athens and Sparta, if not between all of their allies. Unfortunately, in the succeeding years, Nicias could not match the political skills of his rival Alcibiades, who wished to reopen the hostilities with Sparta and widen the war by sending a major expedition to Sicily.

After losing the initial debate on the Sicilian question, Nicias attempted to undermine support for the expedition by exaggerating the number of men and ships necessary for such an effort. That rhetorical ploy failed utterly when the Athenian assembly enlarged the expedition and named Nicias a leader along with Alcibiades and Lamachus. After Alcibiades was recalled in 415 to face charges of sacrilege and Lamachus died in battle, Nicias found himself sole leader on a mission with which he disagreed utterly. Frustrated in his efforts to take the city of Syracuse by force or subterfuge and debilitated by kidney disease, he asked in 414 to be relieved of command, but the Athenian assembly ordered him to maintain the attack and sent him more men, ships, and co-commanders.

With his fleet bottled up and rapidly deteriorating, Nicias finally attempted a breakthrough of the Syracusan naval blockade in 413. That plan had an excellent chance of success, but a lunar eclipse led Nicias to delay action on the advice of his seers. The Syracusans, however, forced the battle. In a subsequent effort to escape overland, Nicias saw his entire force slaughtered or captured by the Syracusans, who executed Nicias after his surrender.

James T. Chambers

See also: Alcibiades; Peloponnesian War, Overview; Pericles; Sicily, Athenian Expedition Against

References

Kagan, Donald. *The Peloponnesian War*. New York: Penguin, 2003.

Munn, Mark. *The School of History: Athens in the Age of Socrates*. Berkeley, CA: University of California Press, 2000.

Strassler, Robert B., ed. *The Landmark Thucydides: A Comprehensive Guide to the Peloponnesian War*. New York: Free Press, 1998.

Tritle, Lawrence A. *A New History of the Peloponnesian War*. Malden, MA: Wiley-Blackwell, 2010.

P

Pelopidas

Pelopidas was one of the Theban generals and politicians most responsible for the emergence of Theban hegemony from 371 to 362 BCE, when Thebes established itself briefly as the preeminent power in Greece. Pelopidas and his friend Epameinondas were responsible for many of the military and political victories of Thebes during that era.

Pelopidas, the son of Hippoclus, was born into a wealthy and influential Theban family in the late fifth century. Little is known with certainty of his education although it was probably typical of elite Greeks. In 384, Pelopidas fought and was wounded while serving in a Theban unit sent to assist Sparta at Mantinea.

A pro-Spartan faction took control of Thebes in 382 and exiled Pelopidas along with others deemed dangerous. Pelopidas organized the exiles to return secretly to the city in 379 where they killed the leaders of the pro-Spartan party and forced the Spartan garrison to surrender. Pelopidas gathered Theban defenses against an immediate Spartan counterattack. In recognition for his part in liberating Thebes, the Thebans elected him one of seven magistrates (*boeotarchs*), the highest office in the city, which he held 13 times during his career. In addition, he also served several years as the commander of the Sacred Band, an elite Theban unit made up of 150 male couples.

In 375, Pelopidas scored an important victory at Tegyra. Encountering a considerably larger Spartan force, Pelopidas ordered an immediate attack into the enemy center. The Thebans broke through the middle of the Spartan line, inflicting great casualties. In 371, employing Epameinondas' new tactics at Leuctra, Theban infantry including Pelopidas and the

Sacred Band shattered the Spartan ranks, breaking Spartan power as Thebes emerged preeminent. The following year Pelopidas and Epameinondas led a Theban invasion of Spartan territory and freed the Messenians.

In 369, Thebes sent Pelopidas north to drive Alexander of Pherae and a Macedonian garrison out of Larissa. He then marched to Macedonia where he settled rival claims to the throne and took hostages including Philip who would become king of Macedon. A year later, he was taken prisoner by Alexander of Pherae but was later freed after Epameinondas led an army into Pherae.

Later he returned to Thessaly where his army defeated Alexander of Pherae in 364 during the Battle of Cynoscephalae, although Pelopidas was killed in the fighting. Pelopidas may not have been a tactical genius, but he was critical to the emergence of the Theban hegemony.

Ryan Hackney

See also: Epameinondas; Leuctra, Battle of; Sparta; Thebes

References

Buckler, John. *The Theban Hegemony.* Cambridge, MA: Harvard University Press, 1980.

Laforse, Bruce. "The Greek World 371–336." In *A Companion to the Classical Greek World*, ed. Konrad Kinzl, 544–59. Malden, MA: Wiley-Blackwell, 2006.

Strassler, Robert B., ed. *The Landmark Xenophon's Hellenika.* New York: Pantheon Books, 2009.

Peloponnesian League

Notable for its longevity, the Peloponnesian League is the modern name for a loose network of military alliances between Sparta and a number of other cities within and outside of the Peloponnesus that lasted from the sixth to fourth centuries BCE. League membership varied over time, but dissolved after the defeat of Sparta at Leuctra in 371.

At some point prior to 500 (the date is unknown), Sparta had arranged for treaties of mutual friends and enemies (*symmachia*) with other cities, most of which were in the Peloponnesus. League members also promised that in the event of joint action, they would follow Spartan leadership.

League members had one vote each in assembly when it was called, and any decision for action was by majority vote, but Sparta could veto any proposal. This was what had happened when Corinth appealed to the league in the years prior to the Peloponnesian War. Membership in the league included Elis, Tegea, Sicyon, Corinth, and Thebes, but not every city in the Peloponnese joined. The league provided Sparta with a buffer of sorts and allies to draw on in the event of a major campaign.

A fundamental way in which the Peloponnesian League differed from other such alliances is that member cities could generally pursue their own foreign policy, even fighting other members of the league. Only when an assembly was called did the allies have to respond. The additional advantage to the allies was that they could call an assembly.

When Darius I sent envoys to Greece prior to the Persian campaign of 490, all members of the league deferred to Sparta. The league fought as part of the Hellenic Alliance until 478 when Sparta and its allies withdrew and Athens established the Delian League. During the fifth century, the Peloponnesian League was often belligerent toward Athens and finally in 431 after a series of provocations war broke out against the Delian League. The Peloponnesian War finally ended in 404 when Athens surrendered.

In the aftermath of the war, Sparta failed to destroy Athens as the leaders of Thebes and Corinth desired. As a result, these two cities left the league. Faced with strong opposition during the Corinthian War from a coalition of anti-Spartan city-states led by Thebes, Sparta's King Agesilaus II sought to reorganize and strengthen the Peloponnesian League. He forced Corinth and some smaller cities to "join" the league again and he continued maneuvering against Thebes. Despite its efforts to defend its hegemony over Greece, Thebes defeated Sparta at the Battle of Leuctra in 371. Later that same year the league ceased to exist.

Lee L. Brice

See also: Agesilaus II; Athens; Corinthian War; Delian League; Greco-Persian Wars, Overview; Hellenic Alliance; Leuctra, Battle of; Peloponnesian War, Consequences of

References

Harrison, Thomas. "The Greek World, 478–432." In *A Companion to the Classical Greek World*, ed. Konrad Kinzl, 509–525. Malden, MA: Wiley-Blackwell, 2006.

Kennel, Nigel M. *Spartans: A New History.* Malden, MA: Wiley-Blackwell, 2010.

Tritle, Lawrence A. *A New History of the Peloponnesian War.* Malden, MA: Wiley-Blackwell, 2010.

Tritle, Lawrence A. and Brian Campbell, ed. *The Oxford Handbook of Classical Military History.* Oxford: Oxford University Press, 2012.

Peloponnesian War, Causes of

Scholars continue to debate the actual trigger of the Peloponnesian War from 434 to 404 BCE, but the chief contemporary source, Thucydides, believed that the Athenian Empire had incurred the anger of other Greek city-states threatened by its power. He wrote that some states had lost their independence to Athens, and others feared that they might as well, especially Sparta, one of the more powerful rivals of Athens. The incident that triggered fighting was the Theban attack on Plataea in 431, but the most likely actual causes of the war are to be found in the events of the fifth century that followed creation of the Delian league in 478 BCE.

During the 50-year period after 480 (sometimes called the *pentacontateia*), Athens had become increasingly powerful, mainly by drawing on the Delian League, an alliance network that had evolved into an empire. At the same time Sparta had some internal difficulties, but remained leader of the loose alliance called the Peloponnesian League. A period of conflict between members of the Delian and Peloponnesian leagues that began in 461 over Athenian expansion on the mainland ended without serious result in 446 with the Thirty Years' Peace. In the years that followed, free to strengthen its control over its allies, Athens grew even stronger and wealthier under Pericles' leadership. All of this concerned other Greek city-states, including several allies of Sparta. This growing fear of Athens was the general cause of the war, but it still required a series of incidents to actually trigger the conflict.

The first incident started in a small Greek city on the Adriatic coast, Epidamnus. A civil war between pro-oligarchy and pro-democracy supporters in Epidamnus—a colony of ancient Corcyra—broke out in 435. The pro-democracy side sought support and ended up turning to Corinth, the city that had originally founded Corcyra. Corinth was an oligarchy, but it was also a long-term enemy of Corcyra, so it came to their support. The Corcyreans resented what they perceived as meddling and armed conflict broke out between the two cities. Corcyra fared poorly and eventually made an alliance with Athens despite the risk of breaking the Thirty Years' Peace should Athens engage in battle against Corinth. In 433, Corcyra, with Athenian assistance, defeated Corinth at sea. Corinth, already afraid of Athenian influence, saw Athenian intervention for the threat that it was (in helping Corcyra, Athens gained an even larger navy) and complained to Sparta. The Spartans did not declare war yet.

The second flashpoint occurred in the northern Aegean at Potidaea. The city in the Chalcidice peninsula was a former colony of Corinth, but also a member of the Delian League. Despite its alliance with Athens, Potidaea and Corinth maintained close political and economic ties. During 433–432 the Athenians demanded in decrees that Potidaea dismiss its Corinthian magistrates and submit to Athenian authority. When their demand was rebuffed the Athenians laid siege to their ally. With active support from Corinth and Perdiccas, king of Macedonia, the Potidaeans held out for two years. In support of its former colony Corinth again appealed to Sparta repeatedly for the league to start war against Athens, but to no avail.

The final trigger occurred in Megara when Athens moved against its neighbor and former ally. A city-state just west of Athenian territory and east of Corinth, Megara had been an early member of the Peloponnesian League, but in 460 it joined the Delian League and remained a member until 446. In 432, probably under Pericles' direction, Athens issued the Megarian Decrees that included several restrictions, most importantly banning Megarian merchants from Delian League ports. The advantage of such a measure on Pericles' part is that it allowed Athens to cause harm to a member of the Peloponnesian League without violating the peace treaty. Megara was reliant on maritime trade for its success and needed access to all the important ports were in the Delian League so this decree was particularly damaging. Despite repeated requests Athens would not rescind the decrees. As a result Megara joined Corinth's previous appeals to Sparta for Peloponnesian League action. Although the decree appears extraordinarily provocative, Thucydides saw it as a mere pretext for the later war.

The combination of Megarian and Corinthian appeals finally stirred Sparta to decide that the combination of provocations had violated the peace treaty. Negotiations toward a resolution with Athens dragged on over the winter of 432–431. Then in 431 the city of Thebes, a member of the Peloponnesian League, without warning attacked the city of Plataea—an old Athenian ally—and the war was underway. As with so many wars, neither side expected the war to last as long as it did or to have such far-reaching consequences.

The state of matters often appears to modern readers, as it did to later ancient authors, that Athens held the bulk of advantages and should have won and so may have provoked a war at a time of strength. It is important to remember, however, that for contemporaries the outcome was not a foregone conclusion. Also, much of our knowledge of these events comes from Thucydides' account in which despite his Athenian bias, the account he constructs is a superb literary construction that builds the drama inherent in the conclusion of the war.

Lee L. Brice

See also: Corinth; Delian League; Peloponnesian League; Peloponnesian War, Overview; Pericles; Sparta; Thebes; Thucydides

References

Kagan, Donald. *The Outbreak of the Peloponnesian War*. Ithaca, NY: Cornell University Press, 1969.

Kagan, Donald. *The Peloponnesian War*. New York: Penguin, 2003.

Lazenby, J. F. *The Peloponnesian War: A Military Study*. New York: Routledge, 2004.

Strassler, Robert B., ed. *The Landmark Thucydides: A Comprehensive Guide to the Peloponnesian War*. New York: Free Press, 1998.

Tritle, Lawrence A. *A New History of the Peloponnesian War*. Malden, MA: Wiley-Blackwell, 2010.

Tritle, Lawrence A. and Brian Campbell, ed. *The Oxford Handbook of Classical Military History*. Oxford: Oxford University Press, 2012.

Peloponnesian War, Consequences of

The Peloponnesian War ended in 404 BCE when Athens accepted Spartan terms. Most of the immediate consequences of the treaty were predictable for both sides. Spartan success in the war initiated a 60-year period in which exploiting military success became a problem for every city-state that tried to dominate Greece, ultimately resulting in the end of politically independent Greek city-states.

Although some of Sparta's allies had sought the total destruction of Athens, the treaty was much more lenient either because Sparta held the unlikely belief that Athens was a worthy city or because it actually feared the city that might benefit in the power vacuum. The terms required destruction of the walls around the city and the Piraeus harbor, the surrender of all but a dozen ships, and the recall of all exiles (most of whom were opponents of democracy). Not surprisingly, although it was not a term of the treaty, the Delian League dissolved since it had been all but destroyed already by Lysander. As bad as these measures were, they applied only to Athens. In a sense, much of Greece fared worse during the war.

The other immediate impacts during the war were much more widespread even if impossible to quantify. In addition to the battle deaths on both sides, an unknown number of men, women, and children died violently off the battlefield during the war. A number of city-states including Melos and Delium had been entirely destroyed or depopulated. The plague in Athens did not single out Athenians, but killed many non-Athenians too. Agricultural production had suffered throughout much of the Greek mainland causing additional economic, social, and medical problems. All of this meant an overall decline in the population in Greece, spread unevenly but affecting all economic levels, free and slave. The nonagricultural economy also suffered in every aspect except military-related as the number of expensive ships and mercenaries employed by both sides increased over time. The loss was great, but within 10 years after the war many city-states had rebounded noticeably and were ready for renewed fighting.

In the aftermath of the peace treaty with Athens, Lysander, still in control of the Spartan navy, tried to exploit the advantage and create a Spartan empire. He forced captured cities that had been part of the Athenian Empire to receive garrisons and a board of pro-Spartan political overseers (*decarchies*). In Athens, Lysander installed a garrison and a board of 30 pro-Spartan overseers that came to be called the Thirty Tyrants because of their excesses.

But Lysander and his supporters overreached and the behavior of the Spartans fomented opposition among other city-states including some allied members of the Peloponnesian League. The Spartans also irritated their former source of wealth, Persia, as they went back on the terms of their agreement with Persia. In return for the wealth Sparta received during the war, it had promised to give the Persian king control of the Greek city-states in western Asia Minor. Lysander initially rejected the agreement because he sought to maintain his own control over these cities.

The Athenians restored democracy in 403 and removed the garrison. Then in 395, frustration with the Spartans led to the Corinthian War as

Corinth, Thebes, and Athens joined forces with Persian funding and naval support against Sparta. The war at sea went well with Conon winning a major victory at Cnidus in 394. Conon then returned to Athens where he led the restored democracy in rebuilding its walls and fleet and began to organize a new naval alliance called the Second Athenian League. The war only ended in 386 when the Persian king threw his money behind Sparta and imposed a peace treaty on Greece, which is often called the King's Peace.

Despite the peace treaty, conflict broke out repeatedly between Thebes and Sparta that led to the utter defeat of Sparta at Leuctra in 371. The outcome led to the end of the Peloponnesian League as Thebes invaded Spartan territory several times and freed the helots and Messenia. As Thebes grew powerful and started to create its own "empire," conflict arose between Athens and Thebes culminating in 362 at the Battle of Mantinea where the Theban general Epameinondas was mortally wounded and Theban dominance began to wane. In the years that followed, Athens tried to dominate but had no better luck, facing opposition from Thebes and Persia that culminated in the collapse of the Second Athenian League.

One additional impact of the war was the evolution in warfare, both on land and sea. When the war began, Greek land warfare was still dominated by heavy-infantry—hoplites—fighting in phalanx formations. During the war both sides began using light armed troops and specialists, both allied and mercenaries, including Cretan archers, Rhodian slingers, and Thracian and Arcadian *peltasts*. The first time these appear in a force dominated by heavy infantry is during the Peloponnesian War from the Pylos campaign in 325. By the end of the conflict, Greek land warfare was much more complicated and expensive as any city that wished to dominate could no longer rely on heavy infantry alone and had to be able to hire mercenary specialist units or train its own.

When the war began at sea, Athens dominated Greek naval warfare. A typical sea battle involved maneuvering one's triremes to ram an opponent's ship in the side or rear to sink it. During the war, Corinth developed the tactic of ramming head-on against the prow of Athenian ships. By the end of the war this tactic had become a standard practice and as a result it made building triremes even more expensive and further reduced the number of cities that could afford to build them.

By the mid-fourth century, the Greek city-states were financially and militarily exhausted. The political and military vacuum that had eventually resulted from the Peloponnesian War coincided with the emergence of

Philip II as king of a resurgent Macedon in the north. In 338, the city-states of Greece succumbed to him thus bringing the Classical period of Greek history to an end and initiating an era of expansion under monarchs.

Lee L. Brice

See also: Conon of Athens; Corinth; Corinthian War; Delian League; Epameinondas; Iphicrates; Lysander; Macedon; Peloponnesian League; Peloponnesian War, Causes of; Peloponnesian War, Overview; Philip II of Macedon; Second Athenian League; Thebes; Trireme

References

Buckler, John. *Aegean Greece in the Fourth Century* BC. Leiden: Brill, 2003.

Strassler, Robert B., ed. *The Landmark Xenophon's Hellenika*. New York: Pantheon Books, 2009.

Tritle, Lawrence A. *A New History of the Peloponnesian War*. Malden, MA: Wiley-Blackwell, 2010.

Welwei, Karl-Wilhelm. "The Peloponnesian War and its Aftermath." In *A Companion to the Classical Greek World*, ed. Konrad Kinzl, 526–43. Malden, MA: Wiley-Blackwell, 2006.

Peloponnesian War, Overview

Between 431 and 404 BCE the Peloponnesian War raged throughout Greece and the Aegean Sea and even as far west as Sicily as Sparta and its allies in the Peloponnesian League fought against what had become the Athenian Empire. It was to be an odd war in which the best Greek army faced the best navy, but Athens had the additional advantages of offensive mobility by sea and plenty of cash. Many Greek cities and even Persia became involved in the war so that it had an impact on nearly every part of the Greek world. The war ended in defeat for Athens and dissolution of its empire.

Throughout the period after 478 Athens had become increasingly powerful, mainly by drawing on the Delian League, an alliance network that had evolved into an empire. After a series of what appeared to Spartan allies as provocations, Sparta, led by its king Archidamus, found Athens in violation of the peace treaty and declared war in 432. After a desultory attempt to negotiate peace, the war began in 431 when Thebes attacked Plataea.

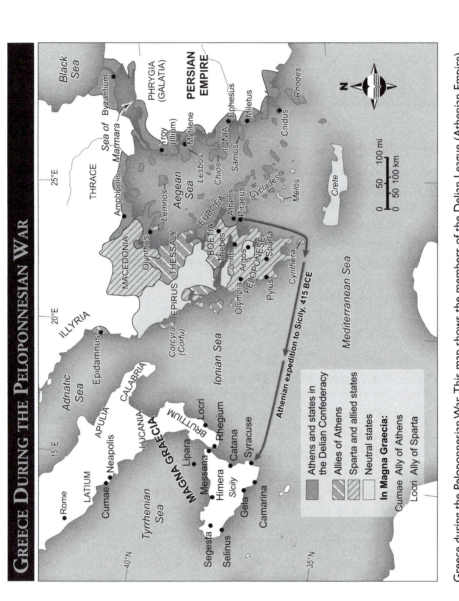

Greece during the Peloponnesian War. This map shows the members of the Delian League (Athenian Empire) and the Peloponnesian League, as well as their allies. Most of Greece joined one side or the other.

Table 3 Key Events of the Peloponnesian War

Event Name	Date	Participants	Key Commanders (if known)	Victor
30-year Peace	446	Sparta and Delian League	Pericles	–
Epidamnus Dispute	435–433	Corinth vs Corcyra	–	Corcyra
Siege of Potidaea	432	Potidaea and Corinth vs Athens	–	Athens
Megarian Decree	432	Athens vs Megara	Pericles	–
Declaration of War	late 432	Peloponnesian League	Archidamus	–
Thebes attacks Plataea	Spring 431	Thebes vs Plataea	–	Plataea
Spartan invasions of Attica	Spring 431, 430, 428, 427, 425	Sparta vs Athens	Archidamus, Agis vs Pericles and others	–
Plague in Athens	430, 429	–	–	–
Attack & Siege of Plataea	429–427	Peloponnesian League vs Plataea	Archidamus and others vs -	Peloponnesians
Battles of Naupactus	429	Peloponnesian League vs Athens	Cnemus, Brasidas, and others vs Phormio	Athens
Revolt of Mytilene	428–427	Mytilene and Peloponnesian League vs Athens	–	Athens
First Sicilian Expedition	427–424	Athens vs Syracuse and Western Greeks	Pythodorus, Sophocles, and Eurymedon vs Hermocrates and others	Syracuse
Corcyraean Revolt	427–425	Corcyra Civil Strife	–	–

(Continued)

Table 3 Key Events of the Peloponnesian War (Continued)

Event Name	Date	Participants	Key Commanders (if known)	Victor
Aetolian campaign	426–25	Delian league vs Aetolians and Peloponnesian League	Demosthenes vs Eurylochus	Athens
Pylos campaign	425	Athens vs Peloponnesian League	Demosthenes and Nicias vs Epitades, Hippagretas and Brasidas	Athens
Battle of Sphacteria	425	Athens vs Peloponnesian League	Demosthenes and Cleon vs Epitades, Hippagretas and Styphon	Athens
Invasion of Cythera	424	Athens vs Sparta	Nicias vs -	Athens
Megarian campaign	424	Athens vs Peloponnesian League	Hippocrates and Demosthenes vs others and Brasidas	Sparta
Boeotian campaign	424	Athens vs Boeotia	Hippocrates and Demosthenes vs -	Athens
Northern Greece campaign	424–422	Peloponnesian League vs Athens	Brasidas vs -	Sparta
Battle of Delium	424	Athens vs Boeotia	Hippocrates vs Pagondas	Boeotia
Capture of Amphipolis	424	Peloponnesian League vs Athens	Brasidas vs Thucydides	Sparta
Battle of Amphipolis	422	Athens vs Sparta	Cleon vs Brasidas	Sparta
Peace of Nicias	Winter 422/21	Athens and Peloponnesian League	–	–
Argive Alliance	419	Argos, Athens, Mantinea, and Elis	Alcibiades	–

Event Name	Date	Participants	Key Commanders (if known)	Victor
Battle of Mantinea	418	Peloponnesian League vs Argive alliance	Agis vs Alcibiades and others	Peloponnesians
Attack on Melos	416	Athens vs Melos	Alcibiades vs -	Athens
Sicilian Expedition	416–413	Athens vs Syracuse, allies, and Peloponnesian League	Alcibiades, Nicias, Lamachus, Eurymedon, and Demosthenes vs Hermocrates, others, and Gylippus	Syracuse
Fortification of Decelea	Spring 413	Sparta vs Athens	Agis vs -	Sparta
Battle of Erineaus	413	Corinth vs Athens	Polyanthes vs Diphilus	Corinth
Revolt of Lesbos, Chios, Miletus, and Ionians	413–11	Peloponnesian League vs Athens	Agis, Alcibiades, and others vs Phrynicus and others	Athens
Sparta and Persia sign treaties of support	412, 411	Sparta and Persia	Tissaphernes	
Oligarchic Coup d'etat	411–410	Athens	–	–
Battle of Eretria	411	Peloponnesian League vs Athens	Agesandridas vs -	Peloponnesians
Revolt of Euboea	411–404	Peloponnesian League vs Athens	- vs -	Peloponnesians
Battle of Cynossema	411	Peloponnesian League vs Athens	Mindarus and others vs Thrasyllus and Thrasybulus	Athens
Battle of Abydos	late 411	Peloponnesian League vs Athens	Mindarus and others vs Thrasyllus and Thrasybulus	Athens

(Continued)

Table 3 Key Events of the Peloponnesian War (*Continued*)

Event Name	Date	Participants	Key Commanders (if known)	Victor
Battle of Cyzicus	410	Peloponnesian League vs Athens	Mindarus and others vs Alcibiades, Thrasybulus and Theramanes	Athens
Ionian campaign	409–408	Athens vs Peloponnesian League and Persia	Thrasyllus, Alcibiades, and others vs – Pharnabazus and Hippocrates	Draw
Chersonese campaign	408	Athens vs Peloponnesian League	Alcibiades vs Clearchus	Athens
Cyrus supports Sparta	407	Persia and Sparta	Cyrus and Lysander	–
Battle of Notium	Late 407 or 406	Athens vs Peloponnesian League	Antiochus vs Lysander	Peloponnesians
Ionian campaign	406	Peloponnesian League vs Athens	Callicratidas vs Conon and others	Peloponnesians
Battle of Mytilene	406	Peloponnesian League vs Athens	Callicratidas vs Conon and Erasinides	Draw
Battle of Arginusae	406	Athens vs Peloponnesian League	Thrasyllos, Pericles, and others vs Callicratidas and Thrasondas	Athens
Battle of Aegospotami	405	Peloponnesian League vs Athens	Lysander and Etionikus vs Conon, Philocles, Adeimantos, and others	Peloponnesians
Capture of Byzantium and Chalcedon	405	Peloponnesian League vs Athens	Lysander vs -	Peloponnesians
Aegean campaign	405	Peloponnesian League vs Athens	Lysander vs -	Peloponnesians
Blockade of Athens	405–404	Peloponnesian League vs Athens	Lysander, Agis, and Pausanias vs -	Peloponnesians

Key Events of the Peloponnesian War. This table provides key events, dates, and participants of the war. When commanders are not known it is left blank.

According to our primary source, Thucydides, both sides had a strategy for victory. Archidamus planned to draw the Athenians out to battle and win a swift victory on land that would result in the collapse of the Delian League. Pericles, the leader in Athens, advised his fellow citizens to remain behind their walls, secure with their large wealth reserves to maintain the fleet and import food, but also raid the coastline of the Peloponnesian League members and cause havoc.

This first phase of the war, sometimes called the Archidamian War, lasted 10 years and began with a Spartan invasion of Athenian territory. Pericles pursued his semi-defensive strategy with great effect. The invasion raided the plain of Attica but left Athens itself untouched and after some desultory destruction the Spartans withdrew. The next year, while the Athenians remained behind their walls a plague struck Athens and reduced its population. This not only affected the numbers of men it could field, but also cost the city-state one of its most capable leaders, Pericles, in 429.

During the early years of the war, there were victories on both sides, but the Athenian occupation of Pylos and capture of some Spartan citizens scared the nearby Spartans into asking for peace in 425. The Athenians, seeing their advantage, refused. Sparta responded by campaigning in the northern Aegean and eventually capturing Amphipolis in 422. This success led directly to the Peace of Nicias that was intended to restore the status quo with both sides returning captured territory.

The island of Sphacteria in the bay of Pylos was site of a major campaign in which Athens captured a Spartan force in 425 BCE. (John W. I. Lee)

The treaty may not have been fully implemented but it initiated a period of uneasy peace during which Athens sought to expand its empire by alliance with Argos, the conquest of Melos, and then a great expedition to Sicily in 415. That campaign in the west proved costly to Athens, as its huge force was defeated at Syracuse in 413. That expedition led to the end of the peace and the beginning of the second phase of the war, called the Decelean War.

During the siege of Syracuse, Sparta was not idle, having invaded Attica again and occupied a fort at Decelea. Sparta also focused on building up its fleet to take advantage of the battered state of the Athenian Navy. A significant portion of the Athenian fleet was destroyed in the attack on Sicily and with it, the men to man the new ships Athens was desperately trying to build. Also, in the aftermath of Syracuse several members of the Delian League revolted and this further occupied Athenian attention. Between 411 and 408, Athens experienced a coup d'état in favor of oligarchy and then a restoration of democracy, the continued rebellion of several allies, and food shortages caused by Spartan naval successes. However, a major Athenian naval victory at the Battle of Cyzicus in 410 decimated the Spartan fleet and revived Athens' hope of winning the war.

Despite the fact that Athens had secured its supply lines and even reclaimed a few of its subject states, political squabbling among the Athenians hampered their military. Meanwhile the Spartans, with wealth provided by the Persians, continued to apply pressure. Athens achieved its last significant victory in the war at the Battle of Arginusae in 406, but even that triumph was marred by the execution of several Athenian generals for reportedly failing to recover and bury their dead. The following year, the Spartan commander Lysander crushed the Athenian fleet at the Battle of Aegospotami. Sparta then cut off Athens' food imports and besieged Athens by land, forcing it to surrender in 404.

Sparta spared Athens from utter destruction, though Corinth and other Spartan allies desired it. Under the conditions of surrender, Athens lost its overseas possessions, its walls, and most of its fleet. The Delian League also dissolved. The Golden Age of Athens and its empire was over. Despite this conclusion Sparta had difficulty exploiting its victory in the decades that followed, so the Peloponnesian War only led to a period of wearing conflict among the Greek city-states.

Jim Emmons

See also: Aegospotami; Alcibiades; Brasidas; Cleon; Corinth; Delian League; Lysander; Nicias; Peloponnesian League; Peloponnesian War,

Causes of; Peloponnesian War, Consequences of; Pericles; Sicily, Athenian Expedition Against; Thebes; Thucydides

References

Kagan, Donald. *The Peloponnesian War*. New York: Penguin, 2003.

Lazenby, J. F. *The Peloponnesian War: A Military Study*. New York: Routledge, 2004.

Strassler, Robert B., ed. *The Landmark Thucydides: A Comprehensive Guide to the Peloponnesian War*. New York: Free Press, 1998.

Tritle, Lawrence A. *A New History of the Peloponnesian War*. Malden, MA: Wiley-Blackwell, 2010.

Tritle, Lawrence A. and Brian Campbell, ed. *The Oxford Handbook of Classical Military History*. Oxford: Oxford University Press, 2012.

Peltasts

Peltasts first appear certainly in a Greek force in 425 BCE at the Pylos campaign in the Peloponnesian War. These light-armed troops made a positive difference to Athens at Sphacteria and were important to Spartan success the following year. They became a part of the changing nature of Greek warfare and remained in use throughout the fourth century and into the Hellenistic period.

The word *peltast* comes from the Greek word for their wicker shields (*pelte*), which Greek artists show as having an iconic crescent shape. They were usually armed with javelins and a light shield, but probably also carried a sword or dagger for self-defense. Other than the shield they usually wore no body armor. The equipment gave the *peltasts* speed and agility that hoplites lacked, making them effective in skirmishing and hit and run attacks, and against cavalry in uneven terrain or in combination with them. Although they often appeared as mercenaries, their light armor was inexpensive so it tended to be favored by the poor and in economically poorer regions as a regular weapon, not just as mercenary gear.

When Greek authors first describe *peltasts* they report them as having come from Thrace, but there was an old tradition of them in Asia Minor and it is probable that they were in Arcadia and Aetolia too in Greece. During the Persian Wars they are part of Xerxes' invasion force in 490 and appear again at the Battle of the Eurymedon River. The next time they appear it is during the Peloponnesian War on both sides. In addition to fighting for Athens at Sphacteria, Thracian *peltasts* were part of Brasidas' force when he pushed north to Amphipolis in 424. From then onward *peltasts* from various areas appear regularly in combat narratives. While these are the earliest appearances of *peltasts* in Greek warfare it seems unlikely that this was their earliest use since they were used so effectively by Athens in this case, and Arcadia in northern Peloponnese seems to have had a tradition of light-armed infantry with which the Spartans would have been familiar.

By the beginning of the fourth century *peltast* use was accepted as a regular part of warfare, a tactical element in any commander's toolbox. During the Corinthian War, the Athenian commander Iphicrates commanded a unit of *peltast* mercenaries that defeated a Spartan hoplite unit by using hit-and-run tactics. Mercenary *peltasts* were among the units described in the *Anabasis*. Epameinondas of Thebes mingled light troops among his cavalry and they played a role at the battles of Leuctra and Mantinea. By the time Philip II of Macedon incorporated *peltasts* into his army there was a well-established practice of using them on flanks and as rapid skirmishers. Alexander the Great continued his father's practices, using light troops effectively throughout his campaigns, often to guard his flanks and to tackle enemy positions in tough terrain. In the aftermath of Alexander's success *peltasts* remained a regular part of Greek warfare.

Lee L. Brice

See also: Alexander the Great; *Anabasis*; Brasidas; Corinthian War; Epameinondas; Eurymedon River, Battle of; Iphicrates; Peloponnesian War, Overview; Philip II of Macedon

References

Anderson, J. K. *Military Theory and Practice in the Age of Xenophon*. Berkeley, CA: University of California Press, 1970.

Best, Jan G. P. *Thracian Peltasts and Their Influence on Greek Warfare*. Groningen: Wolters-Noordhoff, 1969.

Sabine, Philip, Hans van Wees, and Michael Whitby, eds. *The Cambridge History of Greek and Roman Warfare*, vol. 1. Cambridge: Cambridge University Press, 2007.

Penteconter

The *penteconter* was the dominant ship in Greek sea warfare before the invention of the trireme. Invented in the Eastern Mediterranean during the Greek Archaic period, the *penteconter* was so named because it was rowed by 50 oars. It was a long, narrow ship, good in warfare and commerce, capable of carrying men and their equipment.

The type of warfare in which the *penteconter* excelled was carrying fighters who would then fight it out ship to ship or land on shore and engage in battle there. There is no evidence that the *penteconter* was equipped with a proper ram. Although it was used by the Phoenicians, it was also employed by all Greek city-states with fleets.

The trireme evolved out of the *penteconter* during the Late Archaic period. The trireme with its better speed and manpower would eventually supersede the *penteconter*, but it was still being used in the early fifth century. During the Ionian Revolt when Miletus requested aid, Athens sent 20 *penteconters* while Eretria sent 5 triremes, an indication of where Athens had its ship priorities in 499. The advantage of the *penteconter* was that it was less expensive to build and man since it had an estimated complement of less than 55 or so men as opposed to the 200 necessary for a trireme. The trireme did dominate naval warfare after 499, but there is evidence from historians of Rome that *penteconters* were still used in some western Greek cities in the third century.

Lee L. Brice

See also: Ionian Revolt; Trireme

References

Morrison, J. S., J. F. Coates, and N. B. Rankov. *The Athenian Trireme*, 2nd edition. Cambridge: Cambridge University Press, 2000.

van Wees, Hans. *Greek Warfare: Myths and Realities*. London: Duckworth, 2004.

Pericles

Greek statesman and leader of Athens, Pericles was born around 495 BCE in Athens where his father was a prominent political figure. Pericles was one of the leading figures behind renunciation of the Spartan alliance and the new league with Argos and Thessaly in 461 that led to the so-called First Peloponnesian War of 460–445. Pericles became the most prominent figure in the Athenian political arena after the assassination of Ephialtes and the ostracism of Cimon. On several occasions, and certainly during 444–429, he held the office of commanding general (*strategos*) and to the end of his life was acknowledged as the most influential speaker in the popular assembly.

Known as an imperialist, Pericles pushed the expansion of the city-state's power overseas. In 459 he sent about 200 triremes to support Egypt against Persia. In Greece, Athens also fought against Corinth. In 457 Pericles distinguished himself in battle against the Spartans at Tanagra in Boeotia. Although the Spartans won they did not press their advantage, and shortly thereafter Athens secured the submission of much of Boeotia. In 454 Pericles led a force to Oeniadae at the mouth of the Gulf of Corinth. After the Peace of Callias that ended the Persian Wars, Pericles supported moving the Delian League treasury to Athens and using it for rebuilding the Acropolis.

This is an idealistic portrait of Pericles, a general, who was one of the most significant figures of Athens during the fifth century BCE. He sought to expand both Athenian power and democracy, and he was one of the principal figures behind the start of the Peloponnesian War (431–404 BCE) although he died in 429 due to plague. (Library of Congress)

When Athens lost at Coroneia in 447, it lost control of Boeotia. The following year Pericles supported the Thirty Years' Peace with Sparta. From that point on, he had a free hand to focus on internal matters. He abandoned external adventure, and his chief preoccupation became the Athenian Empire including maintenance of a powerful Athenian fleet. He successfully turned the city's Delian League allies into subjects. He began installing military garrisons called *cleruchies* in league cities. Any member city that tried to withdraw from the league was attacked. When Samos revolted in 440 Pericles himself led a fleet out against it. He won one engagement but then divided his fleet, allowing one portion of it to be defeated before taking Samos itself. Within Athens his policy was to introduce full democracy, and under his rule the city experienced its greatest commercial prosperity.

In his last years, Pericles sought to resume western expansion by maintaining a strong fleet and securing alliances with states on the trade routes to Sicily and Italy. By 433, he was apparently convinced that a renewal of the Peloponnesian War was increasingly likely, and due to provocations that he supported the troops of Athens and Corinth soon came to blows. He seems to have been the architect of the Megarian decrees that had finally provoked the war with Sparta and he refused to withdraw them. In 431 the Second Peloponnesian War began.

According to Thucydides, our primary source for the war, Pericles advised the Athenians to stay inside the walls when the Spartans invaded, trust the fleet to import food and harass the Peloponnesian League, and not expand the empire. Some modern authors have tried to see in Pericles' advice a wholly defensive policy, but it is clear from the way events preceded in the first years of the war that his strategy was to pursue an aggressive raiding policy by sea while avoiding pitched battle by land. It was also a policy that trusted in Spartan inability to siege Athens.

Pericles evacuated Attica and moved the inhabitants into Athens itself and the protection of its Long Walls connecting the city with the port of Piraeus and the sea. With these walls and as long as Athens controlled the seas, the city was assured of adequate food. This policy was unpopular with landowning citizens, however, who saw their holdings destroyed by enemy invaders.

In early 430, Pericles made a moving appeal to the pride of the people of Athens in his famed funeral oration. A great plague erupted in the crowded city that summer, ultimately killing off more than a quarter of the population. Pericles led a naval expedition to the Peloponnese the same year but met with little success.

On his return, the Athenian people voted for peace, relieving Pericles of his post of the magistracy and fining him. Soon returned to office with extraordinary powers, Pericles could do little to affect the war effort and became a victim of the plague himself in 429. His death produced a great leadership void that his successors were unable to fill, and Athens was finally defeated in 404.

Spencer C. Tucker

See also: Athens; Corinth; Delian League; Long Walls; Peloponnesian League; Peloponnesian War, Causes of; Peloponnesian War, Overview; Sparta; Trireme

References

Formara, Charles W. and Loren J. Samons II. *Athens from Cleisthenes to Pericles.* Berkeley, CA: University of California Press, 1991.

Kagan, Donald. *The Peloponnesian War.* New York: Viking, 2003.

Strassler, Robert B., ed. *The Landmark Thucydides: A Comprehensive Guide to the Peloponnesian War.* New York: Free Press, 1998.

Tritle, Lawrence A. *A New History of the Peloponnesian War.* Malden, MA: Wiley-Blackwell, 2010.

Persian Empire

The largest empire in the ancient world before 336 BCE, the Persian kingdom started out in the area of the Southern Zagros Mountains in the area of modern-day Iran. In the mid-sixth century the Persian realm expanded under the Achaemenids to include much of Southwest Asia thus giving the empire the alternative name Achaemenid Empire. Its location and size made it immensely wealthy and powerful, but it was also generally stable for much of the period before Alexander's conquest.

Long subject to other local powers including the Babylonians and Medes, what began as the Anshan kingdom became the Persian Empire with the conquests of Cyrus II the Great in about 550. Cyrus was a member of the royal Achaemenid line giving the dynasty name to the empire through 330. The basis of the Achaemenid Empire's strength was their effective use of cavalry to move quickly and strike before enemies could properly prepare. The Persian Empire was the first to use cavalry so

Persian Empire, c. 500 BCE

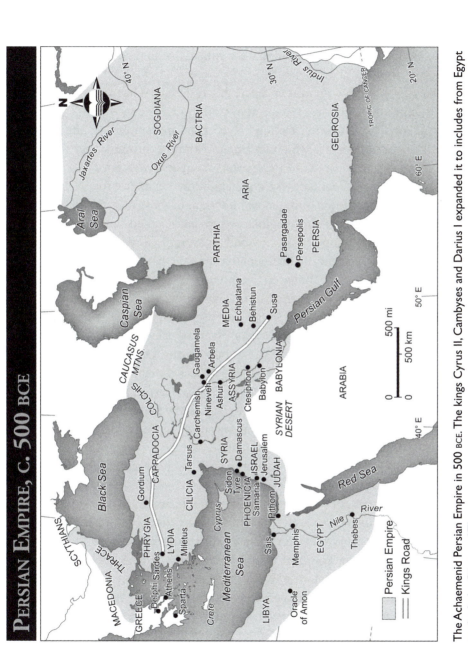

The Achaemenid Persian Empire in 500 BCE. The kings Cyrus II, Cambyses and Darius I expanded it to includes from Egypt to the Indus River and Thrace.

successfully and on such a scale. Cyrus conquered Media and then swept into Anatolia conquering as far west as Lydia before returning to conquer Mesopotamia and Babylonia. It was in Asia Minor that the Persian Empire first encountered the Greek cities of Ionia when Cyrus conquered Croesus' Lydian kingdom. Cyrus died pushing the limits of his domains further east and north of the Persian homelands.

After Cyrus formed an empire under his rule, the Achaemenids continued to build their empire. Cyrus' son, Cambyses II, conquered Egypt but died there. The next king, Darius I, succeeded immensely despite the reportedly irregular way in which he became king. A strong leader with vision, he built a new capital at Persepolis, conquered western India and Thrace, and created or regularized many institutions necessary for efficient government and trade. One of the most important of these reforms was his organization of the empire into regions or provinces called satrapies governed by someone (satrap) chosen by and answerable to the king. These satrapies were often culturally distinct areas as was the case in Egypt and Bactria, and they were not forced to assimilate.

Despite his significant conquests in Thrace and the eastern empire, Darius is more famous militarily for the campaign that ended at Marathon. Regardless of its importance to the Greeks, given the scale of the empire, the loss at Marathon was a minor incident for the Persians. Darius' son, Xerxes I, invaded Greece in 480, but despite burning Athens the campaign ended up in defeat at Salamis and then again in 479 at Plataea. Despite having to withdraw from Greece and losing several more battles, the Persian Wars continued intermittently until 450 when Persian successes made peace possible.

The Persian Empire continued to thrive and grow wealthy through most of the fifth and early fourth centuries as it benefited from several long-lived, stable kings including Artaxerxes I (465–424), Darius II (423–405), and Artaxerxes II (404–359). It was during the reign of Artaxerxes I that Zoroastrianism became a sort of state religion. The most serious threat to stability in this period was the breakaway of Egypt from 399 to 343 and the revolt of Cyrus the Younger against his brother Artaxerxes II. Cyrus hired a large army that included Greek mercenaries, but when he met his brother in battle at Cunaxa he died and the revolt ended. The Ten Thousand mercenaries had to fight their way out of the empire. Their success may have inspired others to consider the empire vulnerable.

Although the Persians were officially at peace with the Greeks after 450, they used the opportunity of the Peloponnesian Wars to give Sparta money to build and man a fleet, thus destroying the Athenian Empire. In exchange for the aid the Persians had hoped to regain control of Ionia.

After the conflict, Sparta was erratic in meeting its commitments to Artaxerxes II and even declared war against Persia. During the early fourth century the Persians used their money to support first one Greek city and then another, playing them off each other and contributing to the overall weakness of the Greek city-states and ensuring that no threat could emerge. At several points in the early fourth century the Persian king even mediated in disputes between Greek cities and imposed peace, the most famous instance of which was the King's Peace.

Several Greek leaders had tried to take up the notion of a Panhellenic campaign against Persia but the first to do so with vigor was Philip II of Macedon. He planned a war against Persia and was elected leader of the League of Corinth for that purpose. He sent an expeditionary force into Ionia, but it achieved little. Then in 336 his son, Alexander III, invaded Persia.

Regional satraps responded by trying to stop Alexander at the Granicus River and tried to attack Greece by sea, but both efforts failed. Alexander pushed through Asia Minor freeing the Greek cities en route and defeated Darius III at Issus in 333. After that defeat Darius gathered a new army while Alexander captured the Phoenician coast and Egypt, but this new force failed at Gaugamela in 331. While Darius tried to marshal a new army Alexander captured Babylon and Persepolis. The burning of Persepolis marked the official end of the Greek campaign of revenge. When Darius III died while fleeing in 330 the Achaemenid line ended and Alexander called himself king of Persia thereafter. Alexander then pushed east pacifying all the satrapies and continuing to employ Persian administrative institutions to control territory. When he died in 323 the Persian Empire was a wealthy, unified realm in which Alexander had already begun to assimilate Persians into his army and administration.

Lee L. Brice

See also: Alexander the Great; *Anabasis*; Darius I; Greco-Persian Wars, Consequences of; Greco-Persian Wars, Overview; Herodotus; King's Peace; Marathon, Battle of; Mycale, Battle of; Peloponnesian War, Consequences of; Peloponnesian War, Overview; Philip II of Macedon; Plataea, Battle of; Salamis, Battle of; Thucydides; Wars of Alexander the Great, Causes of; Xenophon; Xerxes I

References

Briant, Pierre. *From Cyrus to Alexander: A History of the Persian Empire*. Winona Lake, IN: Indiana University Press, 2005.

Cawkwell, George. *The Greek Wars: The Failure of Persia*. Oxford: Oxford University Press, 2005.

Heckel, Waldemar, and Lawrence A. Tritle, eds. *Alexander the Great: A New History*. Malden, MA: Wiley-Blackwell, 2009.

Kuhrt, Amélie. *The Ancient Near East*, 2 vols. New York: Routledge, 1995.

Phalanx, Hoplite

By the time the Battle of Marathon occurred in 490 BCE, Greek warfare had evolved from the individualistic combat of the *Iliad* into a form that relied heavily on a clash of heavy infantry. Such infantry was organized into a phalanx formation that although imperfect was effective enough to dominate Greek warfare from before Marathon down to Chaeronea in 338.

The basic unit of hoplite warfare was each citizen being similarly armed and armored. The infantryman's gear was called a panoply and included a large, concave shield (*aspis*) of about three feet diameter, bronze helmet, chest protection, greaves, and a spear of between six and eight feet length and sword. Shields were made of wood wrapped in bronze or with just a bronze edging. The most common helmet originally seems to have been the iconic enclosed Corinthian although there were a variety of helmet types used throughout Greece. Chest protection could be a bronze chest plate or leather with metal reinforcement or even layered linen sheets. Greaves protected the fighter's vulnerable shins. The spear was carried underhand into the line and then turned for overhand use, over the shoulder for stabbing down onto the opponent. The sword was for pursuit and hand-to-hand combat if the battle came to that point. Initially equipment was undoubtedly expensive, but as it became more regularized in each community the cost would have come down somewhat thereby increasing the number of men able to afford some of it and participate. The only citizens required to participate were the elite and better off farmers. Others would be called upon to serve as required, but only the more wealthy were required to serve as hoplites.

The phalanx is the formation created when the men array for battle. In the phalanx men would line up in files and ranks. The word "files" is used to describe the men standing in a single file, while "ranks" describes the lines of men standing side-by-side. A typical battle array would be six or eight ranks deep, but commanders would spread the line thinner if the opponent's line was longer, as occurred at Marathon in 490. Deeper formations do not usually occur until the fourth century. The physically prime, experienced fighters would be in the front several ranks with the novices behind them and finally, the most senior and experienced men in the rear ranks to steady the phalanx and hold the novices in place.

As they lined up in ranks each man would overlap his shield a bit with the shield of the man to his right. Then as Thucydides reports for the 418 Battle of Mantinea, as the ranks of men marched forward across the field each man would seek to maintain shield coverage on his right side so that the entire line would gradually move a bit to the right. Experienced commanders needed to plan accordingly and make sure the men on their left would be steady since they were likely to be outflanked. The position of honor was always the right end of the phalanx because that was where a phalanx had the best chance of beating the opponent first.

In some battles one or both lines would charge at a run, but it was more common for the sides to approach at a steady pace so as to maintain their formation. Spartans used flute music to keep pace. Once the two lines engaged the spear thrusting began as both sides tried to defeat the other. There is great debate over whether men in a hoplite phalanx fought in close order, a tight formation, or in more open order with a bit more space around each man to allow more room for fighting and for men in the ranks behind to step forward when a man needed to be replaced. Given the nature of hoplite warfare it is difficult to perceive how an over-close formation would function in practice. The "shoving" (othismos) that ancient authors mention as occurring should probably be thought of more as a general pushing off the field of battle by continuous combat rather than a literal pushing. Regardless, combat would continue until one side or the other broke and ran. Pursuit then occurred for a limited distance. When one side broke was when the most casualties occurred as men's unguarded sides became exposed.

The hoplite phalanx was strong and the men well protected on their front. Although not especially maneuverable, the nature of hoplite battle was such that maneuverability often did not matter. Mantinea in 418 is one of the few battles of which we know where a commander was able to maneuver a smaller unit of men during the battle to achieve victory. The phalanx was vulnerable on its flanks and rear. Thus it was common for commanders to array their lines with cavalry or some other obstacle on the flanks for protection. Later as more armies began to include light infantry and cavalry, it became common to place the units on the flanks for protection or use them as skirmishers between the armies as Epameinondas did at Leuctra (371) and Mantinea (362).

Hoplite phalanx combat was typically limited. The heavy armor meant casualties tended to be low unless there was an early panic. The goals of hoplite combat were also usually limited to control of land or enforcement of hegemony. Hoplite warfare could not normally result in annihilation of an enemy force or capture of a city. Because maintaining the phalanx formation was so important to success, battles were often fought in country as open and level as possible and could not occur until both sides conceded. If one side did not come out to fight the opponent would often provoke a response by burning or damaging crops and property. There was no need to completely destroy crops as ancient agriculture was such that merely reducing the crop for one season represented considerable hardship for most farmers. No doubt many battles ended before the phalanges met as one side was so intimidated that it panicked and conceded the battle.

Whichever city held the field of battle at the end of the day could call itself victorious. Afterward it was common for the victors to set up on the battlefield a trophy made of captured enemy arms. Both sides usually agreed to a truce in which they would recover the wounded and dead men and negotiate a peace. The matter was then decided until one side or the other broke the terms of the agreements.

Lee L. Brice

See also: Chaeronea, Battle of; Delium, Battle of; Epameinondas; Herodotus; Leuctra, Battle of; Mantinea, Battles of; Marathon, Battle of; Sparta; Thucydides

References

Anderson, J. K. *Military Theory and Practice in the Age of Xenophon.* Berkeley, CA: University of California Press, 1970.

Hanson, Victor D., ed. *Hoplites: The Ancient Greek Battle Experience.* London: Routledge, 1991.

Pritchett, W. Kendrick. *The Greek State at War*, 5 vols. Berkeley, CA: University of California Press, 1971–1991.

Sabine, Philip, Hans Van Wees, and Michael Whitby, eds. *The Cambridge History of Greek and Roman Warfare*, vol. 1. Cambridge: Cambridge University Press, 2007.

van Wees, Hans. *Greek Warfare: Myths and Realities.* London: Duckworth, 2004.

Phalanx, Macedonian

In the months after he became king of Macedon in 359 BCE, Philip II began securing his throne by reforming the Macedonian Army. The first result of his reforms was the creation of the Macedonian phalanx. The phalanx was the backbone of his military and made many Macedonian victories possible.

Macedonian kings had a long tradition of leading infantry supported by cavalry. In 359 when Philip became king of Macedonia he was reacting to the loss of his brother along with much of the army in the loss to Bardylis of Illyria. He called up men for the army, trained them, and then defeated Bardylis soundly in 358. He then set about reforming the Macedonian Army completely. The stages and process by which the Macedonian phalanx emerged are unclear because the sources are so incomplete, but by 352 Philip had reformed the phalanx and the results were clear.

Philip armed each member of the phalanx with a long pike or *sarissa* of 14 to 18 feet in length (the length varied over time). It was tipped with a sharp iron point and at the butt end had a sharp, weighted iron spike for balance. This spear was made in two shafts that could be assembled with an iron socket sleeve in the middle. The spear was so long it had to be carried with two hands so Philip gave his men smaller shields (*pelta*) of about 24 inches diameter that could be strapped to their left shoulder. The phalanx was organized into smaller units (*taxeis*) based on regional recruitment. The phalanx as a whole was called the foot companions (*pezhetairoi*) to demonstrate their importance to the king.

In addition to the new weapons, Philip increased training and discipline among his men to make sure his infantry could use them effectively. Long pack marches and obedience to commands became key elements of Macedonian army service. There may have been a matrix of rules and penalties regulating military behavior before Philip, but the only evidence for them is during his reign and later. Given the reforms and his success it seems unlikely that discipline was regular in the Macedonian Army before Philip II. Among the tactics he introduced to Macedon was the oblique line with the refused left. This arrangement meant that the enemy right had to march further across the battlefield to engage and in the process risked losing cohesion and opened gaps that would invite a cavalry charge. Philip also had units feign retreat in order to draw poorly disciplined enemy units out of position in the line.

The dynamics of how the phalanx worked come primarily from sources for Alexander's campaigns. During marches the soldier held the *sarissa* vertically. Before battle the men were arrayed in ranks by unit much like hoplites, but deeper. When they went into battle the men in the front ranks lowered their pikes to the horizontal for the impact. The phalanx approached at a steady pace in order to make sure the line remained steady and cohesive. The *sarissa* was so much longer than opponents' weapons that when the Macedonians hit the enemy line it was difficult for the enemy to even reach the Macedonians. Even if they knocked down the first line of spear tips there were still three more lines to go through before reaching the men holding the spears. The *phalangites* did not hold their spears stationary but appear to have jabbed with them too. Enemy lines often shattered against such a phalanx, but even where the enemy did not break immediately the *sarissa* line pinned down the enemy and created gaps as different parts of the enemy line reacted. The result was that few infantry lines could stand up against a steady Macedonian assault.

The phalanx was not invulnerable. Because of the lighter shields and the two-handed nature of the *sarissa* the units were vulnerable in their rear and on the flanks. The Persian attack on Alexander's left at Gaugamela in 331 demonstrates how important this weakness could be. Philip and Alexander were careful to use terrain or station units of light-armed cavalry or the elite *hypaspists* on the flanks of the phalanx, an arrangement that usually worked well.

The extent to which the combination of weapons, tactics, training, and discipline made the Macedonian phalanx so formidable is demonstrated not only by the numerous victories of Philip and Alexander, but even more so by the way in which the phalanx succeeded even when battlefield conditions worked against it. During the Battle of Granicus River, the phalanx had to march down one bank of the river, cross the swift stream and then attack up the opposite bank, all under fire from the Persians. They succeeded in doing so and contributed to victory. At Issus, the phalanx marched across the river and found that the uneven ground led to the formation losing cohesion. Despite the Persian attack into the gap that resulted, the phalanx continued to maintain discipline and drove the Persian units on its left off the battlefield.

Philip's reforms constituted a Revolution in Military Affairs. The phalanx that he created and perfected in less than a generation rendered all other forms of regional warfare obsolete. It would anchor Alexander's conquests and completely dominate Greek warfare until 197.

Lee L. Brice

See also: Alexander the Great; Chaeronea, Battle of; Gaugamela, Battle of; Granicus River, Battle of; Hydaspes, Battle of; Issus, Battle of; Philip II of Macedon; Wars of Alexander the Great, Overview

References

Brice, Lee L. "Philip II, Alexander the Great, and the Question of a Macedonian Revolution in Military Affairs (RMA)." *Ancient World* 42 (2) (2011): 137–47.

Romm, James, ed. *The Landmark Arrian: The Campaigns of Alexander*. New York: Pantheon, 2010.

Sabine, Philip, Hans Van Wees, and Michael Whitby, eds. *The Cambridge History of Greek and Roman Warfare*, vol. 1. Cambridge: Cambridge University Press, 2007.

Sekunda, Nick V. "The Macedonian Army." In *A Companion to Ancient Macedonia*, eds. Joseph Roisman and Ian Worthington, 446–71. Malden, MA: Wiley-Blackwell, 2010.

Worthington, Ian. *Philip II of Macedonia*. New Haven, CT: Yale University Press, 2008.

Philip II of Macedon

Philip II, known as Philip of Macedon, was born in Macedonia in 382 BCE. Little else is known of his early life except that he was held hostage in Thebes in 369 and several years afterward and while there he gained knowledge of Greece, its people, and military changes. He appeared again in the historical record after his older brother, Perdiccas III, died in 359 fighting against Illyrian invaders. Philip thus became leader of the Macedonians and soon, the king. He ruled Macedonia for more than 20 years, from 359 to 336. Philip's reign was made possible by his reorganizing the army and then moving against and defeating the Illyrians in 358.

A key element of Philip's success was his reform and enlargement of the Macedonian Army. Initially, he raised the army after the defeat of his brother and trained it into a superb fighting instrument. After securing his kingdom he gave Macedonian infantrymen new, longer spears called *sarissa* and extended training. The result was some of the finest infantry the Greek world had seen—the Macedonian phalanx. Additional heavy infantry included the *hypaspists*, the elite units who were armed like hoplites. There was also a bodyguard unit similarly armed. Later he added light troops, both allies and mercenaries, armed as *peltasts*, archers and slingers.

Gold stater of Philip II of Macedon featuring the head of Apollo. Philip's expansion into Chalkidike and capture of Amphipolis (357 BCE) and Krenides (356) provided access to rich gold and silver mines at Mt. Pangaion that made possible his continued military activity. (Bibliothéque Nationale, Paris, France; Giraudon/Art Resource, NY)

Philip did not limit his reforms to infantry. Macedonian cavalry had long been drawn from among the noble and elite families and were called king's companions (*hetairoi*). He continued the prior Macedonian practice of using cavalry on the flanks, but later armed them with longer javelins and trained them to ride into gaps created in the opposing line. Philip also hired engineers and maintained a group of them so that his capability at siege surpassed any other Greek army. His engineers invented the torsion catapult. The Macedonian Army became a highly trained, coordinated, combined-arms military capable of any kind of action including complicated siege warfare. The process of reforming the army took a number of years and was only completed after Philip II gained control of the mines in Chalcidice.

Philip used the army first to defeat the Illyrians soundly in 358. He then moved to bring Upper Macedonia directly under his control by tying the nobility to him, probably through connections of land, title, and wealth. He then entered into an ambitious program of expansion by both conquest and diplomacy. An aggressive and bold commander, he moved first to the north and to the east, bringing Paeonia under his control and moving into the Chalcidice. During 355–352, he extended his hegemony into Thessaly in wars with the Thessalians, Phocians, and Athenians, losing an eye in battle at Methone in 354. Philip turned out to be a master of diplomacy and deception as well as armed conflict. He negotiated when he could, bribed enemies at times, and sealed some of his arrangements through marriages. Ancient sources provide a better account of his diplomacy than his military activity.

Philip's demands for manpower during his expansion were such that he gave land to foreign men who would enlist in his army. These land grants made these settlers loyal to the king rather than local Macedonian elites and reinforced the kings hold on the kingdom, a significant political development that ensured stability. With the extra manpower and the funds from the mines in the Chalcidice, Philip was able to transform his phalanx into a professional force capable of fighting all year round. While it is important to not ignore the role of this new wealth in Philip's military reforms, one must recognize also that the reforms began in earnest before he had access to these mines.

The coasts of northeastern Greece had long been an Athenian preserve. Leader of Athens and famed orator Demosthenes became Philip's chief antagonist, delivering the first of his many orations of warning, known as the *Philippics*, to the Greeks about Macedon in 351. Philip continued to push Macedonian influence, and by 348 he was involved in a struggle over control of the Delphic Oracle. By the terms of a peace agreement in 346, he became a member of the Delphic Amphictiony with a recognized position in Greece.

During 346–340, Philip successfully campaigned in Illyria and Thrace, adding these regions to his subjects. Demosthenes continued to attack Philip's aggressive policies, and after Philip absorbed the European side of the Bosporus straits and the Hellespont (Dardanelles) during 344–343, Athens and Thebes moved closer to war against him in 339. The Fourth Sacred War in which Philip was to move against Amphissa resulted in open hostilities between Philip and an alliance of Thebes and Athens. Philip was victorious over the allied Greeks in the 338 Battle of Chaeronea, becoming the recognized master of all Greece. He set up garrisons in key cities including Ambracia, Corinth, and Thebes in order to control military movement. He then established the League of Corinth to provide him the means to maintain his hegemony in Greece. The League named him its leader (*hegemon*) and its military commander (*strategos*) in the war of revenge against Persia. He thus ended the political independence of the Greek cities.

Philip was making preparations for his war after 337 when he sent an expeditionary force to Persia in 336. While celebrating his seventh wedding, Philip was assassinated by a member of his own bodyguard in 336.

Although some modern authors have sought to blame various figures for his death including Darius III, or Olympias and Alexander, the sources are sufficiently flawed to make any accusation possible and plausible.

Philip's consolidation of his kingdom and spread of his hegemony over the rest of Greece were significant components of his son Alexander's success. Most importantly, Philip was the genius behind the Macedonian Army and had trained many of Alexander's most capable generals. Philip's military reforms would revolutionize warfare in the Aegean.

Spencer Tucker and Lee L. Brice

See also: Alexander the Great; Athens; Chaeronea, Battle of; Corinth, League of; Persian Empire; Phalanx, Macedonian; Sacred Wars; Thebes; Wars of Alexander the Great, Overview

References

Brice, Lee L. "Philip II, Alexander the Great, and the Question of a Macedonian Revolution in Military Affairs (RMA)." *Ancient World* 42 (2) (2011): 137–47.

Fox, Robin Lane, ed. *Brill's Companion to Ancient Macedon*. Leiden: Brill, 2011.

Hammond, Nicholas G. L. *Philip of Macedon*. London: Duckworth, 1994.

Heckel, Waldemar and Lawrence A. Tritle, eds. *Alexander the Great: A New History*. Malden, MA: Wiley-Blackwell, 2009.

Roisman, Joseph and Ian Worthington, eds. *A Companion to Ancient Macedonia*. Malden, MA: Wiley-Blackwell, 2010.

Worthington, Ian. *Philip II of Macedonia*. New Haven, CT: Yale University Press, 2008.

Piraeus

The primary harbor of Athens after 490 BCE, the Piraeus became during the fifth century the most important military and commercial port in the Eastern Mediterranean.

Although Phaleron had been the original harbor of Athens, it lost preeminence to Piraeus as a result of Themistocles' expansion of the fleet in the early fifth century. Piraeus was a peninsula with three good harbors, Zea, Munichia, and Kantharos, the first two of which were used exclusively for the fleet while the third handled commerce and the fleet. Themistocles began the process of fortifying the harbor, but the chain of walls and moles would not be complete and linked to Athens by the

Long Walls until 456. These walls secured Athens' access to imported food and supplies while also providing protection to the fleet's home base and shipyards.

During the fifth century the Piraeus became the largest and most important port in the Delian League and then the Eastern Mediterranean. When the Peloponnesian War ended in 404, Sparta pulled down the walls and reduced the fleet stationed there. During the periods of Athenian oligarchy, 411–410 and 404–403, the Piraeus became the center of opposition and led the restoration of democracy. Conon of Athens rebuilt the walls, probably with Persian financial support, ca. 393. The port regained some of its former glory during the first half of the fourth century as a result of the anti-Spartan conflicts and the Second Athenian League. Finally, after Macedonian control extended to Athens in 338 and remained strong, Piraeus lost its preeminence in the Aegean. The port continued to be important to Athens, but as a broader economic and military center Piraeus would never recover.

Lee L. Brice

See also: Athens; Delian League; Pericles; Second Athenian League; Themistocles; Trireme

References

Garland, Robert. *The Piraeus*. Ithaca, NY: Cornell University Press, 1988.

Munn, Mark. *The School of History: Athens in the Age of Socrates*. Berkeley, CA: University of California Press, 2000.

Plataea, Battle of

The Battle of Plataea was a major victory won by the Hellenic Alliance over Persian forces under the command of Mardonius in 479 BCE. That triumph combined with another Greek victory that same season at Mycale brought an end to Xerxes I's invasion as the Persian forces had to withdraw from the Greek mainland.

In 480, Xerxes finally followed up on Darius' failed effort of 10 years earlier and invaded Greece. Although the invasion initially met with some success, Xerxes suffered a devastating naval defeat at the Battle of Salamis in late September of 480. That setback forced Xerxes to return to Persia, but he left a large army in Greece under the commander Mardonius, who was one of his top generals, to maintain control of the conquered Greek territory.

Mardonius, who had been a nephew of Darius I, withdrew northward to Thessaly and Macedonia where he could be certain of logistical support from his allies. The following year he moved the army south and recaptured Athens. After sacking it again he withdrew after learning that King Pausanias of Sparta was approaching with a large force including members of the Hellenic Alliance. Mardonius set out to confront the Greek forces at the centrally located city of Plataea in Boeotia.

The city was located on the route from the Peloponnesus to northern Greece and there was open country, perfect for Persian cavalry. By that time, Pausanias had linked up his troops with the Athenians and other allies. Troop numbers are notoriously difficult to pin down for ancient warfare, but modern authors estimate that the combined Greek force was probably around 40,000 strong. In comparison, Mardonius' force, which included Greek allies, is believed to have numbered at least double that, as much as between about 80,000 and 100,000, including about 10,000 cavalry.

The battle of Plataea was fought in 479 BCE between the Persian army and the Hellenic Alliance. The Greeks moved into the low hills to defend against the Persian cavalry, a strategy that worked and allowed the Greeks to win and begin pushing the Persians out of central Greece. (John W. I. Lee)

In the summer of 479, the two armies faced off south of Thebes near the Asopus River. Mardonius had set up a fortified camp in the valley. The allied army approached through the foothills of Mount Cithaeron and after skirmishing for several days, Pausanias, whom the alliance had agreed to place in charge of the allied Greek army, moved his forces into the high ground of the foothills near Plataea to minimize the effectiveness of the Persian cavalry. In the process of maneuvering, allied communications broke down and the Spartans became separated from the Athenians. Seeing his chance to crush the two groups in detail, Mardonius launched an attack on the Greek forces and initially gained the upper hand. However, the Athenian and Spartan troops held off the Persians long enough to enable the other Greek forces to reinforce their defensive lines. The Greeks counterattacked, and the Spartans managed to kill Mardonius, turning the tide of the battle. The Persian troops were soon in disarray; Greek soldiers killed thousands of them in the valley and the camp.

The Greek victory at Plataea, combined with destruction of the remaining Persian naval forces at the Battle of Mycale around the same time, forced the Persians to withdraw. The surviving Persian forces retreated to Asia Minor. The allies dedicated some of the spoils from the Persian camp to making bronze statues at Olympis, Isthmia, and Delphia and also forged a serpent column with a tripod on top and set it up in Delphi with the names of the 31 alliance members. Hostilities continued until 450, but the victory at Plataea was still decisive in that never again would the Persian empire invade Greece.

Lee L. Brice

See also: Athens; Greco-Persian Wars, Overview; Hellenic Alliance; Herodotus; Mardonius; Mycale, Battle of; Salamis, Battle of; Sparta; Xerxes I

References

Burn, A. R. *Persia and the Greeks: The Defence of the West.* Stanford, CA: Stanford University Press, 1984.

Cawkwell, George. *The Greek Wars: The Failure of Persia.* Oxford: Oxford University Press, 2005.

Strassler, Robert B., ed. *The Landmark Herodotus: The Histories.* New York: Anchor Books, 2009.

S

Sacred Wars

The Sacred Wars were four Greek conflicts that took place between the sixth and the fourth centuries BCE. They originated when the authority in charge of Delphi, the Delphic Amphictiony, charged a city-state with sacrilege against Apollo. Membership in the Amphictiony varied, but included many different cities around Greece. Although the first two conflicts did not have wide repercussions, the last two Sacred Wars resulted in Philip II gaining entry into the military for the first time and political rivalries in central Greece.

The First Sacred War occurred in the early sixth century and resulted in the destruction of Cirrha due to sacrilegious treatment of pilgrims. The military force, sometimes called the Amphictionic League, annihilated the city and cursed the land. The second war started in the mid-fifth century when Athens and Sparta disagreed over Phocian control of Delphi. Athens put Phocis in control of Delphi, but Sparta disagreed and asserted direct Delphic authority. The Athenians responded by giving control back to Phocis ca. 448, probably by force. The conflict was part of the continuing struggle between Sparta and Athens. Both these conflicts are incompletely attested and do not seem to have had repercussions beyond immediate events.

The Third Sacred War turned out to be much more important. In 357 the Amphictiony, under heavy Theban influence, charged Phocis with sacrilege for cultivating the sacred Crisaean Plain. When the Amphictiony imposed a large fine Phocis ignored the fine. With tacit support from other cities its general, Philomelus, seized the sanctuary. Phocis tried to assert its control over Delphi and the leadership in the Amphictiony in order to

The Delphic Amphictiony oversaw the sanctuary at Delphi. In the fourth century BCE the city of Phocis seized the sanctuary and used the captured wealth to fund a war. The third and fourth sacred wars provided Philip II of Macedonia an opportunity to enter the political affairs of central Greece. View of theater is in the foreground, the temple of Apollo in the centerground, and the small treasury of the Athenians is further down the slope, in the center. (Lee L. Brice)

reverse the fine. The Amphictiony declared war. This activity must be seen in light of the Theban hegemony. Athens and Sparta supported Phocis as a way of hurting Theban ambitions. Phocis used the wealth it controlled to raise an army.

Phocis meddled in Thessaly against Philip II of Macedon with the result that their general, Onomarchus, defeated Philip in 354 or 353 and was then defeated by him the following year at the Battle of the Crocus Field. As a result, Philip II became leader (*archon*) of a united Thessaly. The Sacred War continued as a prolonged conflict between Thebes and Phocis with its numerous mercenaries paid for with wealth looted from Delphi. Finally in 347, Thebes requested aid from Philip II. After some panicked maneuvering by the Athenians he made peace with them and secured the pass at Thermopylae in 346. He imposed a peace on Phocis and let the Amphictiony set the penalty. As a result of ending the Sacred War, Philip received seats in the Delphic Amphictiony, a position that provided him legitimate access to political affairs south of Thessaly. The Third Sacred War thus resulted in Philip gaining control of Thessaly and a legitimate role in the political affairs of central Greece.

The Fourth Sacred War led directly to the end of Greek independence. The conflict began when Athens denounced Amphissa for cultivating the cursed land of Cirrha. When representatives of the Delphic Amphictiony were attacked while imposing a penalty it resulted in the council meeting and declaring a sacred war. Amphissa lost the first exchange but then ignored the fine and penalties imposed. Philip II was called in as military leader (*hegemon*) of the Amphictionic League in the fall of 339 and Athens allied with Amphissa and other states to oppose him. After some maneuvering by both sides over the winter and spring, Philip defeated Amphissa in 338 and then brought his entire army to Chaeronea where he defeated the combined Athenian-Theban force with their allies and imposed peace on Greece through the League of Corinth.

The Sacred Wars were originally limited affairs, but through these conflicts Philip of Macedon gained legitimate access to central Greece and eventually ended the political independence of the Greek city-states. Although in hindsight it seems like the result was inevitable it is important to remember that no participant could have seen how the last two wars would have the impact they did on Greece.

Lee L. Brice

See also: Athens; Chaeronea, Battle of; Philip II of Macedon; Sparta; Xenophon

References

Buckler, John. *Philip II and the Sacred War*. Leiden: Brill, 1989.

Osborne, Robin. *Greece in the Making, 1200–479 BC*, 2nd edition. Routledge: New York, 2006.

Rhodes, P. J. *A History of the Classical Greek World, 478–323 BC*, 2nd edition. Malden, MA: Wiley-Blackwell, 2010.

Worthington, Ian. *Philip II of Macedonia*. New Haven, CT: Yale University Press, 2008.

Salamis, Battle of

The Battle of Salamis in 480 was the largest naval battle ever fought in the ancient world.

When they heard about the defeat at Thermopylae, the Hellenic Alliance's fleet at Artemisium withdrew to Salamis. With no barrier remaining between Athens and the Persian land force, the Athenians sought safety. Some citizens fled to Salamis or the Peloponnese, and some men joined the triremes' crews. When Xerxes and his army arrived at Athens the city was nearly empty, although some troops remained to defend (symbolically) the Acropolis. The Persians soon secured it and burned down the temples.

Athens added to the force their reserve fleet that had not participated at Artemisium. Triremes from other cities, notably Corinth, also joined, giving them about 100 additional ships. The combined fleet at Salamis was thus actually much larger than it had been at Artemisium, comprising about 310 ships, most of which were Athenian.

Herodotus discusses the Persian and Greek preparations, but it is difficult at times to separate fact from legend. Xerxes eventually maneuvered his forces into position. He brought advance elements of his fleet from Phalerum, off Salamis, and sent part of his army toward the Peloponnese in the hope that this action would cause the Greeks of that region to order their ships from the main Greek fleet to return home, allowing him to destroy them at his leisure. Failing that, Xerxes was prepared for a battle in the open waters of the Saronic Gulf that forms part of the Aegean Sea. There his superior numbers would have the advantage.

Themistocles wanted a battle in the Bay of Salamis. Drawing on the lessons of the Battle of Artemisium, he pointed out that a fight in close conditions would be to the advantage of the Greeks. According to Herodotus,

In 480 BCE, the Hellenic Alliance defeated the Persian fleet here, in the narrow channel between Athens' port and the island of Salamis. The straits were too narrow for the Persian fleet to employ its superior numbers. (Lee L. Brice)

with his captains furious at this and with the possibility that the Peloponnesian ships would bolt home, Themistocles resorted to stratagem to bring on battle. He sent a letter to the Persians informing Xerxes that Themistocles had changed sides. Themistocles gave no reason for this decision but said that he now sought a Persian victory. In the letter he affirmed that the Greeks were bitterly divided and would offer little resistance. Furthermore, Themistocles claimed, elements of the fleet intended to sail away during the next night and link up with Greek land forces defending the Peloponnese. Themistocles' letter went on to advise the Persians to bottle up the Greeks to keep them from escaping. This letter contained much truth and was, after all, what Xerxes wanted to hear. Whether this ruse actually occurred in this way or not, the Persians acted to the Greeks' advantage.

Xerxes, not wishing to lose the opportunity, acted swiftly. He ordered Persian squadrons patrolling off Salamis to block all possible escape routes while the main fleet came into position that night. The Persians held their stations all night waiting for the Greek breakout. As Themistocles expected, the Persian king chose not to break off the operation that he had begun.

The Greeks moved out to meet the Persians. Xerxes watched the battle progress from a throne at the foot of nearby Mount Aegaleus across from Salamis. Early in the morning the entire Persian fleet went on the attack, moving up the Salamis Channel in a crowded mile-wide front that precluded any organized withdrawal should that prove necessary. The details of the actual battle are obscure, but the superior discipline and seamanship of the Greeks allowed them to take the Persians in the flank. The confusion created by too many Persian ships in narrow waters combined to decide the issue in favor of the Greeks. The Greeks stationed hoplites on the shore of Salamis to kill any Persians swimming onto shore, and the Persians did the same on the Attic side of the strait.

The Persians lost numerous ships, while the defenders lost only about 40. According to Herodotus, few of the Greeks, even from the lost ships, died because they could swim and went to shore on Salamis when their ships floundered, whereas the Persians drowned or were killed on the shore. The next day the Greeks found the Persian ships gone. Xerxes had ordered them to the Hellespont to protect the bridge there. Xerxes left two-thirds of his forces in garrison in central and northern Greece and marched the remainder to Sardis. The Battle of Salamis meant the end of the year's campaign.

Although Salamis was an important Greek victory, it was not decisive in terms of ending a conflict or even the invasion. The victory forced

Xerxes to retreat, but much of the Persian army did not withdraw from Greece. The following year they again sacked and burned Athens. The Persian fleet suffered at Salamis, but not sufficiently enough to clear the seas for more than a season.

Spencer C. Tucker

See also: Athens; Greco-Persian Wars, Overview; Hellenic Alliance; Herodotus; Themistocles; Trireme; Xerxes I

References

Cawkwell, George. *The Greek Wars: The Failure of Persia*. Oxford: Oxford University Press, 2005.

Hale, John. *Lords of the Sea: The Epic Story of the Athenian Navy and the Birth of Democracy*. New York: Viking Press, 2009.

Morrison, J. S., J. F. Coates, and N. B. Rankov. *The Athenian Trireme*, 2nd edition. Cambridge: Cambridge University Press, 2000.

Strassler, Robert B., ed. *The Landmark Herodotus: The Histories*. New York: Anchor Books, 2009.

Strauss, Barry. *The Battle of Salamis: The Naval Encounter That Saved Greece—and Western Civilization*. New York: Simon and Schuster, 2004.

Second Athenian League

The Second Athenian League or Confederacy emerged during 379–377 BCE when Athens set up a defensive military alliance of Greek city-states not in Asia Minor. This confederacy would be the last successful effort by Athens to set up such a network.

The Second Athenian Confederacy grew out of a desire to ensure that Sparta honored the terms of the King's Peace in 378. When it was set up, the Athenians tried to address many of the most serious concerns that had arisen with the Delian League, so there was to be a deliberative assembly for members, no tribute, and no meddling by Athens. The confederacy started well enough and gathered numerous members during its first few years. The confederacy was successful against Spartan attacks and generally fulfilled its duties for much of the first decade.

Over time, however, the confederacy transformed into an Athenian quasi-Empire as many of the same tactics employed in the Delian League gradually emerged here as well, including political meddling, garrisons, tribute, and warfare against members who tried to withdraw. The Social War, a rebellion instigated by the satrap Mausolus of Caria and led by Byzantium, Chios, and Rhodes left the confederacy crippled after 357. The alliance continued as best it could, unable to stop the rebellion. When Philip II created the League of Corinth in 338 the Athenian Confederacy ended. Although the alliance system was a mere (and at times dark) shadow of the Delian League, it was an element of the fourth-century competition for hegemony among the Greek city-states.

Lee L. Brice

See also: Athens; Corinth, League of; Delian League; King's Peace

References

Buckler, John. *Aegean Greece in the Fourth Century BC.* Leiden: Brill, 2003.

Rhodes, P. J. *A History of the Classical Greek World, 478–323 BC*, 2nd edition. Malden, MA: Wiley-Blackwell, 2010.

Sicily

Sicily, the largest island in the Mediterranean Sea, may have seemed far from the Greek mainland, but once Greeks set colonies on the island in the eighth century BCE it became part of the Greek world. East–west interaction between Sicily and Greece affected warfare in both regions.

Greek traders sailing west were long familiar with Sicily and Southern Italy. By the late eighth century, various Greek cities facing population pressure created colonies in eastern and southern Sicily, the most important of which became the Corinthian colony Syracuse. In the western part of the island Carthaginians established trading colonies. In the interior of the island and along parts of the coast indigenous settlements of Sicel and Elymi peoples continued to exist, occasionally fighting against or siding with one city or another in wars. Trade with Greece, Southern Italy, and Africa as well as agricultural wealth of their own permitted Sicilian coastal settlements to prosper.

In the sixth and fifth centuries, the prosperity led to military conflict among the Greek cities and especially against the Carthaginians in the west. These threats made it possible for leaders to seize power. Tyrants

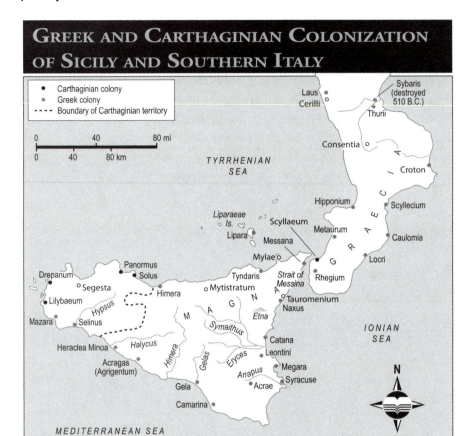

GREEK AND CARTHAGINIAN COLONIZATION OF SICILY AND SOUTHERN ITALY

- Carthaginian colony
- Greek colony
- - - - Boundary of Carthaginian territory

Sicily and Southern Italy in 415. Greece and Carthage had set up colonies in Sicily beginning in the eighth century. The pretext for the Athenian expedition against Sicily was conflict between the towns of Segesta and Selinus. Athens counted on receiving more support in Italy and Sicily than it found.

ruled many of those cities, like Phalaris and Theron of Acragas, Gelon and Hieron of Syracuse. These tyrants used military tactics similar to those employed in Greece such as the hoplite phalanx and cavalry in support. Warfare between cities and against Carthage was sufficiently common in this period that the Sicilian Greeks acquired a reputation for military ability. When the Hellenic League faced Xerxes' invasion in 480 they approached Gelon of Syracuse for assistance, but he was busy preparing to fight Carthaginian forces. In 480, Gelon and Theron won an enormous victory against the Carthaginians at Himera that solidified Gelon's rule, but also brought peace with Carthage.

During the Peloponnesian War Athens made treaties with several Sicilian cities and sent missions there. The first time, during 427–424, they sought assistance in Sicily and Southern Italy and sent a small force west. In 415, after Sicilian allies had requested aid, Alcibiades convinced the Athenian assembly that the conquest of democratic Syracuse would be highly profitable and would hurt the Peloponnesian League. The city sent an enormous force of more than 100 triremes and numerous support ships along with more than 5,000 soldiers. Syracuse successfully appealed to Corinth and Sparta for assistance. The expedition went badly from the start and in the end failed to achieve anything for Athens except enormous loss in men and material.

Beginning in 409, the Carthaginians attempted to conquer the entire island, capturing nearly all except the eastern coastal cities. Dionysius I succeeded in establishing himself as tyrant of Syracuse and used his mercenary armies and improved siege techniques to defeat the Carthaginians and push them back to the west of the island. His innovations in siege warfare had a dramatic impact on the rest of the Greek world as he adopted Near Eastern siege techniques. His victory ushered in an extended period of tyranny in Syracuse (398–367) that ended in more fighting between cities and with Carthage.

Facing a renewed Carthaginian threat, at the request of Syracuse, Corinth sent out Timoleon with a small force. He defeated the Carthaginian forces and with mercenaries established Greek rule over most of Sicily by 340. By the end of the fourth century Syracuse was again under a tyrant.

Sicily may seem a sideshow compared with mainland Greece, but it was an important part of the Greek world and the military activity there had an impact in the Aegean. Athens' failed Sicilian expedition, for example, weakened Athens during the Peloponnesian War and contributed to its eventual defeat. Sicilian tyrant Dionysius I's invention of the torsion catapult and adoption of eastern siege techniques would change sieges in Greece and have a pronounced influence on Philip II's military.

Lee L. Brice

See also: Alcibiades; Artillery; Athens; Corinth; Dionysius I; Peloponnesian War, Overview; Sicily; Sicily, Athenian Expedition Against; Thucydides; Timoleon

References

Asheri, David. "Carthaginians and Greeks." In *Cambridge Ancient History*, vol. 4, 2nd edition, ed. D. Lewis et al., 147–70. Cambridge: Cambridge University Press, 1988.

Asheri, David. "Sicily, 478–431." In *Cambridge Ancient History*, vol. 5, 2nd edition, eds. D. Lewis et al., 739–80. Cambridge: Cambridge University Press, 1988.

Talbert, Richard J. A. "The Greeks in Sicily and South Italy." In *The Greek World in the Fourth Century from the Fall of the Athenian Empire to the Successors of Alexander*, ed. Lawrence A. Tritle, 137–65. New York: Routledge, 1997.

Sicily, Athenian Expedition Against

The Athenian invasion of Sicily, usually called the Sicilian Expedition, began in 415 BCE full of promise. By the time it was over two years later, Athens had lost two fleets and many men in addition to reigniting the Peloponnesian War. Thucydides devotes more of his history to this expedition than to any other event suggesting more than anything else that this failure led to the Athenian defeat in 404.

The Sicilian Expedition began during the Peace of Nicias. An Athenian ally, Segesta, requested aid against a threat by allies of Syracuse. Alcibiades proposed that the city aid its ally and in the process conquer Syracuse and enrich the city. Despite counterarguments by his older political competitor, Nicias, the proposal carried and the assembly appointed both men leaders of the force along with a third man, Lamachus, to balance things out. Athens prepared for an enormous and expensive expedition.

The night before the fleet departed someone defaced herms—anthropomorphic religious markers—in the city. Although this was a crime and Alcibiades was suspect the fleet sailed. The force included more than 134 triremes and warships and over 100 additional support ships. There were also 5,100 hoplites as well as archers, slingers, and *peltasts*. The one aspect in which they were weak was cavalry, which they probably expected to obtain in Sicily or southern Italy. When they arrived in the west they learned that there was less support than expected. In need of a base, they sailed to Catana, on the east coast of Sicily, and captured it by subterfuge.

Syracuse was as large as Athens so it had the potential for a large army, but its commanders and hoplites were inexperienced. Its navy was small, inexperienced and in disrepair, but the Syracusans had begun constructing ships as soon as they learned the Athenians were coming. Two aspects in which the Syracusans had an advantage were in cavalry and allies. They had a numerous and experienced cavalry and many allies on whom they could draw.

Before the invaders could act further, Alcibiades was recalled to Athens to face trial for defacing the herms. During the return he defected to Sparta. According to Thucydides, he alerted the Spartans to the invasion and advised them to send a capable commander and as much support as their allies could to Syracuse. Sparta responded by sending Gylippus with reinforcements.

Despite the setback of losing Alcibiades the campaign continued. Nicias and Lamachus tried diplomacy to secure funds and allies, with little result. Late in 415 they attacked Syracuse. The Athenians won a hoplite engagement, but failed to follow up and then had to withdraw to Catana for the winter. They wrote to Athens requesting assistance and continued diplomacy. Nicias, who had an old connection to Syracuse, may well have been trying to get friends in the city to surrender it to him. Syracuse spent the winter seeking assistance from the Peloponnesian League and in Sicily as well as building up ships and fortifications in the harbor.

The next year started well for Athens. Cavalrymen from Athens and cash arrived to buy horses and supplies. Then in a surprise attack they captured the strategic Epipolae heights west of Syracuse and built a fort. Starting from this fort they built a wall of circumvallation south to cut off Syracuse from the rest of Sicily. If they could finish the encircling wall then with their ships they could cut off the city and starve it to surrender. Syracuse tried to build counterwalls, but the Athenians destroyed these efforts in several battles. During this fighting Lamachus died leaving Nicias in command alone. Afterward, they sailed into Syracuse's Great Harbor and secured a beachhead for a base. Just as events seemed to be going Nicias' way the Spartan commander Gylippus arrived with numerous reinforcements.

Gylippus energized Syracuse and immediately began improving their army. He started fighting the Athenians daily and started a new counterwall on the heights to stop the circumvallation. He was often successful in skirmishing and after some weeks brought his counterwall out across the Athenian path, thus stopping them from cutting off the city. The Athenian fleet also suffered from constant wear and tear on blockade as Syracuse trained its rowers and prepared new ships. Syracuse had the advantage by the end of 414.

Both sides spent winter seeking additional assistance. Nicias asked to be withdrawn or replaced. The Athenians responded by sending out another 75 ships and 5,000 hoplites under the command of Demosthenes. The Peloponnesians sent more ships and soldiers to assist Syracuse. Sicilian allies also provided manpower to Syracuse.

A fleet engagement in the Great Harbor initiated the campaign season of 413. Although Nicias had only 60 triremes against the Syracusan 80, the Athenians' experience told as they won the engagement. While everyone watched the sea battle Gylippus also attacked all the Athenian forts capturing three of the four. These combined actions meant that the sea blockade was broken and the Syracusans now had the Athenian camp cut off from land. A second naval engagement several weeks later went to Syracuse, which had adopted the Corinthian tactic of ramming bow to bow. Soon afterward Demosthenes finally arrived with 73 more ships and 5,000 hoplites.

Demosthenes favored action so he led a night attack against the position on Epipolae. The attack started well, but when Syracuse counterattacked the Athenians became entangled and confused leading to defeat and withdrawal with heavy losses. After this battle Athenian morale declined. They decided to evacuate, but an eclipse of the moon caused Nicias to delay action on religious grounds. When they were finally ready to evacuate Syracuse blocked the harbor and fought hard. The Athenians lost and failed to break out. They tried to retreat under cover via a land route westward. The Syracusan cavalry harassed them, killing many men. The entire force was captured. Nicias and Demosthenes were executed and the remaining captives who could not find a way out worked to death in the quarries.

As a result of the expedition, Athens lost many thousands of men as well as numerous ships, supplies, and wealth. Some Athenian allies revolted when news of the immense defeat made it back to the Aegean. Sparta was unable to capitalize on Athens' loss and the war dragged on for another nine years.

Lee L. Brice

See also: Alcibiades; Athens; Corinth; Nicias; Peloponnesian League; Peloponnesian War, Overview; Sicily; Thucydides; Trireme

References

Brice, Lee L. "The Athenian Expedition to Sicily." In *The Oxford Handbook of Classical Military History*, ed. Lawrence A. Tritle and Brian Campbell. Oxford: Oxford University Press, 2012.

Strassler, Robert B., ed. *The Landmark Thucydides: A Comprehensive Guide to the Peloponnesian War*. New York: Free Press, 1998.

Tritle, Lawrence A. *A New History of the Peloponnesian War*. Malden, MA: Wiley-Blackwell, 2010.

Sparta

The Greek city of Sparta, also known as Lacedaemon, emerged in the region of Laconia during the Early Archaic Period and by the end of the seventh century BCE had become the dominant military power in the Peloponnese. After its conquest of Messenia sometime before 600 BCE, Sparta became a highly militarized society in which citizen males, called the Equals (*homoioi*), were raised in a system of public education called the *agoge*. This incompletely understood institution taught military skills and emphasized duty and discipline. The army was led by one of the two kings. The citizens were supported by nearby communities of free noncitizens called *perioikoi* who also served in the army, and by state-owned helots who worked the land so citizens could focus on warfare. By the late sixth century the Spartans had the dominant land army in Greece and maintained their supremacy until 371 BCE when loss at Leuctra triggered the collapse of their power.

When the Ionian Greeks sought assistance for their revolt in 499 the Spartans declined to join. But when Darius I demanded earth and water from them they declined on behalf of their alliance, the Peloponnesian League, and murdered the envoys. When Athens requested assistance in 490 Sparta arrived too late to contribute. Then in 481 when the Greeks

The ancient city of Sparta was in the fertile Eurotas river valley. Surrounded on all sides by high mountains, the Spartans conquered their neighbors for their land and maintained a militarized society. Little remains of ancient Sparta, but the valley remains populous and fertile. (Lee L. Brice)

formed the Hellenic Alliance to oppose Xerxes' invasion, the Spartans held the position of leadership since they were the acknowledged military experts. Leonidas and his 300 Spartans led the doomed Greek effort at Thermopylae and their fate crystallized Sparta's reputation for steadfast bravery. Sparta was officially in command at Salamis even if Themistocles was the actual commander. The following year at Plataea the Spartan king, Pausanius, led the alliance forces and achieved a surprising victory against Mardonius, driving the Persians out of Greece. The king successfully pressed the Persians in 478, but after disputes over leadership the Spartans and the Peloponnesian League withdrew from the Hellenic Alliance, leaving Athens to establish the Delian League.

Sparta went its separate way focusing its attention on maintaining its hegemony in the Peloponnese. Spartan society had difficulty maintaining population numbers, a situation exacerbated ca. 469 when the city's gymnasium collapsed after an earthquake, killing many young boys. Then in 466 a serious revolt of helots led Sparta to request Athenian assistance in laying siege to Ithome. After Cimon arrived from Athens with an army the Spartans became nervous and sent him home suddenly resulting in his exile. This worsened relations between the cities. The Athenians eventually negotiated a settlement between Sparta and the helots, relocating some helots to the Aetolian port of Naupactus. Tension with Athens during 466–445 continued to result in skirmishes and even open conflict occasionally, sometimes called the First Peloponnesian War.

In 431 after a variety of Athenian provocations of Peloponnesian League members Sparta declared war on Athens. Thucydides blamed the war on Spartan fears of Delian League strength. Sparta waged a desultory effort for much of the Archidamian phase of the war and made little real progress. Sparta was unable to effectively counter the Periclean strategy of keeping the army behind the Long Walls, importing grain, and using its fleet to harass the Peloponnese coast. Sparta's potential manpower crisis is indicated by events during 425–423. Athens seized the initiative by occupying Pylos and forcing a Spartan force on Sphacteria to surrender in 425. Sparta responded by sending Brasidas with an army made up of freed helots and some *perioikoi* to northern Greece where they captured Amphipolis. The ensuing campaign led to the Peace of Nicias.

During the peace, Sparta and its allies resisted Alcibiades' attempts to create an Argive alliance, eventually winning a major victory in 418 at Mantinea. When Alcibiades defected during the Sicilian Expedition they welcomed him in and took his advice to send a commander to Syracuse.

Gylippus went in 414 and effectively led the Syracusans to victory in 413. Despite this victory and the occupation of Decelea inside Attica, and Athenian political troubles, the Spartans were unable to end the war. Lysander eventually secured Persian wealth in exchange for control of the Ionian Greek cities, thus allowing Sparta to build a strong navy. The Spartan fleet victory at Aegospotami in 405 made it possible to cut off Athens' food supply so that the war ended in 404. Sparta tore down Athens' walls and eliminated the Delian League but ignored the demands of several Peloponnesian League members to destroy Athens utterly.

Lysander turned the former Delian League into a Spartan naval empire, but after several years of expansion and hegemony the Corinthian War began when Athens, Corinth, and Thebes resisted with Persian funding. This was the beginning of continuous conflict for Sparta with both Athens and Thebes. Even as it slowly won the war with these cities, there were several campaigns in Ionia against Achaemenid Persia, the largest of which was led by the king, Aegesilaus II. Making little real progress in Ionia, Sparta and Persia, who were becoming concerned about Athenian expansion, negotiated the King's Peace in 387. This treaty ensured Persian funding for Sparta and made it the enforcer of the peace in Greece, in return for the Ionian Greeks, again.

During the peace, Agesilaus took a hard line against Sparta's enemies, especially Thebes. This policy eventually led to open conflict. In 371 the Thebans crushed a Spartan army under Cleombrotus at Leuctra, thus breaking the reputation of Spartan armies. The Peloponnesian League folded soon thereafter. The following year, Epameinondas invaded the Peloponnese and made it into Laconia, but he did not take the city. While there he freed Messenia and established Megalopolis as a free Messenian city to counter Spartan hegemony, thus destroying the basis of Spartan power. During the years afterward, the Spartan economy and much of its military strength collapsed. Theban forces invaded again in 367, but did not attack Sparta. In 362 Sparta organized a broad anti-Theban alliance that fought Epameinondas at Mantinea, but the battle was a draw that failed to change the situation for Sparta.

Leuctra completely changed Sparta's role in the Peloponnese. For much of the rest of the fourth century Sparta limped along and many of its warriors became mercenaries, especially against Persia. Sparta did not contribute to the anti-Macedonian alliance at Chaeronea in 338 and when Philip created the League of Corinth he excluded Sparta, as did Alexander III when he became king. The last time Sparta made a military splash came during 331–330 when its king, Agis III, with Persian funding raised a revolt against Alexander and captured much of Crete before moving to central Greece. There he lost to Antipater and Sparta was further isolated, a position it would hold for much of the rest of its existence.

Lee L. Brice

See also: Aegospotami, Battle of; Agesilaus II; Agis III; Athens; Brasidas; Corinth, League of; Corinthian War; Delian League; Greco-Persian Wars, Consequences of; Greco-Persian Wars, Overview; Hellenic Alliance; Herodotus; Ionian Revolt; King's Peace; Leuctra, Battle of; Lysander; Mantinea, Battles of; Peloponnesian League; Peloponnesian War, Causes of; Peloponnesian War, Overview; Sphacteria; Thebes; Thermopylae, Battle of; Thucydides; Xenophon

References

Buckler, John. *Aegean Greece in the Fourth Century BC.* Leiden: Brill, 2003.

Hodkinson, Stephen and Anton Powell, eds. *Sparta and War.* Swansea: Classical Press of Wales, 2006.

Kennel, Nigel M. *Spartans: A New History.* Malden, MA: Wiley-Blackwell, 2010.

Rhodes, P. J. *A History of the Classical Greek World, 478–323 BC*, 2nd edition. Malden, MA: Wiley-Blackwell, 2010.

Sphacteria

The Battle of Sphacteria in 425 BCE was important because it was the first time a Spartan force surrendered. This battle was the culmination of the Athenian campaign at Pylos and led to Cleon's dominance in Athens and Brasidas' campaign in northern Greece.

The Battle of Sphacteria occurred during the first phase of the Peloponnesian War. The Athenian commander Demosthenes had seized an opportunity to land in Spartan territory at Pylos and established a garrison. The Spartan attempt to dislodge him resulted in an Athenian naval victory in the bay. In the aftermath a group of Spartan soldiers, including 120 Spartan citizens, was stranded on the island of Sphacteria. Spartan policy had always been to never surrender, but in this case city leadership was so concerned at the potential death of so many citizens that they negotiated with Athens for peace. When the negotiations failed due to Cleon's interference Demosthenes tightened the island blockade and requested reinforcements. Cleon, the rising political leader in Athens, was sent to take Sphacteria. In addition to hoplites he employed Thracian *peltasts* for the first time in the war. The combined force was successful in maneuvering the Spartans into an impossible position. The Spartans were ordered by their leaders to surrender rather than be annihilated and did so.

The victory gave Athens significant leverage in negotiations and secured Cleon's primacy in Athens. In response, Brasidas led a campaign north in 424 to take Amphipolis and disrupt Athenian ambitions.

Lee L. Brice

See also: Athens; Brasidas; Cleon; Peloponnesian War, Overview; *Peltasts*; Sparta

References

Strassler, Robert B., ed. *The Landmark Thucydides: A Comprehensive Guide to the Peloponnesian War*. New York: Free Press, 1998.

Tritle, Lawrence A. *A New History of the Peloponnesian War*. Malden, MA: Wiley-Blackwell, 2010.

Strategos

The Greek word *strategos* refers to top military leadership or a general. In the Athenian democratic reforms of ca. 508 BCE the 10 generals (*strategoi*) were established as elected posts, with one from each of the 10 tribes.

The 10 Athenian *strategoi* held equal authority to lead, but often one or two would emerge as most capable. At Marathon each general took turns for the day. Miltiades had no more authority than any of other *strategos*. By the time of Xerxes' invasion the *strategoi* had become the only elected posts in the Athenian democracy so that they attracted the most ambitious men. The *strategos* became the platform for leading the city-state. Themistocles, Cimon, Pericles, Cleon, Demosthenes, Nicias, Alcibiades, and Iphicrates were all important Athenian generals even though they were not all interested in political dominance.

There is poor evidence for how other cities selected their generals. A general would usually be called a *strategos*, although some cites used other words. Epameinondas and Pelopidas were generals of Thebes, called *boeotarchs*.

Lee L. Brice

See also: Athens; Cimon; Conon of Athens; Herodotus; Iphicrates; Marathon, Battle of; Miltiades the Younger; Nicias; Pericles; Themistocles; Thucydides

References

Munn, Mark. *The School of History: Athens in the Age of Socrates.* Berkeley, CA: University of California Press, 2000.

Pritchett, W. Kendrick. *The Greek State at War*, 5 vols. Berkeley, CA: University of California Press, 1971–1991.

Sabine, Philip, Hans Van Wees, and Michael Whitby, eds. *The Cambridge History of Greek and Roman Warfare*. Vol. 1. Cambridge: Cambridge University Press, 2007.

T

Thebes

The city of Thebes was an important Greek center in the Bronze Age, but had declined somewhat afterward. Located on a strategic site on the Boeotian Plain, Thebes had long tried to assert its primacy among the cities in Boeotia, with mixed success. Given our limited sources for Thebes, little is known with certainty about its history before 490 BCE. There is little doubt that although militarily it was a notch below Athens and Sparta for much of the period between 490 and 323, Thebes was still an important city that continued to influence Greek affairs.

By 490 Thebes was a member of the Peloponnesian League. When Darius I sent envoys to Greece it deferred to Sparta. The city played no role at Marathon. Thebes was part of the Hellenic Alliance in 480 and sent men to Thermopylae. Herodotus suggests that the city would defect to Persia at the first opportunity, but this impression is likely due to his *History* having been written in Athens when it was in conflict with Thebes. The Theban troops at Thermopylae died fighting in the pass along with the Spartans and Thespians. Thebes also contributed men to the fight at Plataea.

During the period after 479, Thebes does not appear to have played a strong role outside Boeotia. It fought against Athens in several engagements before 457, but failed to keep it out of Boeotia where Athens dominated for a decade. Thebes contributed in 447 to ejecting Athens from the region and then formed the Boeotian Confederacy. Thebes attacked Plataea in 431 thus igniting the Peloponnesian War. During the war it often asserted dominance in the Boeotian Confederacy by defeating other regional cities. When Sparta declined to destroy Athens at the end of the war Thebes left the Peloponnesian League and remained at odds with Sparta.

The Boeotian plain as seen from Orchomenos. Epameinondas, the Theban general in the fourth century, called it the "dancing floor of war" because of all the battles that occurred on or around it, including Plataea, Delium, Leuctra, and Chaeronea. (John W. I. Lee)

During the fourth century Thebes was one of several cities competing for hegemony. It was a major participant and the primary loser in the Corinthian War ended by the King's Peace in 387. The terms of the Peace declared all Greek cities autonomous, a condition Sparta interpreted as requiring dismantling of the Boeotian Confederacy. Although they chafed at Spartan meddling and a garrison, under Pelopidas' leadership the Thebans ejected the garrison and prepared for war. Thebes and Sparta met in 371 at Leuctra where the Thebans won a great victory that broke Sparta's reputation for invincibility.

The victory at Leuctra ushered in a period of Theban hegemony in Greece. In 370 Epameinondas led a Theban force into the Peloponnese where he invaded Spartan territory, and although not taking the city, he freed the Messenian helots and dismantled Spartan power. Thebes under Epameinondas' leadership used the opportunity to meddle in the politics of Thessaly and the Peloponnese as well as intimidate other parts of Greece for the next several years. The hegemony lasted until 362 when a large alliance led by Sparta and Athens met Thebes at Mantinea. The battle ended in a draw when Epameinondas died, but it was the effective end of the Theban hegemony.

During the next several decades, Thebes was impotent as no Greek city was able to become dominant. In the Third Sacred War when Phocis used its looted wealth to dominate central Greece, Thebes invited Philip II of Macedon to assist in 347 and he settled the war the following year. During the Fourth Sacred War Thebes opposed Philip II and allied with Athens at the Battle of Chaeronea at which they lost to Macedon. Afterward Thebes became a member of the League of Corinth. When Alexander became king of Macedon and confirmed his leadership of the League of Corinth in 336, Thebes agreed. While Alexander was securing his northern frontier, Thebes revolted since it believed he had died. Learning of the revolt, Alexander marched south and after a brief engagement he sacked the city and with league permission razed it to the ground as punishment.

Thebes had once been one of the most important cities of Greece, but by the late fourth century it was destroyed. Later, at the end of his career, Alexander regretted having destroyed the city and in the Hellenistic Period it was rebuilt.

Lee L. Brice

See also: Alexander the Great; Athens; Chaeronea, Battle of; Epameinondas; Greco-Persian Wars, Overview; Hellenic Alliance; Herodotus; King's Peace; Pelopidas; Peloponnesian League; Peloponnesian War, Causes of; Peloponnesian War, Consequences of; Peloponnesian War, Overview; Sparta; Thermopylae, Battle of; Wars of Alexander the Great, Overview; Xenophon

References

Buckler, John. *Aegean Greece in the Fourth Century BC.* Leiden: Brill, 2003.

Buckler, John. *The Theban Hegemony.* Cambridge, MA: Harvard University Press, 1980.

Kinzl, Konrad, ed. *A Companion to the Classical Greek World.* Malden, MA: Wiley-Blackwell, 2006.

Strassler, Robert B., ed. *The Landmark Herodotus: The Histories.* New York: Anchor Books, 2009.

Strassler, Robert B., ed. *The Landmark Thucydides: A Comprehensive Guide to the Peloponnesian War.* New York: Free Press, 1998.

Strassler, Robert B., ed. *The Landmark Xenophon's Hellenika.* New York: Pantheon Books, 2009.

Tritle, Lawrence A. *A New History of the Peloponnesian War.* Malden, MA: Wiley-Blackwell, 2010.

Themistocles

The Athenian leader Themistocles was born in 525 or 524 BCE into a wealthy family in Athens. He grew up to be both outspoken and practical. A champion of the recently established Athenian democracy, he also saw that Darius I of Persia intended to conquer European Greece.

Elected a magistrate (archon) in 493 on the platform of a hard line toward Persia, Themistocles began the fortification of the Piraeus coastal district and its transformation into a naval and commercial harbor. He sought to make its defenses sufficiently strong that a small garrison could hold it, releasing more men for the fleet. In 490 he participated as one of 10 Athenian commanders (*strategoi*) in the Battle of Marathon and was in the thick of this fight that defeated the first Persian invasion of Greece.

Unlike many of his countrymen, Themistocles was certain that Persia would again invade Greece and with a larger force. When workers at the state-owned mines discovered a rich silver vein at Laurium in 482, Themistocles persuaded Athenians to spend the windfall on the navy, increasing the fleet from about 50 triremes to 200. His justification was that they needed the ships to wage war on Aegina, a commercial rival in the Saronic Gulf.

When Xerxes I of Persia did invade in 480, Themistocles devised the naval strategy that would defeat it, leading a combined Hellenic Alliance fleet in battles at Artemisium and Salamis. In the decisive engagement at Salamis in 480, the Athenian fleet made up about half of the Greek fleet that crippled a larger Persian force after Themistocles tricked Xerxes into attacking the Greeks in narrow waters disadvantageous to his more numerous ships. Themistocles had not only made it possible for the Greeks to avoid Persian domination, but he also laid the basis for the Athenian naval empire that would dominate the Aegean for decades to come.

Despite these accomplishments, Themistocles soon found himself in political difficulty. More conservative Athenian leaders such as Aristeides and Cimon led a naval offensive against Persia and advocated friendly relations with Sparta, while Themistocles urged rapprochement with Persia and took an aggressive stance toward the Spartans. Accused of collaboration with the Persians, he was ostracized (exiled) from Athens in 471. He eventually took up residence in Asia Minor, where Xerxes' successor, Artaxerxes I, made him governor of Magnesia. Themistocles died there around 460.

Spencer C. Tucker

See also: Artemisium, Battle of; Athens; Darius I; Hellenic Alliance; Herodotus; Marathon, Battle of; Salamis, Battle of; Trireme; Xerxes I

References

Burn, A. R. *Persia and the Greeks: The Defense of the West*. Stanford, CA: Stanford University Press, 1984.

Frost, Frank J. *Plutarch's Themistocles: A Historical Commentary*. Princeton, NJ: Princeton University Press, 1980.

Lazenby, J. F. *The Defense of Greece, 490–479 BC*. Warminster: Aris and Phillips, 1993.

Strassler, Robert B., ed. *The Landmark Herodotus: The Histories*. New York: Anchor Books, 2009.

Strauss, Barry. *The Battle of Salamis: The Naval Encounter That Saved Greece— and Western Civilization*. New York: Simon and Schuster, 2004.

Thermopylae, Battle of

When the Persian king, Xerxes I, invaded Greece in 481 BCE, he commanded an enormous invasion force. The Persian army quickly occupied Thrace and Macedonia. Northern Greek city-states surrendered to Xerxes' authority and added soldiers to Xerxes' army. Only Plataea, Thespiae, and Thebes in Boeotia prepared to fight.

Given the mountainous nature of northern Greece the Hellenic Alliance initially planned to make a stand in one of the narrow passes in northern Greece, the Vale of Tempe, and sent forces northward. When they realized this would be too easily turned by Persia they decided to blockade the enemy advance at the Thermopylae Pass. It was a narrow track between the waters of the Gulf of Malis and steep mountains wide enough for only two carts to pass side by side. A small force could hold off a much larger one and there was even a wall there built originally for that purpose. Nearby, there was a narrow strait between Artemisium on the island of Euboea and the mainland such that a small naval force could blockade that too, so the Persians could not resupply or get around the land blockade.

The mostly Athenian fleet arrived first at Artemisium. When the time came to assemble soldiers, the Spartans were in the middle of a religious ceremony that prohibited most of the citizens from going, so King Leonidas set out with 300 Spartans accompanied by perhaps 900 helots to carry their gear. Leonidas reportedly chose only citizens with sons so that no Spartan family line would be extinguished.

Around 4,000 Hellenic Alliance troops assembled at Thermopylae under Leonidas' command. The same day that the fleets clashed at Artemisium, Xerxes launched his first attack against the Greek defenders at

In 480 BCE the Hellenic Alliance army took position in the narrow pass at Thermopylae between the mountains and the sea. Although it has silted in now, during the battle the narrow space was only wide enough for two carts to pass. The sea would have covered the modern road in this image. (John W. I. Lee)

Thermopylae. They were driven back. Xerxes committed his famous Immortals, but they too were forced back in disorder with heavy casualties. Xerxes tried again the next day, but the defenders repelled this assault as well.

After two days a local shepherd, Ephialtes of Malis, revealed to Xerxes an indirect route over the mountains that would put the Persians behind Leonidas' position. Ephialtes then led a Persian force by that approach, routing a lightly held Phocian outpost that guarded this route.

Learning that the Persians would turn his position, Leonidas released the rest of the Hellenic Alliance force to reassemble at the isthmus. Hoplites from Thespiae and Thebes declined to withdraw and remained with the Spartans and their helots. On the third day after much fighting the remaining soldiers succumbed and Xerxes' army marched for Athens. Only two Spartans are said to have survived; Leonidas sent one badly wounded man back to guide a battle-blind fellow Spartan soldier. When the fleet at Artemisium learned the outcome they withdrew to Athens.

The Hellenic defeat at Thermopylae made little military difference in the war, but has become famous as an example of glorious defeat. Over the tomb of the Spartans was placed the famous Greek epitaph: "Go, stranger, and tell the Lacedamonians [Spartans] we lie here in obedience to their laws."

Spencer C. Tucker

See also: Artemisium, Battles of; Greco-Persian Wars, Overview; Hellenic Alliance; Herodotus; Phalanx, Hoplite; Sparta; Xerxes I

References

Cartledge, Paul. *Thermopylae: The Battle that Changed the World*. New York: Overlook Press, 2006.

Cawkwell, George. *The Greek Wars: The Failure of Persia*. Oxford: Oxford University Press, 2005.

Rawson, Elizabeth. *The Spartan Tradition in European Thought*. Oxford: Oxford University Press, 1991.

Strassler, Robert B., ed. *The Landmark Herodotus: The Histories*. New York: Anchor Books, 2009.

Thucydides

Thucydides was a Greek soldier and author who lived through and subsequently chronicled the Peloponnesian War (431–404 BCE) in a detailed history called *The Peloponnesian War*. Thucydides has sometimes been regarded as the creator of modern historiography, as he claimed to strive for accuracy and impartiality.

Born sometime between 460 and 455, Thucydides was from a wealthy Athenian family that owned property and mines in Thrace. An eyewitness to many of the important events during the later fifth century, Thucydides caught but survived the plague that ravaged Athens between 430 and 427 when he was a naval commander stationed in the North Aegean. When Brasidas was active in the north and captured Amphipolis, the Athenians blamed Thucydides and exiled him from Athens. He apparently spent the remainder of the war writing his history. When Athens surrendered to Sparta in 404, Thucydides returned home.

His method in writing was remarkable for its time as he rejected mythology, tried to interview participants, and attempted to record the original "spirit" of speeches. He also edited the account thoroughly. Most

Mourning Athena, after a Greek relief sculpture from around 465 BCE, located at the Acropolis Museum. The sculpture's subject is uncertain; some scholars hold that the goddess is reading a stele carved with names of Athenian casualties of war. This sculpture and Pericles' "Funeral Oration" by Thucydides provide examples of how the city commemorated those men who died in war. (Hartemink/ Dreamstime)

historians consider his account of the war the most reliable, although it is now also recognized as biased and carefully composed to present a particular vision of events.

Thucydides' history of the Peloponnesian War encompassed eight books but was never completed. The history ends abruptly in the middle of events that occurred in the winter of 411. Since his account makes no mention of events past 400, historians concluded that he died around 404. His work on the war is the only text he is known to have written.

Lee L. Brice

See also: Amphipolis; Athens; Brasidas; Peloponnesian War, Causes of; Peloponnesian War, Overview; Strategos

References

Hornblower, Simon. *A Commentary on Thucydides*, 3 vols. Oxford: Oxford University Press, 1991, 1996, and 2010.

Kagan, Donald. *Thucydides: The Reinvention of History*. New York: Viking Press, 2009.

Strassler, Robert B., ed. *The Landmark Thucydides: A Comprehensive Guide to the Peloponnesian War*. New York: Free Press, 1998

Timoleon

Timoleon of Corinth was sent out to Syracuse in 345 BCE to drive out Dionysius II, the tyrant. While there he also defeated the Carthaginians at Crimisus, drove numerous other tyrants out, and was credited with re-founding the Corinthian colony.

Little is known of Timoleon's background and career prior to 345. He is reported to have assassinated his brother Timophanes who apparently ca. 365 made himself tyrant in Corinth. This was during the period of Theban hegemony when Corinth was militarily impotent. Timoleon reappears in 345 when Corinth received a request for aid in Syracuse. The Corinthians elected Timoleon *strategos* and sent him. The resources they provided him—nine ships without crews and little money—demonstrate how little they were willing to venture on this effort. Timoleon recruited 700 or so mercenaries and crews and sailed for Syracuse.

He was well received in Tauromenium in 344 and defeated the tyrant of Leontinoi before pushing on against Dionysius II of Syracuse. Corinth committed greater resources as he showed promise of winning. They sent him 2,000 hoplites, 200 cavalry, 10 ships and silver. Two of the Corinthian commanders sent with the reinforcements were associated with Philip II of Macedon, so it has for long been suggested that he was the source of the Corinthian wealth (evident in its increased coinage) that underwrote this external activity. Regardless, the reinforcements enabled him to defeat Dionysius and his allies in 343 and send him back to Corinth.

The chronology for Timoleon's career after the capture of Syracuse remains impossible to assemble. At some point after the fall of Syracuse, but before 339, Carthaginian forces landed in Sicily and pushed east against Syracuse. Timoleon with his new forces including Corinthian reinforcements defeated them at the Crimisus River and sent much booty back to Corinth. He then defeated other tyrants in Sicily and made a peace treaty with the Carthaginians securing them to the western part of the island. His final acts refounded the city of Syracuse by attracting numerous new settlers and he also had a new constitution created. He probably retired from office in 337 and died in Syracuse where he was buried with honors. Timoleon's career is important for the light it sheds on Sicilian and

Corinthian affairs in a period when both cities seem to otherwise have been less important.

Lee L. Brice

See also: Corinth; Mercenaries; Philip II of Macedon; Sicily; Strategos

References

Asheri, David. "Sicily, 478–431." In *Cambridge Ancient History*, vol. 5, 2nd edition, ed. D. Lewis et al., 739–80. Cambridge: Cambridge University Press, 1988.

Salmon, J. B. *Wealthy Corinth*. Oxford: Clarendon Press, 1984.

Talbert, Richard J. A. "The Greeks in Sicily and south Italy." In *The Greek World in the Fourth Century from the Fall of the Athenian Empire to the Successors of Alexander*, ed. Lawrence A. Tritle, 137–65. New York: Routledge, 1997.

Talbert, Richard J. A. *Timoleon and the Revival of Greek Sicily 344–317 BC*. Cambridge: Cambridge University Press, 1974.

Training, Military

Although most hoplites were amateurs that need not mean they were untrained. Fighting in formation such as in a hoplite phalanx or in support of it required training both in weapon use and in working together. There is plenty of evidence that in the period 490–323 BCE all hoplites were trained and some received or invested in more training than others.

The city-state that exceeded all others in training of all sorts was Sparta. The public educational system (*agoge*) trained Spartan young men from ages 7 to 29 for military prowess. The exact training regimen is lost, but it trained young men to be skilled in weapons, obedient to command, able to work as a unit, and disciplined enough to stand firm in battle. Among the exercises employed were certainly physical exercise, dance, and especially drills of all sorts. The men learned to stand in files, move in unison to command, and march to music. Just as the Spartan system trained its young men to fight it also trained its officers to lead steadily in the midst of battle. Spartans were, for example, sufficiently disciplined that in 480 at Thermopylae they could use the tactic of feigned retreat to draw their opponents out of line and then turn to fight them. The combination of training for men and officers and their professionalism meant that the Spartan Army had the advantage over all other militaries in Greece, a condition that intimidated most of its opponents well before the battle even began.

There were more general training regimes in other cities for which we have evidence. Men were encouraged in every city-state to engage in physical training in the gymnasia. Those exercises that developed agility were prized for those wishing to improve their military skill. There were also common dances that trained men in particular weapon movements as well as agility. The poorer men and communities who specialized in archery, slings, and javelins practiced often throughout life since their livelihood and even their life could depend on such skills. Men who were wealthy enough to do so could and often did invest in individual military training in weapon skills and horsemanship. Specialists in military training (*hoplomachoi*), in weapons skills, tactics, and generalship (*strategika*) appear during the late fifth century.

More formal training at the level of cities is poorly attested, but given the importance of the formation and forming into battle lines there must have been some regular training for all men eligible for military service. Thucydides has Pericles make much of Athenian amateurism in military preparation, but it is clear from Herodotus' and Thucydides' descriptions of battles that the Athenians and other Greeks were trained to line up for battle and fight together. Indeed, in his account of the Sicilian Expedition, the Syracusan hoplites of 415 are poorly led and poorly trained in the initial engagement, but by 413 when Demosthenes led the night assault the Syracusans have grown better in every respect through their training as well as experience. If there was one aspect that does not seem to have been heavily emphasized in non-Spartan armies it was discipline in the sense of standing firm in the battle line.

The same is true of men serving on the ships. Athens prided itself on well-trained and disciplined rowers and officers. The kinds of tactics employed in trireme combat required skilled and disciplined crews to be effective. These strengths contributed to Greek success at Salamis as well as to Athenian success in the fifth century. When the Spartans built fleets they had to offer higher pay to attract skilled rowers and officers, but their naval successes were few until they became more experienced.

During the fourth century some new developments emerged in training. More cities recognized the importance of regular training and anchoring a battle line on specialized, highly trained units. In the aftermath of the Peloponnesian War more cities seem to have adopted specialized units that were professional or nearly so in serving year round and receiving much more training and regular discipline. The Sacred Band of Thebes was merely one of several examples. The *hoplomachoi* become more common and acceptable. A number of cities may have developed an institution similar to Athens' ephebate—common training for all young men approaching full citizenship. Young men received training in working and serving together. In Athens they served on the frontiers as garrison troops.

Forging his new army, Philip II of Macedon employed vigorous training and regular discipline as well as training different kinds of units to work together in support of each other. A Macedonian *phalangite* needed skill to employ his lengthy *sarissa* effectively in unison with his comrades and sufficient discipline to stand in battle line. Philip used the oblique line of battle and the feigned retreat to create gaps in his opponents' battle line. He also trained his infantry to stand apart to allow opponents to ride or hurl objects harmlessly over them. Philip also armed his cavalry with *sarissa* and often employed a wedge formation that required skill and discipline to employ in battle. Alexander continued throughout his campaigns the training and disciplinary regimes employed by his father. Before his death Alexander began teaching Macedonian training to his Persian subjects. By the end of the fourth century all leaders sought to ensure that their armies were as well trained as they could afford.

Lee L. Brice

See also: Alexander the Great; Athens; Phalanx, Hoplite; Phalanx, Macedonian; Mercenaries; Philip II of Macedon; Salamis, Battle of; Sparta; Thermopylae, Battle of; Thucydides; Xenophon

References

Anderson, J. K. *Military Theory and Practice in the Age of Xenophon*. Berkeley, CA: University of California Press, 1970.

Pritchett, W. Kendrick. *The Greek State at War*, vol. 2. Berkeley, CA: University of California Press, 1974.

Sabine, Philip, Hans van Wees, and Michael Whitby, eds. *The Cambridge History of Greek and Roman Warfare*, vol. 1. Cambridge: Cambridge University Press, 2007.

Trireme

The trireme was a long, low, and narrow galley warship. It derived its name from the fact that its oars were ranged in three banks on each side of the vessel with rowers, one man to an oar, pulling up to 200 oars. Seaworthiness, comfort, cargo capacity, and range were deliberately sacrificed

The trireme was the dominant ship in eastern Mediterranean naval warfare. Long and slim, it was built for speed and maneuverability. *The Olympias,* a replica of an ancient Athenian trireme off the Greek island of Poros in 1987. Note ram at bow. (Time & Life Pictures/Getty Images)

to achieve speed, power, and maneuverability. In addition to its oars, the trireme carried sails on its two masts as a means of auxiliary power.

Probably invented by Phoenicians or Ionian Greeks, little is actually known about the triremes, but they were said to be sturdy in battle and very fast. Although thousands of triremes were sunk in antiquity, no wreck has been identified. What we know of the trireme comes from paintings or contemporary descriptions, none of these detailed. Although modern experts built a full-scale copy of a trireme, they failed to discover how it could move so fast.

The Athenian trireme was approximately 100–120 feet in length and normally had a crew of 200, of whom 170 were rowers. Oarsmen were drawn from the poorer classes and sometimes included slaves whose owners contracted with the state. Because of stability and speed issues the complement of nonrowing fighters was usually small. At Salamis, each ship had 10 marines and 4 archers. The crew also included a flutist who piped time for the rowers. This left 15 deck hands.

The chief weapon of the trireme was its bronze ram at the bow. The captain of the trireme would attempt to place his own vessel perpendicular to an enemy ship; then, using his oarsmen, he would drive his own ship into the opposing vessel at high speed, sinking it. The Athenians also successfully used naval bowmen during the Peloponnesian War. Although far less frequent, crewmen could also take an opposing vessel by storm with swords, axes, and other small arms.

Triremes were expensive ships, but they so dominated naval warfare that every city wishing to be a power had to build them. They also had to be taken out of the water occasionally to avoid rot so it was common to beach the ships, both for easy unloading and security. Thucydides reports that one talent of gold was required to pay all of a trireme's maintenance cost for a month. In the fourth century, even larger ships such as quinquiremes emerge, some of which were employed by Alexander the Great, but the trireme remained the workhorse of Mediterranean navies.

Spencer C. Tucker

See also: Aegospotami, Battle of; Athens; Corinth; Delian League; Hellenic Alliance; Peloponnesian War, Overview; Salamis, Battle of; Sicily, Athenian Expedition Against; Themistocles

References

Hale, John. *Lords of the Sea: The Epic Story of the Athenian Navy and the Birth of Democracy*. New York: Viking Press, 2009.

Morrison, John S., John F. Coats, and N. Boris Rankov. *The Athenian Trireme: The History and Reconstruction of an Ancient Greek Warship*, 2nd edition. Cambridge: Cambridge University Press, 2000.

Murray, William. *The Age of Titans: The Rise and Fall of Great Hellenistic Navies*. Oxford: Oxford University Press, 2012.

Tyre, Siege of

Alexander the Great's siege of Tyre during 333–332 BCE is one of the great military operations of his short career. In 333 he defeated Persian king Darius III at Issus, then turned south to conquer Egypt. Securing the Phoenician coastal city-states would also open those ports for his own ships and deny them to the Persian fleet, preventing a Persian naval attack on Greece.

Tyre was the most important of the Phoenician coastal city-states. Old Tyre was located on an island about three miles in circumference, separated from the mainland city by a half mile of water. The channel between the island and mainland was more than 20 feet deep. The island citadel was reputedly impregnable, protected by massive walls at the edge of the sea. Alexander wanted to bypass Tyre, but he had to reduce it before he could move against Egypt. Alexander expected that once Tyre fell the Phoenician ships, deprived of their bases, would defect to the winning side.

Determined to hold out, the Tyrians rejected Alexander's overtures. They were confident in their defenses and believed that a protracted siege would give Darius time to mobilize a new army and campaign in Asia Minor. Alexander sent heralds to urge a peaceful resolution, but when Tyrian leaders killed the heralds that cemented Alexander's resolve and won him solid support from his military.

Alexander took mainland Tyre without difficulty and initiated siege operations against the island in January 332. He ordered construction of a causeway, about 200 feet wide, out from the land and to reach the island and bring up siege engines. The Macedonians secured wood from the forests of Lebanon for the piles of the mole, while the structures of mainland Tyre were demolished for the fill.

The Tyrians sent ships from the island filled with archers to attack the Macedonians working on the mole. To counter such forays, Alexander ordered his men to construct two great siege towers, each 150 feet in height. As the mole advanced, the towers moved with it. One night the Tyrians successfully used a fireship to destroy the towers. At the same time, a flotilla of smaller Tyrian craft arrived and attacked Alexander's men on the mole and destroyed other siege equipment that had escaped destruction in the fire.

Alexander's men constructed two more towers. Alexander then traveled to Sidon to secure ships to operate against the island and protect those working on the mole. Soon he had gathered 223 ships from Sidon, Cyprus, Rhodes, and other Eastern Mediterranean city-states. Alexander placed in them some 4,000 hoplites recruited from the Peloponnese by Cleander. This flotilla then sailed for Tyre. Alexander commanded its right wing, and Pinitagoras commanded its left wing.

The Tyrians learned of Alexander's activities and planned to give battle at sea, but noting the size of the approaching fleet, the Tyrian admiral changed his mind; he chose instead to protect the two narrow entrances to the island's harbor. A number of ships sunk side by side were sufficient to block both. Alexander concentrated offensive actions against Sidonian Harbor, the smaller of these entrances and about 200 feet wide, but he was unsuccessful. Subsequently the Tyrians substituted heavy iron chains for their block ships.

Tyrians then employed catapults against both the mole and the Macedonian siege towers as the latter came within range. Alexander's catapults replied. Although the Macedonians suffered setbacks, the mole gradually advanced and ultimately reached the island. Under the protection of the towers, the Macedonians employed battering rams against the citadel's walls, but the Tyrian defenses stood firm.

Alexander had also ordered construction of naval battering rams. Each was mounted on a large platform lashed between two barges. Other barges carried catapults. Finally, this naval assault opened a breach in the walls; unfortunately, a gale then arose. Some of Alexander's vessels were sunk, and others were badly damaged.

The Tyrians tried a number of defensive measures. They dropped masonry over the walls to keep Alexander's naval rams at a distance, devised drop beams which could be swung out against the ships by derricks, and, at the end of lines, grappling irons or barbed hooks known as crows that could be dropped on the Macedonians. They tipped onto the attackers bowls of red-hot sand. Finally, Alexander's naval rams broke down a section of the wall. Infantry were sent into the breach on boarding ramps as the defenders continued their resistance in the city center.

Tyre fell at the end of July. Frustration over the length and ferocity of the siege gave way to rage, and the Macedonian troops extended no quarter to the inhabitants. Reportedly 8,000 Tyrians died during the siege; the Macedonians slew another 7,000 afterward as the city became one large abattoir. Another 30,000 inhabitants, including women and children, were sold into slavery. With Tyre destroyed, the Macedonian Army set out on foot in July or early August for Egypt.

Spencer C. Tucker

See also: Alexander the Great; Darius III; Gaza, Siege of; Issus, Battle of; Phalanx, Macedonian; Wars of Alexander the Great, Overview

References

Bloedow, Edmund F. "The Siege of Tyre, 332 BC: Alexander at the Crossroads in His Career." *La Parola del Passato* 301 (1998): 255–93.

Bosworth, A. B. *Conquest and Empire: The Reign of Alexander the Great*. Cambridge: Cambridge University Press, 1988.

Heckel, Waldemar and Lawrence A. Tritle, eds. *Alexander the Great: A New History*. Malden, MA: Wiley-Blackwell, 2009.

Murray, William. *The Age of Titans: The Rise and Fall of Great Hellenistic Navies*. Oxford: Oxford University Press, 2012.

Wars of Alexander the Great, Causes of

The campaigns of Alexander before his invasion of Persia in 334 BCE were part of his becoming king, but the causes of his war against the Achaemenid Empire must be sought in the reign of Philip II. The pretext for the war was a Panhellenic campaign of revenge for Xerxes' burning of Athens in 480, but the actual cause(s) remain a matter of considerable debate.

Before Alexander planned to invade Persia his father had planned the same war. Philip created the League of Corinth during 338–337 to impose peace and his hegemony on Greece, but an open pretext for creating it was a Panhellenic war of revenge on Persia. The idea for the war had not originated with Philip's actions in 338. The idea had been suggested by the Athenian philosopher Isocrates in the early fourth century and proposed to Agesilaus II, Dionysius I, and Alexander of Pherae, son of Jason who had also publicly cited a war of revenge as pretext for his ambitions. Isocrates composed and disseminated in 346 a call for Philip II of Macedon to take up the war, but he was not ready before Chaeronea. Regardless of where the idea originated, the goal of uniting all the Greeks behind a war of revenge for Xerxes' burning of Athens was the pretext Philip and Alexander used. Alexander repeatedly refers to his war as revenge, especially after Granicus in 334 and the burning of Persepolis in 330.

Ancient and modern historians of the period have cited various similar causes to explain Philip's actual motives for war. Polybius, writing in the second century BCE, blamed the war on Philip's perception of the apparent weakness of Persia as exposed by the *Anabasis* and Agesilaus II's campaigns in Asia Minor. Another popular theory has been that Philip and Alexander needed to invade because they were financially bankrupt and needed new sources of funding. Perhaps connected to that, some historians have seen the war as having always been intended to be blatant imperialism, a war of conquest. There is certainly no evidence that Philip or Alexander ever envisioned limited gains. Other possible causes include Philip's need to keep his nobles and army active away from Macedon or a desire for personal glory. This last suggestion fits Alexander better than Philip II as a cause for the war. Indeed Alexander had the additional incentive of trying to exceed the reputation of his talented father. Several ancient sources suggest that revenge actually played into Alexander's invasion since he blamed Persia for assassinating his father, but no modern authors give much weight to this incentive. Neither Philip nor Alexander left any explanation of their motives so the genuine cause must remain a matter of conjecture.

The pretext for Alexander's war against the Achaemenid Empire was certainly revenge, but the actual cause in 334 must in large part have been his own desire for personal glory that would demonstrate his skill and exceed his father's reputation.

Lee L. Brice

See also: Agesilaus II; Alexander the Great; *Anabasis*; Chaeronea, Battle of; Corinth, League of; Darius III; Greco-Persian Wars, Consequences of; Jason of Pherae; Macedon; Phalanx, Macedonian; Philip II of Macedon

References

Bloedow, Edmund F. "Why Did Philip and Alexander Launch a War against the Persian Empire?" *L'Antiquite Classique* 72 (2003): 261–74.

Briant, Pierre. *From Cyrus to Alexander: A History of the Persian Empire*. Winona Lake, IN: Indiana University Press, 2005.

Fox, Robin Lane, ed. *Brill's Companion to Ancient Macedon*. Leiden: Brill, 2011.

Heckel, Waldemar and Lawrence A. Tritle, eds. *Alexander the Great: A New History*. Malden, MA: Wiley-Blackwell, 2009.

Roisman, Joseph and Ian Worthington, eds. *A Companion to Ancient Macedonia*. Malden, MA: Wiley-Blackwell, 2010.

Worthington, Ian. *Philip II of Macedonia*. New Haven, CT: Yale University Press, 2008.

Wars of Alexander the Great, Consequences of

When Alexander III of Macedon died in June 323 BCE he left an enormous legacy. His war against the Achaemenid Empire (334–323) ushered in a period of cultural change, now called the Hellenistic world, which continues to reverberate today. In terms of its military consequences, however, the impact on the region was more destabilizing and chaotic than anything else as his generals competed for dominance.

The new Macedonian Army created by Philip and adjusted by Alexander had a profound impact on military action in the period after 323. The reforms made every other form of regional warfare obsolete. Every ambitious leader or state in the post-Philip Greco-Persian world had to adopt the Macedonian method of warfare or suffer defeat. Over the course of the next couple of decades after 323, the phalanx dominated tactical thinking while the cavalry charge gradually became secondary in many armies until Rome introduced a different type of warfare.

A second consequence was chaos as Alexander's generals and satraps competed for dominance in 75 years of warfare throughout Alexander's former empire. This series of conflicts on land and sea led to shifting alliances, uprooted populations, death and disease, military and political exhaustion and the emergence of new kingdoms in the region. Alexander effectively turned a stable political situation in the Greco-Persian world of 336 into instability and warfare post-323.

Alexander made possible the constant warfare in several ways. The large armies of Macedonians, indigenous peoples, and mercenaries he employed both in Greece and on campaign meant there were many men trained and equipped for combat and in need of a livelihood. The wealth he released from Persia and spread around provided the incentive for those seeking service and the economic means for ambitious leaders and states to raise mercenary armies and fleets. The numerous generals Alexander employed, such as Antipater, were ambitious for power in the wake of Alexander's achievement and there was no one to keep them united.

One other military impact of Alexander's wars has been the model of brilliant generalship he created. All his successors sought initially to emulate Alexander's military achievements. Eventually when they realized such conquests were out of their reach some of these kings were content with living up to the model he provided. Roman generals also openly emulated Alexander. In the first century BCE, Pompey was called "the Great" in mocking of Alexander and Julius Caesar also openly modeled some of his actions on Alexander. After the Roman Empire emerged in 27 BCE Alexander was a model for numerous emperors, especially Nero, Domitian, Trajan, and Caracalla. This emulation creeps into Roman historians' works on Alexander's life, so readers must be careful to separate later accretions from the original life.

The cultural consequences of Alexander's wars were numerous and mostly positive in the short and long run throughout his former empire and the broader Mediterranean world. In terms of Greek warfare, his legacy is much less positive. The pedantic part of Alexander's legacy can still be found in ancient to modern essays and books seeking to discern the skills or even recipe Alexander employed for greatness. There is little point in speculating on counterfactual history such as the "what ifs" had he survived. He changed the world to an extent few individuals do in any period.

Lee L. Brice

See also: Antipater; Corinth, League of; Mercenaries; Phalanx, Macedonian; Persian Empire; Philip II of Macedon

References

Bosworth, A. Brian. *The Legacy of Alexander: Politics, Warfare, and Propaganda under the Successors*. Oxford: University of Oxford Press, 2002.

Brice, Lee L. "Philip II, Alexander the Great, and the Question of a Macedonian Revolution in Military Affairs (RMA)." *Ancient World* 42 (2) (2011): 137–47.

Erskine, Andrew, ed. *A Companion to the Hellenistic World*. Malden, MA: Wiley-Blackwell, 2005.

Hammond, Nicholas G. L. *The Genius of Alexander the Great*. Chapel Hill, NC: The University of North Carolina Press, 1997.

Heckel, Waldemar and Lawrence A. Tritle, eds. *Alexander the Great: A New History*. Malden, MA: Wiley-Blackwell, 2009.

Roisman, Joseph and Ian Worthington, eds. *A Companion to Ancient Macedonia*. Malden, MA: Wiley-Blackwell, 2010.

Wars of Alexander the Great, Overview

The wars of Alexander the Great occupied most of his life after 336 BCE. His wars started in Greece and would stretch north to the Danube, west to Illyria, and east as far as the Hyphasis River. By the time these wars ended the world was changed in ways that would reverberate for centuries and seal Alexander's reputation.

Alexander's first act after being confirmed king in 336 by the army assembly was to ride to Thessaly where he was confirmed as their leader (*archon*) and to Corinth where he was confirmed as leader and general (*hegemon* and *strategos*) of the League of Corinth. The following spring

Alexander mosaic pulled from the floor of Cassa del Fauno at Pompeii. The Roman mosaic, possibly based on a Hellenistic original, depicts the Battle of Issus between Alexander the Great and Darius III in 333 BCE. Darius III has panicked and is fleeing in this image. (Museo Archeologico Nazionale, Naples, Italy/Alinari/The Bridgeman Art Library)

Alexander the Great became king. Aigai (modern Vergina) was one of the capital cities of the kingdom of Macedonia. After Philip's death in 336 BCE, Alexander the Great became king at the palace built there by his father. Philip II was buried in the nearby necropolis. (Lee L. Brice)

Table 4 Numbers of men and losses in the Wars of Alexander the Great

Event	Date	Number	Source
Philip's Advance Force	336	10,000 total	Polyaenus 5.44.4
Macedonian Invasion Force	334	43,000 infantry 5,500 cavalry	Anaximenes of Lampsachus *FGrH* 72 F29
		30,000 infantry 5,000 cavalry	Ptolemy son of Lagos *FGrH* 138 F4
		30,000 infantry 4,000 cavalry	Aristobulus of Cassandreia *FGrH* 139 F4
		32,000 infantry 5,100 cavalry	Diodorus Siculus 17.17.3-4
		30–43,000 infantry 4-5,000 cavalry	Plutarch *Alexander* 15.1
		40,000 total	Frontinus *Stratagemata* 4.2.4
		32,000 infantry 4,500 cavalry	Justin 11.6.2
Persian strength at Granicus R.		100,000 infantry 10,000 cavalry	Diodorus *Siculus* 17.19.4
		c.20,000 cavalry, c.20,000 mercenaries	Arrian *Anabasis* 1.14.4
		600,000 total	Justin 11.6.11
Persian losses at Granicus		20,000 infantry, 2500 cavalry	Plutarch *Alex.* 16.7
		1000 cavalry, c.20,000 mercenaries	Arrian *Anab.* 1.16.1
Alexander's losses at Granicus		9 infantry, 25 cavalry	Plutarch *Alex.*16.7
		30 infantry, 60 cavalry	Arrian *Anab.* 1.16.4
		9 infantry, 120 cavalry	Justin 11.6.12
Persian strength at Issus	333	400,000 infantry, 100,000 cavalry	Diodorus Siculus 17.31.2 & Justin 11.9.1
		600,000 total	Oxyrhinchus Historian *FGrH* 148/*POxy* Arrian *Anab.* 2.8.8 & Plutarch *Alex.* 18.6

194

Event	Date	Number	Source
Persian losses at Issus		250,000 infantry, 62,200 cavalry	Curtius 3.2.4-9
		Included 30,000 mercenaries	Arrian *Anab.* 2.8.8 & Curtius 3.9.2
		100,000, 10,000 cavalry	Diodorus Siculus 17.36.6, Plutarch *Alex.* 20.5, Curtius 3.11.27
		100,000 including 10,000 cavalry	Arrian *Anab.* 2.11.8
		61,000 infantry, 10,000 cavalry and 40,000 captured	Justin 11.9.10
Alexander's losses at Issus		300 infantry, 150 cavalry	Diodorus Siculus 17.36.6
		150 dead, 302 missing, 4500 wounded	Curtius 3.11.27
		120 Macedonians	Arrian *Anab.* 2.10.7
		130 infantry, 150 cavalry	Justin 11.9.10
Phoenician losses at Tyre	332	7000+ dead, 2000 crucified, 13,000 + prisoners	Diodorus Siculus 17.46.4
		6000 dead, 2000 crucified	Curtius 4.4.16-17
		8000 dead, 30,000 prisoners	Arrian *Anab.* 2.24.4-5
Alexander's dead at Tyre		400 dead	Arrian *Anab.* 2.24.5
Persian strength at Gaugamela	331	800,000 infantry, 200,000 cavalry	Diodorus Siculus 17.39.4, 53.3, Plutarch *Alex.* 31.1
		200,000 infantry, 45,000 cavalry	Curtius 4.12.13
		1,000,000 infantry, 40,000 cavalry, 200 chariots	Arrian *Anab.* 3.8.6
		500,000 total	Justin 11.12.5
Alexander's strength at Gaugamela		40,000 infantry, 7,000 cavalry	Arrian *Anab.* 3.12.5

(Continued)

Table 4 Numbers of men and losses in the Wars of Alexander the Great (*Continued*)

Event	Date	Number	Source
Persian losses at Gaugamela		53,000 total	Oxyrhinchus Historian *POxy* 1798
		90,000 total	Diodorus Siculus 17.61.3
		40,000 total	Curtius 4.16.26
		300,000 total	Arrian *Anab.* 3.15.6
Alexander's losses at Gaugamela		1000 infantry, 200 cavalry	Oxyrhinchus Historian *POxy* 1798
		500 dead, many wounded	Diodorus Siculus 17.61.3
		300 dead	Curtius 4.16.26
		100 dead	Arrian *Anab.* 3.15.6
Agis III forces in revolt in Greece	330	20,000 infantry, 2000 cavalry	Diodorus Siculus 17.62.7
Antipater's strength in response		40,000 total	Diodorus Siculus 17.63.1
Agis' losses at Megalopolis		5300 total	Diodorus Siculus 17.63.3 and Curtius 6.1.16
Antipater's losses at Megalopolis		3500 total	Diodorus Siculus 17.63.3
		1000+ total	Curtius 6.1.16

Event	Date	Number	Source
Indian strength at Hydaspes	326	50,000 infantry, 3000 cavalry, 1000 chariots, 130 elephants	Diodorus Siculus 17.87.2
		30,000 infantry, 300 chariots, 85 elephants	Curtius 8.13.6
		30,000 infantry, 4000 cavalry, 300 chariots, 200 elephants	Arrian *Anab.* 5.15.4
Alexander's strength at Hydaspes		6000 or 8000 infantry, 5000 cavalry	Arrian *Anab.* 5.14.1, 18.3
Indian losses at Hydaspes		12,000 dead, 9000 prisoners, 80 elephants captured	Diodorus Siculus 17.89.1-2
		20,000+ infantry, 3000 horse, 300 chariots destroyed	Arrian *Anab.* 5.18.3
		12,000 infantry, 80 elephants captured	Metz *Epitome* 61
Alexander's losses at Hydaspes		700 infantry, 280 cavalry	Diodorus Siculus 17.89.3
		80 infantry, 230 cavalry	Arrian *Anab.* 5.18.3
		900 infantry, 300 cavalry	Metz *Epitome* 70
Macedonians released at Opis	324	10,000 men	Diodorus Siculus 17.109.1 and Arrian *Anab.* 7.12.1
		9870 men	Curtius 10.2.9-11

Numbers of men and losses in Wars of Alexander the Great. This table is intended to provide a sense of how ancient sources reported the size of Alexander's and his opponents' armies and losses. Accurate numbers would have been extremely difficult for sources to learn and really did not matter to ancient authors as much as the scale the numbers convey.

after making preparations he assembled the army and moved north against Thrace, Triballi, and Getae whom he defeated and forced to make peace that included providing soldiers for the campaign in Persia. Learning of trouble in Illyria, he turned west in the late summer and moved against the Illyrians whom he forced to make peace. Then sudden revolt in central Greece resulted in a remarkable surprise march of less than two weeks from Illyria to Thebes. Alexander received league support for razing the city and enslaving the survivors. With the home front and frontiers pacified, Alexander made preparations for the invasion of Asia. He designated Antipater as guardian of Greece during the campaign and left him a large force and orders to train reinforcements.

In the spring of 334, Alexander invaded Persia with a force of around 32,000–40,000 Macedonians, Greeks, and subject peoples. The size of Alexander's army has been variously estimated, but probably included about 12,000 heavy infantry from Macedonia, at least 7,000 hoplites, more than 7,000 light troops of various types, and 5,000 cavalry. It was a large force for Greece, but insignificant in comparison to the potential resources on which Persia could draw. He was joined in Asia by the advance force of several thousand men under Parmenio that had been sent out in 336.

The first battle occurred at the Granicus River where a satrapal force of cavalry and Greek mercenaries sought to stop Alexander's advance. The

In 334 BCE Alexander the Great laid siege to Hallicarnassus (modern Bodrum). The fortified citadel was located in the superb harbor where later rulers built the castles in this image. (Lee L. Brice)

Table 5 Key Events in the Wars of Alexander the Great

Event Name	Date	Alexander's Key Officers	Opposition Leadership
King Alexander III proclaimed	336	Antipater	–
Confirmation Leader of the League of Corinth	336	–	–
Sack of Thebes	Sept. 335	Antipater, Cleitus the Black, Craterus	
Crossing the Hellespont	334	Parmenio and Calas	
Battle of Granicus River	May 334	Cleitus the Black and Parmenio	Arsites, Arsames, Rhoesaces, Spithridates, Memnon of Rhodes
Siege of Miletus	334	Nicanor	Glaucippus
Siege of Halicarnassus	334-332	Perdiccas, Ptolemy, Ada of Caria vs	Memnon of Rhodes, Orontobates, Ephialtes, Thrasybulus
Persian Campaign in the Aegean	334-333	Proteas and Amphoterus	Memnon, Pharnabazus, and Datames
Gordium Knot	Winter 333	–	–
Battle of Issus	Nov. 333	Parmenio	Darius III
Siege of Tyre	Jan.–Jul./Aug. 332	Coenus, Diades of Thessaly	Tyrians
Siege of Gaza	Oct. 332	Hephaistion,	Batis
Revolt of Agis III	331	Corrhagus, Antipater	Agis III
Battle of Gaugamela	Oct. 331	Parmenio, Craterus, Philotas	Dariu III, Mazaeus, Bessus
Battle of Megalopolis	331	Antipater	Agis III

(Continued)

Table 5 Key Events in the Wars of Alexander the Great (*Continued*)

Event Name	Date	Alexander's Key Officers	Opposition Leadership
Capture of Susa and Babylon	331	Philoxenus	Mazaeus, Abulites
Battle of the Persian Gates	Winter 331	Ptolemy, Craterus, Philotas	Ariobarzanes
Capture and Burning of Persepolis	Jan–March 330	Parmenio	Tiridates
Capture of Ecbatana	330	Parmenio	Bisthanes
Murder of Darius III	330		Bessus, Satibarzanes, Barsaentes, Nabarzanes
Revolt of Bessus	330–329	Ptolemy, Stasanor, Erigyius	Bessus, Nabarzanes, Satibarzanes, Spitamenes, Dataphernes, and Brazanes, Sisicottus
Conspiracy of Philotas	330	Philotas, Parmenion, Craterus, Hephaestion, Coenus, and Cleander	
Subjugation of Bactria & Sogdiana	329–327	Craterus, Coenus	Spitamenes, Dataphernes, Sisimithres, Ariazmazes
Pages Conspiracy	327		Hermolaus, Callisthenes

Event Name	Date	Alexander's Key Officers	Opposition Leadership
Conquest of India	327–325	Hephaesteion, Perdiccas Craterus	
Bajaur, Swat, and Kophen river campaigns	Summer 327–Spring 326	Craterus, Coenus, Hephaestion, Perdiccas, Ptolemy	Aspasians, Assacenus, Cleophis, Astis
Battle of the Hydaspes	May 326	Craterus, Meleager, Coenus	Porus, Spitaces
Halt at the Hyphasis	Summer 326	Coenus	–
Descent of the rivers	Sept. 326	Craterus, Hephaistion, Philip, Nearchus, Ptolemy	–
Mallian Campaign	Lt 326–Spring 325	Perdiccas, Peucestas	–
Descent of the Indus	Spring 325	Nearchus, Peithon	Oxycanus, Sambus, Musicanus,
Craterus to Carmania	Summer 325	Craterus	
Gedrosian and Makran March	Autumn–Dec. 325	Nearchus, Hephaistion, Leonnatus	
Reunion in Carmania	Dec. 325	Nearchus, Craterus, Cleander	
Arrival at Susa	Mar. 324		
Opis Mutiny	June 324	Seleucus	
Alexander Dead	June 11, 323		

Key Events in the Wars of Alexander the Great. This table lists events with the date and both sides' officers if known.

battle was over swiftly, and the dead Macedonians were honored, spoils sent back to Athens, and Greek prisoners sent to the mines in Macedon. Alexander then moved south along the Aegean coast inviting the Greek communities to join him and freeing those with garrisons still. Some communities, including the satrapal capital Sardis, surrendered without a fight in the hope of better treatment. Alexander had to siege Miletus and Halicarnassus where Memnon of Rhodes, the regional Persian military commander, organized opposition, but they both were reduced and Alexander dismissed much of his fleet. The campaign then meandered through Asia Minor reducing strong points and stopping in key cities like Gordium and reaching Tarsus in 333. Memnon organized naval raids that year and captured Chios and Lesbos temporarily, but his death at Mytilene ended the last Persian counterstroke in the Aegean.

The Achaemenid king Darius III assembled a large army and marched west to destroy Alexander when he emerged from Cilicia. Delayed by illness in Tarsus, Alexander continued his march down the coast of Cilicia only to discover that the Persian army had maneuvered behind him. He turned back and met Darius at the favorable site of Issus. Alexander's victory was complete as he drove Darius from the field and captured the Persian camp and baggage along with Darius' family. Alexander ignored Darius' flight and continued south capturing Phoenician cities as he moved toward the island city of Tyre. He needed to capture the Phoenician ports in order to deny the Persians any chance of launching naval raids behind him or in Greece. The siege took more than seven months as the Macedonians built a causeway and gathered naval support from the rulers on Cyprus. Once Gaza—the next stronghold to the south—was reduced, Alexander moved into Egypt with ease and became its king and rested his men. The entire eastern coast of the Mediterranean was now in his control.

Alexander set out for Babylon and Darius in the spring of 331 with his army rested, supplied, and in good spirits. Darius had raised a new army at least double the size of Alexander's and prepared to meet him at Gaugamela. Alexander's army and tactical genius again proved victorious and Darius fled once again. Babylon, Susa, and other nearby cities surrendered without a fight as Alexander moved on around the Persian Gates to Persepolis, the capital city Darius I had built. After wintering there and stripping its wealth, Alexander burned it down in the spring of 330 and declared the Panhellenic war of revenge complete. The Greek soldiers from the League of Corinth were given the option of returning home or reenlisting as mercenaries, which many did. A revolt in Greece led by Agis III had delayed Alexander's advance as he awaited news, but Antipater crushed it after settling affairs in Thrace. Now in control of the eastern half of the empire, Alexander set out after Darius on a campaign to subjugate the rest of the Persian Empire.

Darius had fled north with some satraps, but by the time Alexander caught up he was dead, assassinated in flight. The assassins led by Bessus, satrap of Bactra, fled to that region and Sogdiana. Alexander chased them relentlessly in 330/329 into the central Asian regions. Despite having captured and punished Bessus, Alexander found himself fighting a guerilla war for nearly three years trying to pacify the region and capture the opposition leadership. During this period, the constant fighting wore down the army and the first signs of serious indiscipline showed up in the form of two conspiracies and numerous smaller incidents. The most serious conspiracy led to the execution of Parmenion and his son Philotas. The warfare was only calmed by more lenient treatment of local leaders and the marriage of Alexander to Roxane. An indication of Alexander's success in pacifying the region can be found in his having left 10,000 mercenaries in various settlements and colonies to hold the territory.

Alexander moved in 327 across the mountains and into the most easterly satrapies of the Persian Empire—India. There Alexander found some local leaders inclined to surrender and others resisting strongly. The fighting was difficult from the start and few sites were more difficult than the nearly impregnable Rock of Aornus, which eventually fell. Alexander continued to push east in 326 finding some local rulers like Taxiles willing to surrender in return for assistance against their own local enemies so that his army swelled with indigenous soldiers. In his last major battle of the campaign Alexander met the local king, Porus, with an enormous army at the Hydaspes River. Through some surprising maneuvers across the river and some lucky breaks in the weather Alexander won a significant tactical victory. Afterward, he confirmed Porus as his satrap and continued to move east through the monsoon season. At the Hydaspes River, the furthest east of the Indus tributaries in this region, the army expressed displeasure with the notion of continuing east and after several days of inactivity Alexander conceded and turned back to the Hydaspes where he had a fleet under construction.

Beginning in late 326 the army moved south, down the Indus, by ship and by land. The march down the Indus was not easy, the worst fighting occurred in the territory of the Mallians where Alexander was badly wounded. By mid-325 the army had reached the mouth of the Indus and

Alexander made preparations for returning to Babylon. He sent part of the army with Craterus along a more northern route, and part of the force with the navy led by Nearchus to sail the Indian Ocean and Arabian Gulf. The rest of the army marched through the Gedrosian desert. Why Alexander decided to take the torrid route across the desert remains a mystery, although the most likely explanation is that it seemed an insurmountable task. In 324 Alexander reached Pasargadae and then met the navy at Susa in the heart of his Persian Empire before finally reaching Babylon.

Alexander rewarded his soldiers and officers with immense gifts of wealth and marriage opportunities with Persian women. He began to introduce Persian units into his army and dismissed the overage and wounded Macedonians, sending them back home. These actions resulted in a mutiny at Opis that Alexander responded to swiftly and directly. At the same time Alexander reviewed his satrapal appointments and considered how best to rule the empire. This period of assessment and reorganization marks the end of Alexander's wars.

The following year on June 11, 323, Alexander died, probably of disease. Among his final papers there were supposedly plans for campaigns against Carthage and Rome, but these were added by later authors seeking to build up Alexander's reputation with hindsight awareness. Alexander's failure to secure an heir well in advance meant that his empire was unstable and quickly collapsed into war between ambitious generals.

Lee L. Brice

See also: Agis III; Antipater; Cavalry; Chaeronea, Battle of; Corinth, League of; Darius III; Gaugamela, Battle of; Gaza, Siege of; Granicus River, Battle of; Hydaspes, Battle of the; Issus, Battle of; Mutiny; Phalanx, Macedonian; Philip II of Macedon; Thebes; Tyre, Siege of

References

Bosworth, A. Brian. *Alexander and the East: The Tragedy of Triumph*. Oxford: Oxford University Press, 2001.

Bosworth, A. Brian. *Conquest and Empire: The Reign of Alexander the Great*. Cambridge: Cambridge University Press, 1988.

Fox, Robin Lane, ed. *Brill's Companion to Ancient Macedon*. Leiden: Brill, 2011.

Hammond, Nicholas G. L. *Alexander the Great: King, Commander, and Statesman*. London: Duckworth, 1981.

Heckel, Waldemar and Lawrence A. Tritle, eds. *Alexander the Great: A New History*. Malden, MA: Wiley-Blackwell, 2009.

Roisman, Joseph and Ian Worthington, eds. *A Companion to Ancient Macedonia.* Malden, MA: Wiley-Blackwell, 2010.

Romm, James, ed. *The Landmark Arrian: The Campaigns of Alexander.* New York: Pantheon, 2010.

Tritle, Lawrence A. and Brian Campbell, eds. *The Oxford Handbook of Classical Military History.* Oxford: Oxford University Press, 2012.

X

Xenophon

Xenophon was a Greek soldier and historian in the fourth century BCE. He wrote a number of works on various subjects including horses, hunting, government, and the life and philosophy of Socrates, but is also important as a source for military history of the early fourth century.

Xenophon was born in Athens ca. 431. His family was fairly wealthy, and Xenophon was a member of the aristocratic cavalry. In his youth, he studied with Socrates. Xenophon matured as a supporter of democracy, so when Athens was under the oligarchs in 404 he left the city.

Xenophon enlisted in the Greek Army raised by the Persian prince Cyrus to fight Artaxerxes II. Xenophon fought in the Battle of Cunaxa, but when the satrap Tissaphernes executed the Greek commanders, Xenophon got himself elected a commander of the Greek mercenaries. He helped lead the Ten Thousand north to the Black Sea and eventually back to Ionia, an adventure he recorded as *Anabasis*.

Xenophon continued to fight for the Spartans even after they went to war with Athens. He fought against the Persians with the Spartan commander Agesilaus II. In 394, he went back to Greece with Agesilaus and fought with him against Athens in the Battle of Coronea. After that battle the Spartans allowed him to stay in Sparta with his family. His children were educated in Sparta, and Xenophon was himself elected a Spartan official (*proxenos*) in charge of entertaining Spartans who visited Olympia.

After his travels and his fighting, Xenophon spent much of his time writing. He was prolific and used a simple, eloquent style. His most famous work is *Anabasis*. He also wrote numerous other works including *Hellenika*, which contains much that is of interest to military historians.

Lee L. Brice

See also: Agesilaus II; *Anabasis*; Athens; Greco-Persian Wars, Consequences of; Mercenaries; Persian Empire; Sparta

References

Anderson, J. K. *Military Theory and Practice in the Age of Xenophon*. Berkeley, CA: University of California Press, 1970.

Buckler, John. *Aegean Greece in the Fourth Century BC*. Leiden: Brill, 2003.

Strassler, Robert B., ed. *The Landmark Xenophon's Hellenika*. New York: Pantheon Books, 2009.

Xerxes I

Xerxes I was the king of Persia early in the fifth century BCE. He is best remembered for his massive, failed invasion of Greece in 480. Although his attempted conquest of Greece failed, Xerxes successfully defeated rebellions and kept his multinational empire together.

Xerxes was born around 519. His father was the Persian king Darius I. When Darius died in 486, Xerxes succeeded him with a minimum of disorder. One of his priorities was to settle his father's planned second campaign on Greece.

Before he was able to punish the Greeks, however, Xerxes had to contend with several internal revolts. He successfully put down a revolt in Egypt in 485, and in 481 resolved trouble in Babylonia. In both cases, he punished the leaders and stabilized the situation within the empire.

By 480, Xerxes gathered a large army drawn from all parts of the empire. Herodotus' account makes identifying trustworthy numbers of combatants difficult, but it was a ginormous army, at least 2–3 times the strength of the Hellenic Alliance force. The invasion required extensive logistical planning. A fleet sailed along the coast protecting the army from surprise attack and carrying supplies and his engineers bridged the Hellespont.

Although he was held up for a few days at Thermopylae, Xerxes reached Athens where he found and eliminated a small force on the Acropolis.

Xerxes then had his army sack and burn Athens. When he learned that much of the populace had fled to Salamis he decided a naval battle was likely. Themistocles, the Athenian naval leader, used stratagem to draw Persia into a battle in the straits of Salamis where advantage in numbers did not matter. Xerxes insisted on watching the battle to see who performed well and who shirked duty. As he watched, the Greeks destroyed part of his fleet and won the battle. As a result, Xerxes immediately returned to Persia to ensure his throne. He left behind a large army under Mardonius to complete the conquest of Greece. When Mardonius was defeated by a Hellenic Alliance army in 479 at Plataea, Xerxes' invasion ended.

Xerxes withdrew from active campaigning after his return to Persia. He concentrated on building projects such as roads and public buildings, which employed many workers. Xerxes died in 465, having kept the empire stable and prosperous despite the losses in Greece.

Tim Watts

See also: Artemisium, Battles of; Darius I; Greco-Persian Wars, Overview; Hellenic Alliance; Herodotus; Persian Empire; Plataea, Battle of; Salamis, Battle of; Thermopylae, Battle of

References

Briant, Pierre. *From Cyrus to Alexander: A History of the Persian Empire.* Winona Lake, IN: Indiana University Press, 2005.

Burn, A. R. *Persia and the Greeks: The Defence of the West.* Stanford, CA: Stanford University Press, 1984.

Cawkwell, George. *The Greek Wars: The Failure of Persia.* Oxford: Oxford University Press, 2005.

Strassler, Robert B., ed. *The Landmark Herodotus: The Histories.* New York: Anchor Books, 2009.

Documents

1. Herodotus, Account of the Battle of Marathon

The battlefield account here is of the first battle of the Persian Wars, Marathon. The Athenian army assembled and marched out soon after the Persian force landed at the Marathon plain in 490 BCE. A force from Plataea reinforced the Athenians. After several days as each of the 10 Athenian commanders (*strategoi*) and the military magistrate (*polemarch*) took turns in charge, Miltiades' turn came and seeing that the Persians were preparing to depart he favored battle. He set the line of battle, made a sacrifice and read the signs for support from the gods, and then ordered a charge.

In his descriptions of ancient battles Herodotus invented what we now recognize as battlefield narratives. While historians may prefer that he recorded battles in minute detail, Herodotus' accounts were intended to entertain as well as to explain what happened. He may also have been able to interview participants or witnesses to what happened and use those details to improve his account of a battle that his audience already knew. This description is important not only because it is the earliest historical description of hoplites in battle, but because it adds details like the order of battle and the importance of sacrifices. On the other hand, much that it describes is sufficiently informal that it has resulted in a confusing and debated portrait of hoplite tactics. In the passage below the translator has exchanged the Greek word *barbaroi* for the English word "foreigner" because Greeks referred to all non-Greek speakers as barbarians. The word did not carry connotations of uncivilized.

By saying this Miltiades won over Callimachus. The polemarch's vote was counted in, and the decision to attack was resolved upon. Thereafter the generals who had voted to fight turned the presidency over to Miltiades as each one's day came in turn. He accepted the office but did not make an attack until it was his own day to preside.

When the presidency came round to him, he arrayed the Athenians for battle, with the polemarch Callimachus commanding the right wing, since it was then the Athenian custom for the polemarch to hold the right wing. He led, and the other tribes were numbered out in succession next to each other. The Plataeans were marshalled last, holding the left wing. Ever since that battle, when the Athenians are conducting sacrifices at the festivals every fourth year, the Athenian herald prays for good things for the Athenians and Plataeans together.

As the Athenians were marshalled at Marathon, it happened that their line of battle was as long as the line of the Medes. The center, where the line was weakest, was only a few ranks deep, but each wing was strong in numbers. When they had been set in order and the sacrifices were favorable, the Athenians were sent forth and charged the foreigners at a run. The space between the armies was no less than eight stadia.

The Persians saw them running to attack and prepared to receive them, thinking the Athenians absolutely crazy, since they saw how few of them there were and that they ran up so fast without either cavalry or archers. So the foreigners imagined, but when the Athenians all together fell upon the foreigners they fought in a way worthy of record. These are the first Hellenes whom we know of to use running against the enemy. They are also the first to endure looking at Median dress and men wearing it, for up until then just hearing the name of the Medes caused the Hellenes to panic.

They fought a long time at Marathon. In the center of the line the foreigners prevailed, where the Persians and Sacae were arrayed. The foreigners prevailed there and broke through in pursuit inland, but on each wing the Athenians and Plataeans prevailed. In victory they let the routed foreigners flee, and brought the wings together to fight those who had broken through the center. The Athenians prevailed, then followed the fleeing Persians and struck them down. When they reached the sea they demanded fire and laid hold of the Persian ships.

In this labor Callimachus the polemarch was slain, a brave man, and of the generals Stesilaus son of Thrasylaus died. Cynegirus son of Euphorion fell there, his hand cut off with an ax as he grabbed a ship's figurehead. Many other famous Athenians also fell there.

In this way the Athenians overpowered seven ships. The foreigners pushed off with the rest, picked up the Eretrian slaves from the island where they had left them, and sailed around Sounion hoping to reach the city before the Athenians. There was an accusation at Athens that they devised this by a plan of the Alcmaeonidae, who were said to have arranged to hold up a shield as a signal once the Persians were in their ships.

They sailed around Sounion, but the Athenians marched back to defend the city as fast as their feet could carry them and got there ahead of the foreigners. Coming from the sacred precinct of Heracles in Marathon, they pitched camp in the sacred precinct of Heracles in Cynosarges. The foreigners lay at anchor off Phalerum, the Athenian naval port at that time. After riding anchor there, they sailed their ships back to Asia.

Source: Herodotus. *History*, Book 6.110–116, with an English translation by A. D. Godley. Cambridge: Harvard University Press, 1920.

2. Mardonius, the Persian General, on Greek Warfare

In 480 BCE as he prepared to invade Greece, Xerxes I called his military advisors together for advice on whether to launch the war. Mardonius, the Persian commander who had led a failed invasion of Macedonia in 492, gave his opinion on why they should attack and how they would fare. In his *History* of the Persian Wars, Herodotus invented speeches for his historical characters. It was common for ancient historians to invent such speeches and while they can be informative we should not forget that these speeches are fictional in the sense that the speaker did not speak that way. The speeches fit either what the author needed a character to say or convey the author's views. The passage here is a good example of one such speech. In the speech Herodotus has Mardonius give, he provides a characterization of contemporary Greek hoplite warfare that is useful for getting a sense of what hoplite warfare had been like in the early fifth century and how futile it could seem at times to contemporaries like Herodotus.

"What have we to fear from them? Have they a massive population or abundance of wealth? Their manner of fighting we know, and we know how weak their power is; we have conquered and hold their sons, those who dwell in our land and are called Ionians and Aeolians and Dorians. I myself have made trial of these men, when by your father's command I marched against them. I marched as far as Macedonia and almost to Athens itself, yet none came out to meet me in battle.

"Yet the Greeks are accustomed to wage wars, as I learn, and they do it most senselessly in their wrongheadedness and folly. When they have declared war against each other, they come down to the fairest and most level ground that they can find and fight there, so that the victors come off with great harm; of the vanquished I say not so much as a word, for they are utterly destroyed. Since they speak the same language, they should end their disputes by means of heralds or messengers, or by any way rather than fighting; if they must make war upon each other, they should each discover where they are in the strongest position and make the attempt there. The Greek custom, then, is not good; and when I marched as far as the land of Macedonia, it had not come into their minds to fight.

"But against you, O king, who shall make war? You will bring the multitudes of Asia, and all your ships. I think there is not so much boldness in Hellas as that; but if time should show me wrong in my judgment, and those men prove foolhardy enough to do battle with us, they would be taught that we are the greatest warriors on earth. Let us leave nothing untried; for nothing happens by itself, and all men's gains are the fruit of adventure."

Source: Herodotus. *History*, Book 7.9a–c, with an English translation by A. D. Godley. Cambridge: Harvard University Press, 1920.

3. Herodotus, Account of the Battle of Thermopylae

Xerxes I invaded Greece in 480 BCE with an immense force. The Hellenic Alliance army assembled at the narrow pass of Thermopylae where the mountains met the sea, leaving a gap wide enough for only two carts to pass. This gap was reinforced by an ancient wall. The Greek units were organized by city and took turns blockading the pass and fighting. Once their position was turned, Leonidas sent most of the army home. The passage here describes Persian failure and finally the end of the battle in a dramatic style that gave birth to the tradition of glorious defeat. In the passage below the translator has exchanged the Greek word *barbaroi* for the English word "foreigner" because Greeks referred to all non-Greek speakers as barbarians. The word did not carry connotations of uncivilized.

As already noted, Herodotus invented the battlefield narrative. The selection here describes how the Greeks blocked the Persian assaults in the gap. This passage is important for providing a sense of battlefield tactics by both sides as well as a sense of what the battle may have been like for the Greeks. Herodotus also described how the Spartans used feigned retreat, a tactic in which the antagonist retreats to draw the opponent out of line, and then turns back and attacks suddenly. It was extremely effective, but useful only to the best-trained and disciplined soldiers, a measurement of Spartan prowess.

While they debated in this way, Xerxes sent a mounted scout to see how many there were and what they were doing. While he was still in Thessaly, he had heard that a small army was gathered there and that its leaders were Lacedaemonians, including Leonidas, who was of the Heracleid clan. Riding up to the camp, the horseman watched and spied out the place. He could, however, not see the whole camp, for it was impossible to see those posted inside the wall which they had rebuilt and were guarding. He did take note of those outside, whose arms lay in front of the wall, and it chanced that at that time the Lacedaemonians were posted there. He saw some of the men exercising naked and others combing their hair. He marvelled at the sight and took note of their numbers. When he had observed it all carefully, he rode back in leisure, since no one pursued him or paid him any attention at all. So he returned and told Xerxes all that he had seen.

. . .

He let four days go by, expecting them to run away at any minute. They did not leave, and it seemed to him that they stayed out of folly and lack of due respect. On the fifth day he became angry and sent the Medes and Cissians against them, bidding them take them prisoner and bring them into his presence. The Medes bore down upon the Hellenes and attacked. Many fell, but others attacked in turn, and they made it clear to everyone, especially to the king himself, that among so many people there were few real men. The battle lasted all day.

When the Medes had been roughly handled, they retired, and the Persians whom the king called Immortals, led by Hydarnes, attacked in turn. It was thought that they would easily accomplish the task. When they joined battle with the Hellenes, they fared neither better nor worse than the Median army, since they used shorter spears than the Hellenes and could not use their numbers fighting in a narrow space. The Lacedaemonians fought memorably, showing themselves skilled fighters amidst unskilled on many occasions, as when they would turn their backs and feign flight. The barbarians would see them fleeing and give chase with shouting and noise, but when the Lacedaemonians were overtaken, they would turn to face the barbarians and overthrow innumerable Persians. A few of the Spartans themselves were also slain. When the Persians could gain no inch of the pass, attacking by companies and in every other fashion, they withdrew.

It is said that during these assaults in the battle the king, as he watched, jumped up three times from the throne in fear for his army. This, then, is how the fighting progressed, and on the next day the barbarians fought no better. They joined battle supposing that their enemies, being so few, were now disabled by wounds and could no longer resist. The Hellenes, however, stood ordered in ranks by nation, and each of them fought in turn, except the Phocians, who were posted on the mountain to guard the path. When the Persians found nothing different from what they saw the day before, they withdrew.

The king was at a loss as to how to deal with the present difficulty. Ephialtes son of Eurydemos, a Malian, thinking he would get a great reward from the king, came to speak with him and told him of the path leading over the mountain to Thermopylae. In so doing he caused the destruction of the Hellenes remaining there.

. . .

The Persians crossed the Asopus and travelled all night along this path, with the Oetaean mountains on their right and the Trachinian on their left. At dawn they came to the summit of the pass. In this part of the mountain one thousand armed men of the Phocians were on watch, as I have already shown, defending their own country and guarding the path. The lower pass was held by those I have mentioned, but the Phocians had voluntarily promised Leonidas to guard the path over the mountain.

The Phocians learned in the following way that the Persians had climbed up: they had ascended without the Phocians' notice because the mountain was entirely covered with oak trees. Although there was no wind, a great noise arose like leaves being trodden underfoot. The Phocians jumped up and began to put on their weapons, and in a moment the barbarians were there.

When they saw the men arming themselves, they were amazed, for they had supposed that no opposition would appear, but they had now met with an army. Hydarnes feared that the Phocians might be Lacedaemonians and asked Ephialtes what country the army was from. When he had established what he wanted to know with certainty, he arrayed the Persians for battle. The Phocians, assailed by thick showers of arrows and supposing that the Persians had set out against them from the start, fled to the top of the mountain and prepared to meet their destruction. This is what they intended, but the Persians with Ephialtes and Hydarnes paid no attention to the Phocians and went down the mountain as fast as possible.

The seer Megistias, examining the sacrifices, first told the Hellenes at Thermopylae that death was coming to them with the dawn. Then deserters came who announced the circuit made by the Persians. These gave their signals while it was still night; a third report came from the watchers running down from the heights at dawn. The Hellenes then took counsel, but their opinions were divided. Some advised not to leave their post, but others spoke against them. They eventually parted, some departing and dispersing each to their own cities, others preparing to remain there with Leonidas.

It is said that Leonidas himself sent them away because he was concerned that they would be killed, but felt it not fitting for himself and the Spartans to desert that post which they had come to defend at the beginning.

. . .

Those allies who were dismissed went off in obedience to Leonidas, only the Thespians and Thebans remaining with the Lacedaemonians. The Thebans remained against their will and desire, for Leonidas kept them as hostages. The Thespians very gladly remained, saying they would not abandon Leonidas and those with him by leaving; instead they would stay and die with them. Their general was Demophilus son of Diadromes.

Xerxes made libations at sunrise and waiting till about mid-morning, made his assault. Ephialtes had advised this, for the descent from the mountain is more direct, and the way is much shorter than the circuit and ascent. Xerxes and his barbarians attacked, but Leonidas and his Hellenes, knowing they were going to their deaths, advanced now much farther than before into the wider part of the pass. In all the previous days they had sallied out into the narrow way and fought there, guarding the defensive wall. Now, however, they joined battle outside the narrows and many of the barbarians fell, for the leaders of the companies beat everyone with whips from behind, urging them ever forward. Many of them were pushed into the sea and drowned; far more were trampled alive by each other, with no regard for who perished. Since the Hellenes knew that they must die at the hands of those who had come around the mountain, they displayed the greatest strength they had against the barbarians, fighting recklessly and desperately.

By this time most of them had had their spears broken and were killing the Persians with swords. Leonidas, proving himself extremely valiant, fell in that struggle and with him other famous Spartans, whose names I have learned by inquiry since they were worthy men. Indeed, I have learned by inquiry the names of all three hundred. Many famous Persians also fell there, including two sons of Darius, Abrocomes and Hyperanthes, born to Darius by Phratagune daughter of Artanes. Artanes was the brother of king Darius and son of Hystaspes son of Arsames. When he gave his daughter in marriage to Darius, he gave his whole house as dowry, since she was his only child.

Two brothers of Xerxes accordingly fought and fell there. There was a great struggle between the Persians and Lacedaemonians over Leonidas' body, until the Hellenes by their courageous prowess dragged it away and routed their enemies four times. The battle went on until the men with Ephialtes arrived. When the Hellenes saw that they had come, the contest turned, for they retired to the narrow part of the way, passed behind the wall, and took their position crowded together on the hill, all except the Thebans. This hill is at the mouth of the pass, where the stone lion in honor of Leonidas now stands. In that place they defended themselves with swords, if they still had them, and with hands and teeth. The barbarians buried them with missiles, some attacking from the front and throwing down the defensive wall, others surrounding them on all sides.

This then is how the Lacedaemonians and Thespians conducted themselves, but the Spartan Dieneces is said to have exhibited the greatest courage of all. They say that he made the following speech before they joined battle with the Medes: he had learned from a Trachinian that there were so many of the barbarians that when they shot their missiles, the sun was hidden by the multitude of their arrows. He was not at all disturbed by this and made light of the multitude of the Medes, saying that their Trachinian foreigner brought them good news. If the Medes hid the sun, they could fight them in the shade instead of in the sun. This saying and others like it, they claim, Dieneces the Lacedaemonian left behind as a memorial.

Source: Herodotus. *History*, Book 7.208, 210–213.1, 217–220.1, 222–226, with an English translation by A. D. Godley. Cambridge: Harvard University Press, 1920.

4. Herodotus, Account of Cavalry and Light Infantry versus Hoplites at the Battle of Plataea

During the winter after Salamis, Mardonius remained in northern Greece, but moved south in 479 BCE and sacked Athens again. The Persians then marched into Boeotia and met the Hellenic Alliance force near Plataea. After several days of maneuvering, the Hellenic force under command of the Spartan king, Pausanias, had become dispersed during the night. Mardonius caught the Spartans and Athenians in the open in groups separated from each other and charged. The results did not go well for the Persians.

Cavalry was always important to Persian success and Herodotus highlights its importance in his account of Plataea. The ability of cavalry to harass and defeat unprotected hoplites is clear in the opening. The Persians used the cavalry to block springs and limit foragers and supply. Eventually the Spartans were able to close with the cavalry and demonstrate their skill and the advantage of their superior armor to defeat Mardonius, and then they charged the light infantry. Even after the initial defeat the cavalry of Persia and its allies protected Mardonius' troops as they fled from battle to their fort. Herodotus' unfair criticism of the Spartans for their inability to assault the Persian stockade was pro-Athenian bias, but it shows the importance of being flexible in battle. The narrative ends with the sharing out of the spoils.

The armies had already lain hidden opposite each other for eight days when he gave this counsel. Mardonius perceived that the advice was good, and when night had fallen, he sent his horsemen to the outlet of the pass over Cithaeron which leads towards Plataea. This pass the Boeotians call the Three Heads, and the Athenians the Oak's Heads. The horsemen who were sent out did not go in vain, for they caught five hundred beasts of burden which were going into the low country, bringing provisions from the Peloponnese for the army, and men who came with the wagons. When they had taken this quarry, the Persians killed without mercy, sparing neither man nor beast. When they had their fill of slaughter, they encircled the rest and drove them to Mardonius and his camp.

After this deed they waited two days more, neither side desiring to begin the battle, for although the barbarians came to the Asopus to test the Greeks intent, neither army crossed it. Mardonius' cavalry, however, kept pressing upon and troubling the Greeks, for the Thebans, in their zeal for the Persian part, waged war heartily, and kept on guiding the horsemen to the encounter; thereafter it was the turn of the Persians and Medes, and they and none other would do deeds of valor.

. . .

Mardonius was overjoyed and proud of this semblance of victory, and sent his cavalry to attack the Greeks. The horsemen rode at them and shot arrows and javelins among the whole Greek army to its great hurt, since they were mounted archers and difficult to deal with in an encounter; they spoiled and blocked the Gargaphian spring, from which the entire Greek army drew its water. None indeed but the Lacedaemonians were posted near the spring, and it was far from the several stations of the other Greeks, whereas the Asopus was near; nevertheless, they would always go to the spring, since they were barred from the Asopus, not being able to draw water from that river because of the horsemen and the arrows.

When this happened, seeing that their army was cut off from water and thrown into confusion by the horsemen, the generals of the Greeks went to Pausanias on the right wing, and debated concerning this and other matters; for there were other problems which troubled them more than what I have told. They had no food left, and their followers whom they had sent into the Peloponnese to bring provisions had been cut off by the horsemen and could not make their way to the army.

. . .

Now Amompharetos at first supposed that Pausanias would never have the heart to leave him and his men, and he insisted that they should remain where they were and not leave their post. When Pausanias' men had already proceeded some distance, he thought that they had really left him. He accordingly bade his battalion take up its arms and led it in marching step after the rest of the column, which after going a distance of ten furlongs, was waiting for Amompharetos by the stream Molois and the place called Argiopium, where there is a shrine of Eleusinian Demeter. The reason for their waiting was that, if Amompharetos and his battalion should not leave the place where it was posted but remain there, they would then be able to assist him. No sooner had Amompharetos' men come up than the barbarians' cavalry attacked the army, for the horsemen acted as they always had. When they saw no enemy on the ground where the Greeks had been on the days before this, they kept riding forward and attacked the Greeks as soon as they overtook them.

. . .

With that, he led the Persians with all speed across the Asopus in pursuit of the Greeks, supposing that they were in flight; it was the army of Lacedaemon and Tegea alone which was his goal, for the Athenians marched another way over the broken ground, and were out of his sight. Seeing the Persians setting forth in pursuit of the Greeks, the rest of the barbarian battalions straightway raised their standards and also gave pursuit, each at top speed, no battalion having order in its ranks nor place assigned in the line.

So they ran pell-mell and shouting, as though they would utterly make an end of the Greeks. Pausanias, however, when the cavalry attacked him, sent a horseman to the Athenians with this message: "Men of Athens, in this great contest which must give freedom or slavery to Hellas, we Lacedaemonians and you Athenians have been betrayed by the flight of our allies in the night that is past. I have accordingly now resolved what we must do; we must protect each other by fighting as best we can. If the cavalry had attacked you first, it would have been the duty of both ourselves and the Tegeans, who are faithful to Hellas, to aid you; but now, seeing that the whole brunt of their assault falls on us, it is right that you should come to the aid of that division which is hardest pressed. But if, as may be, anything has befallen you which makes it impossible for you to aid us, do us the service of sending us your archers. We are sure that you will obey us, as knowing that you have been by far more zealous than all others in this present war."

When the Athenians heard that, they attempted to help the Lacedaemonians and defend them with all their might. But when their march had already begun, they were set upon by the Greeks posted opposite them, who had joined themselves to the king. For this reason, being now under attack by the foe which was closest, they could at the time send no aid. The Lacedaemonians and Tegeans accordingly stood alone, men-at-arms and light-armed together; there were of the Lacedaemonians fifty thousand and of the Tegeans, who had never been parted from the Lacedaemonians, three thousand. These offered sacrifice so that they would fare better in battle with Mardonius and the army which was with him. They could get no favorable omen from their sacrifices, and in the meanwhile many of them were killed and by far more wounded (for the Persians set up their shields for a fence, and shot showers of arrows). Since the Spartans were being hard-pressed and their sacrifices were of no avail, Pausanias lifted up his eyes to the temple of Hera at Plataea and called on the goddess, praying that they might not be disappointed in their hope.

While he was still in the act of praying, the men of Tegea leapt out before the rest and charged the barbarians, and immediately after Pausanias' prayer the sacrifices of the Lacedaemonians became favorable. Now they too charged the Persians, and the Persians met them, throwing away their bows. First they fought by the fence of shields, and when that was down, there was a fierce and long fight around the temple of Demeter itself, until they came to blows at close quarters. For the barbarians laid hold of the spears and broke them short. Now the Persians were neither less valorous nor weaker, but they had no armor; moreover, since they were unskilled and no match for their adversaries in craft, they would rush out singly and in tens or in groups great or small, hurling themselves on the Spartans and so perishing.

Where Mardonius was himself, riding a white horse in the battle and surrounded by a thousand picked men who were the flower of the Persians, there they pressed their adversaries hardest. So long as Mardonius was alive the Persians stood their ground and defended themselves, overthrowing many Lacedaemonians. When, however, Mardonius was killed and his guards, who were the strongest part of the army, had also fallen, then the rest too yielded and gave ground before the men of Lacedaemon. For what harmed them the most was the fact that they wore no armor over their clothes and fought, as it were, naked against men fully armed.

. . .

This flight of theirs which took place before the actual closing of battle and was prompted because they saw the Persians flee, proves to me that it was on the Persians that the fortune of the barbarians hung. They accordingly all fled, save the cavalry, Boeotian and other; this helped the fleeing men in so far as it remained between them and their enemies and shielded its friends from the Greeks in their flight.

So the Greeks, now having the upper hand, followed Xerxes' men, pursuing and slaying. During this steadily growing rout there came a message to the rest of the Greeks, who were by the temple of Hera and had stayed out of the fighting, that there had been a battle and that Pausanias' men were victorious. When they heard this, they set forth in no ordered array, those who were with the Corinthians keeping to the spurs of the mountain and the hill country, by the road that led upward straight to the temple of Demeter, and those who were with the Megarians and Philasians taking the most level route over the plain. However, when the Megarians and Philasians had come near the enemy, the Theban horsemen (whose captain was Asopodorus son of Timander) caught sight of them approaching in haste and disorder, and rode at them; in this attack they trampled six hundred of them, and pursued and drove the rest to Cithaeron.

So these perished without anyone noticing. But when the Persians and the rest of the multitude had fled within the wooden wall, they managed to get up on the towers before the coming of the Lacedaemonians; then they strengthened the wall as best they could. When the Athenians arrived, an intense battle for the wall began. For as long as the Athenians were not there, the barbarians defended themselves and had a great advantage over the Lacedaemonians who had no skill in the assault of walls. When the Athenians came up, however, the fight for the wall became intense and lasted for a long time. In the end the Athenians, by valor and constant effort, scaled the wall and breached it. The Greeks poured in through the opening they had made; the first to enter were the Tegeans, and it was they who plundered the tent of Mardonius, taking from it besides everything else the feeding trough of his horses which was all of bronze and a thing well worth looking at. The Tegeans dedicated this feeding trough of Mardonius in the temple of Athena Alea. Everything else which they took they brought into the common pool, as did the rest of the Greeks. As for the barbarians, they did not form a unified body again once the wall was down, nor did anyone think of defense because the terrified men in the tiny space and the many myriads herded together were in great distress. Such a slaughter were the Greeks able to make, that of two hundred and sixty thousand who remained after Artabazus had fled with his forty thousand, scarcely three thousand were left alive. Of the Lacedaemonians from Sparta ninety-one all together were killed in battle; of the Tegeans, seventeen and of the Athenians, fifty-two.

. . .

Then Pausanias made a proclamation that no man should touch the spoils, and ordered the helots to gather all the stuff together. They, spreading all over the camp, found there tents adorned with gold and silver, and couches gilded and silver-plated, and golden bowls and cups and other drinking-vessels; and sacks they found on wagons, in which were seen cauldrons of gold and silver. They stripped from the dead who lay there their armlets and torques, and golden daggers; as for the embroidered clothing, it was disregarded. Much of all this the helots showed, as much as they could not conceal, but much they stole and sold to the Aeginetans. As a result the Aeginetans laid the foundation of their great fortunes by buying gold from the helots as though it were bronze.

Having brought all the loot together, they set apart a tithe for the god of Delphi. From this was made and dedicated that tripod which rests upon the bronze three-headed serpent, nearest to the altar; another they set apart for the god of Olympia, from which was made and dedicated a bronze figure of Zeus, ten cubits high; and another for the god of the Isthmus, from which was fashioned a bronze Poseidon seven cubits high. When they had set all this apart, they divided what remained, and each received, according to his worth, concubines of the Persians and gold and silver, and all the rest of the stuff and the beasts of burden. How much was set apart and given to those who had fought best at Plataea, no man says. I think that they also received gifts, but tenfold of every kind, women, horses, talents, camels, and all other things also, was set apart and given to Pausanias.

Source: Herodotus. *History*, Book 9.39–40, 49–50, 57, 59–63, 68–70, 80–81, with an English translation by A. D. Godley. Cambridge: Harvard University Press, 1920.

5. Thucydides, Account of the Naval Battles of Patrae and Naupactus

When the Peloponnesian War began in 431 BCE Athens had the foremost trireme fleet in the Aegean. Its rowers, helmsmen, and commanders were experienced and its ships were built for speed and maneuverability. During the early years of the war, Athens sent a force to Naupactus in the Corinthian Gulf to harass Corinthian shipping. The force was under the command of Phormio. In 429 he fought a series of battles against Peloponnesian fleets in the Corinthian Gulf, all of which he won.

The nature of naval combat and ancient familiarity with it means that descriptions of fleet actions tend to be less informative than we might like. The descriptions Thucydides provides of several battles in 429 explain some features of how naval combat worked. In the first passage the defensive tactic of forming a circle (*kuklos*) is illustrated as well as the means to defeat it. In the second passage Thucydides provides an example of the tactic called sailing around (*periplous*). In both cases the Athenians won because of their skill and experience. By the time of the engagements in Syracuse trireme warfare was undergoing significant changes.

Meanwhile the fleet from Corinth and the rest of the confederates in the Crissaean gulf, which was to have co-operated with Cnemus and prevented the coast Acarnanians from joining their countrymen in the interior, was disabled from doing so by being compelled about the same time as the battle at Stratus to fight with Phormio and the twenty Athenian vessels stationed at Naupactus.

. . .

The Peloponnesians ranged their vessels in as large a circle as possible without leaving an opening, with the prows outside and the sterns in; and placed within all the small craft in company, and their five best sailors to issue out at a moment's notice and strengthen any point threatened by the enemy.

The Athenians, formed in line, sailed round and round them, and forced them to contract their circle, by continually brushing past and making as though they would attack at once, having been previously cautioned by Phormio not to do so till he gave the signal. His hope was that the Peloponnesians would not retain their order like a force on shore, but that the ships would fall foul of one another and the small craft cause confusion; and if the wind should blow from the gulf (in expectation of which he kept sailing round them, and which usually rose towards morning), they would not, he felt sure, remain steady an instant. He also thought that it rested with him to attack when he pleased, as his ships were better sailors, and that an attack timed by the coming of the wind would tell best. When the wind came down, the enemy's ships were now in a narrow space, and what with the wind and the small craft dashing against them, at once fell into confusion: ship fell foul of ship, while the crews were pushing them off with poles, and by their shouting, swearing and struggling with one another, made captains' orders and boatswains' cries alike inaudible, and through being unable for want of practice to clear their oars in the rough water, prevented the vessels from obeying their helmsmen properly. At this moment Phormio gave the signal, and the Athenians attacked. Sinking first one of the admirals, they then disabled all they came across, so that no one thought of resistance for the confusion, but fled for Patrae and Dyme in Achaea. The Athenians gave chase and captured twelve ships, and taking most of the men out of them sailed to Molycrium, and after setting up a trophy on the promontory of Rhium and dedicating a ship to Poseidon, returned to Naupactus. As for the Peloponnesians, they at once sailed with their remaining ships along the coast from Dyme and Patrae to Cyllene, the Eleian arsenal; where Cnemus and the ships from Leucas that were to have joined them, also arrived after the battle of Stratus.

The Lacedaemonians now sent to the fleet to Cnemus three commissioners, Timocrates, Brasidas, and Lycophron, with orders to prepare to engage again with better fortune, and not to be driven from the sea by a few vessels; for they could not at all account for their discomfiture, the less so as it was their first attempt at sea; and they fancied that it was not that their marine was so inferior, but that there had been misconduct somewhere, not considering the long experience of the Athenians as compared with the little practice which they had had themselves. The commissioners were accordingly sent in anger. As soon as they arrived they set to work with Cnemus to order ships from the different states, and to put those which they already had in fighting order. Meanwhile Phormio sent word to Athens of their preparations and his own victory, and desired as many ships as possible to be speedily sent to him, as he stood in daily expectation of a battle.

. . .

Such was the exhortation of Phormio. The Peloponnesians finding that the Athenians did not sail into the gulf and the narrows, in order to lead them in whether they wished it or not, put out at dawn, and forming four abreast, sailed inside the gulf in the direction of their own country, the right wing leading as they had lain at anchor. In this wing were placed twenty of their best sailors; so that in the event of Phormio thinking that their object was Naupactus, and coasting along thither to save the place, the Athenians might not be able to escape their onset by getting outside their wing, but might be cut off by the vessels in question. As they expected, Phormio, in alarm for the place at that moment emptied of its garrison, as soon as he saw them put out, reluctantly and hurriedly embarked and sailed along shore; the Messenian land forces moving along also to support him. The Peloponnesians seeing him coasting along with his ships in single file, and by this inside the gulf and close in shore as they so much wished, at one signal tacked suddenly and bore down in line at their best speed on the Athenians, hoping to cut off the whole squadron. The eleven leading vessels, however, escaped the Peloponnesian wing and its sudden movement, and reached the more open water; but the rest were overtaken as they tried to run through, driven ashore and disabled; such of the crews being slain as had not swum out of them. Some of the ships the Peloponnesians lashed to their own, and towed off empty; one they took with the men in it; others were just being towed off, when they were saved by the Messenians dashing into the sea with their armor and fighting from the decks that they had boarded.

Thus far victory was with the Peloponnesians, and the Athenian fleet destroyed; the twenty ships in the right wing being meanwhile in chase of the eleven Athenian vessels that had escaped their sudden movement and reached the more open water. These, with the exception of one ship, all out-sailed them and got safe into Naupactus, and forming close in shore opposite the temple of Apollo, with their prows facing the enemy, prepared to defend themselves in case the Peloponnesians should sail in shore against them. After a while the Peloponnesians came up, chanting the paean for their victory as they sailed on; the single Athenian ship remaining being chased by a Leucadian far ahead of the rest. But there happened to be a merchantman lying at anchor in the roadstead, which the Athenian ship found time to sail round, and struck the Leucadian in chase amidships and sank her. An exploit so sudden and unexpected produced a panic among the Peloponnesians; and having fallen out of order in the excitement of victory, some of them dropped their oars and stopped their way in order to let the main body come up—an unsafe thing to do considering how near they were to the enemy's prows; while others ran aground in the shallows, in their ignorance of the localities.

Elated at this incident, the Athenians at one word gave a cheer, and dashed at the enemy, who, embarrassed by his mistakes and the disorder in which he found himself, only stood for an instant, and then fled for Panormus, whence he had put out. The Athenians following on his heels took the six vessels nearest them, and recovered those of their own which had been disabled close in shore and taken in tow at the beginning of the action; they killed some of the crews and took some prisoners. On board the Leucadian which went down off the merchantman, was the Lacedaemonian Timocrates, who killed himself when the ship was sunk, and was cast up in the harbor of Naupactus. The Athenians on their return set up a trophy on the spot from which they had put out and turned the day, and picking up the wrecks and dead that were on their shore, gave back to the enemy their dead under truce. The Peloponnesians also set up a trophy as victors for the defeat inflicted upon the ships they had disabled in shore, and dedicated the vessel which they had taken at Achaean Rhium, side by side with the trophy.

Source: Thucydides. *The Peloponnesian War*, Book 2.83.1, 83.5–85.4, 2.90–92.5. London: J. M. Dent; New York: E. P. Dutton, 1910.

6. Thucydides, Account of the Battle of Delium

Having begun in 431 BCE, the Peloponnesian War had been a stalemate in its first five years, but by 424 Athens had taken the initiative as a result of its success the previous year at Sphacteria. The Battle of Delium was the culmination of a strategy to detach Boeotia from the Peloponnesian League. Hippocrates, the

Athenian commander, was trying to retreat from Boeotia. Pagondas of Thebes tried to defeat him before he could escape. Although it reads like a traditional hoplite battle initially, when compared to the Greeks at Marathon hoplite warfare had already evolved in complexity.

Delium was the first hoplite-on-hoplite battle that Thucydides, writing in the late fifth century, described in sufficient detail to draw conclusions about hoplite phalanx combat. This battle narrative is one of the few from the war complete enough to provide many different components of a battle. This passage is important for providing a sense of the tactics employed in later fifth century Greece. Notice that in this battle Greeks employed light-armed troops as well as cavalry along with the full hoplite array. Thucydides provides a sense of how the one side might charge into the other to force the opponent's line into disarray. Whereas Mardonius had described battle on a flat plain, this battle was fought on a hillside and Pagondas even used the hill to cover his movements.

In this passage Thucydides also illustrates the commander's role in battle—awareness of terrain and how the action developed as well as the need to communicate. The aftermath demonstrates other important aspects of battle—recovering one's dead and spoiling the enemy. Thucydides' description of the Boeotian siege of the Athenian fort at Delium is full of unique and interesting details about siege tactics.

During the days thus employed the Boeotians were mustering at Tanagra, and by the time that they had come in from all the towns, found the Athenians already on their way home. The rest of the eleven Boeotarchs were against giving battle, as the enemy was no longer in Boeotia, the Athenians being just over the Oropian border, when they halted; but Pagondas, son of Aeolidas, one of the Boeotarchs of Thebes (Arianthides, son of Lysimachidas, being the other), and then commander-in-chief, thought it best to hazard a battle. He accordingly called the men to him, company after company, to prevent their all leaving their arms at once, and urged them to attack the Athenians, and stand the issue of a battle.

. . .

By these arguments Pagondas persuaded the Boeotians to attack the Athenians, and quickly breaking up his camp led his army forward, it being now late in the day. On nearing the enemy, he halted in a position where a hill intervening prevented the two armies from seeing each other, and then formed and prepared for action. Meanwhile Hippocrates at Delium, informed of the approach of the Boeotians, sent orders to his troops to throw themselves into line, and himself joined them not long afterwards, leaving about three hundred horse behind him at Delium, at once to guard the place in case of attack, and to watch their opportunity and fall upon the Boeotians during the battle. The Boeotians placed a detachment to deal with these, and when everything was arranged to their satisfaction appeared over the hill, and halted in the order which they had determined on, to the number of seven thousand heavy infantry, more than ten thousand light troops, one thousand horse, and five hundred targeteers. On their right were the Thebans and those of their province, in the center the Haliartians, Coronaeans, Copaeans, and the other people around the lake, and on the left the Thespians, Tanagraeans, and Orchomenians, the cavalry and the light troops being at the extremity of each wing. The Thebans formed twenty-five shields deep, the rest as they pleased. Such was the strength and disposition of the Boeotian army.

On the side of the Athenians, the heavy infantry throughout the whole army formed eight deep, being in numbers equal to the enemy, with the cavalry upon the two wings. Light troops regularly armed there were none in the army, nor had there ever been any at Athens. Those who had joined in the invasion, though many times more numerous than those of the enemy, had mostly followed unarmed, as part of the levy in mass of the citizens and foreigners at Athens, and having started first on their way home were not present in any number.

. . .

Hippocrates had got half through the army with his exhortation, when the Boeotians, after a few more hasty words from Pagondas, struck up the paean, and came against them from the hill; the Athenians advancing to meet them, and closing at a run. The extreme wing of neither army came into action, one like the other being stopped by the water-courses in the way; the rest engaged with the utmost obstinacy, shield against shield. The Boeotian left, as far as the center, was worsted by the Athenians. The Thespians in that part of the field suffered most severely. The troops alongside them having given way, they were surrounded in a narrow space and cut down fighting hand to hand; some of the Athenians also fell into confusion in surrounding the enemy and mistook and so killed each other. In this part of the field the Boeotians were beaten, and retreated upon the troops still fighting; but the right, where the Thebans were, got the better of the Athenians and shoved them further and further back, though gradually at first. It so happened also that Pagondas, seeing the distress of his left, had sent two squadrons of horse, where they could not be seen, round the hill, and their sudden appearance struck a panic into the victorious wing of the Athenians, who thought that it was another army coming against them. At length in both parts of the field, disturbed by this panic, and with their line broken by the advancing Thebans, the whole Athenian army took to flight. Some made for Delium and the sea, some for Oropus, others for Mount Parnes, or wherever they had hopes of safety, pursued and cut down by the Boeotians, and in particular by the cavalry, composed partly of Boeotians and partly of Locrians, who had come up just as the rout began. Night however coming on to interrupt the pursuit, the mass of the fugitives escaped more easily than they would otherwise have done. The next day the troops at Oropus and Delium returned home by sea, after leaving a garrison in the latter place, which they continued to hold notwithstanding the defeat.

The Boeotians set up a trophy, took up their own dead, and stripped those of the enemy, and leaving a guard over them retired to Tanagra, there to take measures for attacking Delium.

. . .

After these words from the herald, the Athenians sent their own herald to the Boeotians to say that they had not done any wrong to the temple, and for the future would do it no more harm than they could help; not having occupied it originally in any such design, but to defend themselves from it against those who were really wronging them. The law of the Hellenes was that conquest of a country, whether more or less extensive, carried with it possession of the temples in that country, with the obligation to keep up the usual ceremonies, at least as far as possible. The Boeotians and most other people who had turned out the owners of a country, and put themselves in their places by force, now held as of right the temples which they originally entered as usurpers. If the Athenians could have conquered more of Boeotia this would have been the case with them: as things stood, the piece of it which they had got they should treat as their own, and not quit unless obliged. The water they had disturbed under the impulsion of a necessity which they had not wantonly incurred, having been forced to use it in defending themselves against the Boeotians who had first invaded Attica. Besides, anything done under the pressure of war and danger might reasonably claim indulgence even in the eye of the god; or why, pray, were the altars the asylum for involuntary offences? Transgression also was a term applied to presumptuous offenders, not to the victims of adverse circumstances. In short, which were most impious—the Boeotians who wished to barter dead bodies for holy places, or the Athenians who refused to give up holy places to obtain what was theirs by right? The condition of evacuating Boeotia must therefore be withdrawn. They were no longer in Boeotia. They stood where they stood by the right of the sword. All that the Boeotians had to do was to tell them to take up their dead under a truce according to the national custom.

Meanwhile the Boeotians at once sent for darters and slingers from the Malian gulf, and with two thousand Corinthian heavy infantry who had joined them after the battle, the Peloponnesian garrison which had evacuated Nisaea, and some Megarians with them, marched against Delium, and attacked the fort, and after divers efforts finally succeeded in taking it by an engine of the following description. They sawed in two and scooped out a great beam from end to end, and fitting it nicely together again like a pipe, hung by chains a cauldron at one extremity, with which communicated an iron tube projecting from the beam, which was itself in great part plated with iron. This they brought up from a distance upon carts to the part of the wall principally composed of vines and timber, and when it was near, inserted huge bellows into their end of the beam and blew with them. The blast passing closely confined into the cauldron, which was filled with lighted coals, sulphur and pitch, made a great blaze, and set fire to the wall, which soon became untenable for its defenders, who left it and fled; and in this way the fort was taken. Of the garrison some were killed and two hundred made prisoners; most of the rest got on board their ships and returned home.

Soon after the fall of Delium, which took place seventeen days after the battle, the Athenian herald, without knowing what had happened, came again for the dead, which were now restored by the Boeotians, who no longer answered as at first. Not quite five hundred Boeotians fell in the battle, and nearly one thousand Athenians, including Hippocrates the general, besides a great number of light troops and camp followers.

Source: Thucydides. *The Peloponnesian War,* Book 4.91, 93–94.1, 96.1–97.1, 98, 100–101.2. London: J. M. Dent; New York: E. P. Dutton, 1910.

7. Thucydides, Account of the First Battle of Mantinea

This battle narrative covers the First Battle of Mantinea, in 418 BCE. The Peace of Nicias in 421 created an armistice between Athens and Sparta. Alcibiades used the opportunity to forge an anti-Spartan, Peloponnesian alliance centered on Argos. This battle was the culmination of an effort by Sparta to recover its former ally, Mantinea, and crush the Argive alliance. Agis, the Spartan king, was under pressure to succeed after failure the prior year. On the first day the Spartans had withdrawn and begun flooding Mantinean territory. On the second day they were marching to do the same when the Argives surprised them.

In addition to being a large hoplite battle, the account illustrates tactics and battlefield mechanics. As in the case of Delium, Thucydides demonstrated the importance of a competent commander. In addition to the commander, the nature of Spartan organization in warfare comes out as well as the discipline of the Spartan soldiers. Finally, this battle is one of the few to include elite forces of 300 men on both sides. With its large, orderly armies and disciplined engagement this battle is the ultimate expression of ideal hoplite warfare and yet the maneuvers and light-armed skirmishers show that warfare continued to evolve.

The next day the Argives and their allies formed in the order in which they meant to fight, if they chanced to encounter the enemy; and the Lacedaemonians returning from the water to their old encampment by the temple of Heracles, suddenly saw their adversaries close in front of them, all in complete order, and advanced from the hill. A shock like that of the present moment the Lacedaemonians do not ever remember to have experienced: there was scant time for preparation, as they instantly and hastily fell into their ranks, Agis, their king, directing everything, agreeably to the law. For when a king is in the field all commands proceed from him: he gives the word to the Polemarchs; they to the Lochages; these to the Pentecostyes; these again to the Enomotarchs, and these last to the Enomoties. In short all orders required pass in the same way and quickly reach the troops; as almost the whole Lacedaemonian army, save for a small part, consists of officers under officers, and the care of what is to be done falls upon many.

　　In this battle the left wing was composed of the Sciritae, who in a Lacedaemonian army have always that post to themselves alone; next to these were the soldiers of Brasidas from Thrace, and the Neodamodes with them; then came the Lacedaemonians themselves, company after company, with the Arcadians of Heraea at their side. After these were the Maenalians, and on the right wing the Tegeans with a few of the Lacedaemonians at the extremity; their cavalry being posted upon the two wings. Such was the Lacedaemonian formation. That of their opponents was as follows:—On the right were the Mantineans, the action taking place in their country: next to them the allies from Arcadia; after whom came the thousand picked men of the Argives, to whom the state had given a long course of military training at the public expense; next to them the rest of the Argives, and after them their allies, the Cleonaeans and Orneans, and lastly the Athenians on the extreme left, and their own cavalry with them.

Such were the order and the forces of the two combatants. The Lacedaemonian army looked the largest; though as to putting down the numbers of either host, or of the contingents composing it, I could not do so with any accuracy. Owing to the secrecy of their government the number of the Lacedaemonians was not known, and men are so apt to brag about the forces of their country that the estimate of their opponents was not trusted. The following calculation, however, makes it possible to estimate the numbers of the Lacedaemonians present upon this occasion. There were seven companies in the field without counting the Sciritae, who numbered six hundred men: in each company there were four Pentecostyes, and in the Pentecosty four Enomoties. The first rank of the Enomoty was composed of four soldiers: as to the depth, although they had not been all drawn up alike, but as each captain chose, they were generally ranged eight deep; the first rank along the whole line, exclusive of the Sciritae, consisted of four hundred and forty-eight men.

The armies being now on the eve of engaging, each contingent received some words of encouragement from its own commander. The Mantineans were reminded that they were going to fight for their country and to avoid returning to the experience of servitude after having tasted that of empire; the Argives, that they would contend for their ancient supremacy, to regain their once equal share of Peloponnese of which they had been so long deprived, and to punish an enemy and a neighbor for a thousand wrongs; the Athenians, of the glory of gaining the honors of the day with so many and brave allies in arms, and that a victory over the Lacedaemonians in Peloponnese would cement and extend their empire, and would besides preserve Attica from all invasions in future. These were the incitements addressed to the Argives and their allies. The Lacedaemonians meanwhile, man to man, and with their war-songs in the ranks, exhorted each brave comrade to remember what he had learnt before; well aware that the long training of action was of more saving virtue than any brief verbal exhortation, though never so well delivered.

After this they joined battle, the Argives and their allies advancing with haste and fury, the Lacedaemonians slowly and to the music of many flute-players—a standing institution in their army, that has nothing to do with religion, but is meant to make them advance evenly, stepping in time, without breaking their order, as large armies are apt to do in the moment of engaging.

Just before the battle joined, King Agis resolved upon the following manoeuvre. All armies are alike in this: on going into action they get forced out rather on their right wing, and one and the other overlap with this their adversary's left; because fear makes each man do his best to shelter his unarmed side with the shield of the man next him on the right, thinking that the closer the shields are locked together the better will he be protected. The man primarily responsible for this is the first upon the right wing, who is always striving to withdraw from the enemy his unarmed side; and the same apprehension makes the rest follow him. On the present occasion the Mantineans reached with their wing far beyond the Sciritae, and the Lacedaemonians and Tegeans still farther beyond the Athenians, as their army was the largest. Agis afraid of his left being surrounded, and thinking that the Mantineans outflanked it too far, ordered the Sciritae and Brasideans to move out from their place in the ranks and make the line even with the Mantineans, and told the Polemarchs Hipponoidas and Aristocles to fill up the gap thus formed, by throwing themselves into it with two companies taken from the right wing; thinking that his right would still be strong enough and to spare, and that the line fronting the Mantineans would gain in solidity.

However, as he gave these orders in the moment of the onset, and at short notice, it so happened that Aristocles and Hipponoidas would not move over, for which offence they were afterwards banished from Sparta, as having been guilty of cowardice; and the enemy meanwhile closed before the Sciritae (whom Agis on seeing that the two companies did not move over ordered to return to their place) had time to fill up the breach in question. Now it was, however, that the Lacedaemonians, utterly worsted in respect of skill, showed themselves as superior in point of courage. As soon as they came to close quarters with the enemy, the Mantinean right broke their Sciritae and Brasideans, and bursting in with their allies and the thousand picked Argives into the unclosed breach in their line cut up and surrounded the Lacedaemonians, and drove them in full rout to the wagons, slaying some of the older men on guard there. But the Lacedaemonians, worsted in this part of the field, with the rest of their army, and especially the center, where the three hundred knights, as they are called, fought round King Agis, fell on the older men of the Argives and the five companies so named, and on the Cleonaeans, the Orneans, and the Athenians next them, and instantly routed them; the greater number not even waiting to strike a blow, but giving way the moment that they came on, some even being trodden under foot, in their fear of being overtaken by their assailants.

The army of the Argives and their allies having given way in this quarter was now completely cut in two, and the Lacedaemonian and Tegean right simultaneously closing round the Athenians with the troops that outflanked them, these last found themselves placed between two fires, being surrounded on one side and already defeated on the other. Indeed they would have suffered more severely than any other part of the army, but for the services of the cavalry which they had with them. Agis also on perceiving the distress of his left opposed to the Mantineans and the thousand Argives, ordered all the army to advance to the support of the defeated wing; and while this took place, as the enemy moved past and slanted away from them, the Athenians escaped at their leisure, and with them the beaten Argive division. Meanwhile the Mantineans and their allies and the picked body of the Argives ceased to press the enemy, and seeing their friends defeated and the Lacedaemonians in full advance upon them, took to flight. Many of the Mantineans perished; but the bulk of the picked body of the Argives made good their escape. The flight and retreat, however, were neither hurried nor long; the Lacedaemonians fighting long and stubbornly until the rout of their enemy, but that once effected, pursuing for a short time and not far.

Such was the battle, as nearly as possible as I have described it; the greatest that had occurred for a very long while among the Hellenes, and joined by the most considerable states. The Lacedaemonians took up a position in front of the enemy's dead, and immediately set up a trophy and stripped the slain; they took up their own dead and carried them back to Tegea, where they buried them, and restored those of the enemy under truce.

. . .

While the battle was impending, Pleistoanax, the other king, set out with a reinforcement composed of the oldest and youngest men, and got as far as Tegea, where he heard of the victory and went back again. The Lacedaemonians also sent and turned back the allies from Corinth and from beyond the Isthmus, and returning themselves dismissed their allies, and kept the Carnean holidays, which happened to be at that time. The imputations cast upon them by the Hellenes at the time, whether of cowardice on account of the disaster in the island, or of mismanagement and slowness generally, were all wiped out by this single action: fortune, it was thought, might have humbled them, but the men themselves were the same as ever.

Source: Thucydides. *The Peloponnesian War*, Book 5.66–74.2, 75.1–3. London: J. M. Dent; New York: E. P. Dutton, 1910.

8. Thucydides, Account of a Naval Battle at Syracuse

Athens sent an expedition against Sicily in 415 BCE. Their mission was to defeat Syracuse. The land and naval force fared well initially and nearly won in 414, but by 413 Syracuse had seized the initiative on land. The Syracusan navy was initially weak and inexperienced in comparison to the Athenians, but by 413 they had trained extensively and accumulated a large force to fight in the Great Harbor of Syracuse. Learning that Athenian reinforcements were coming they decided to attack at sea. Before engaging they copied Corinthian ships and reinforced the bows for prow-to-prow ramming in the narrow space. They would also try a trick with a lunch break to win the element of surprise.

The account of the battle explains how prow ramming was to Syracuse's advantage and describes naval tactics. The account also mentions an unusual aspect of naval combat, the marketplace. Sailors could not carry food on board during battle so when there was a break they would beach the ship and go to a prearranged marketplace to buy food. Thucydides describes how the Syracusan commander took advantage of this common practice, a tactic that would be used again at Aegospotami.

Meanwhile the Syracusans hearing of their approach resolved to make a second attempt with their fleet and their other forces on shore, which they had been collecting for this very purpose in order to do something before their arrival. In addition to other improvements suggested by the former sea-fight which they now adopted in the equipment of their navy, they cut down their prows to a smaller compass to make them more solid and made their cheeks stouter, and from these let stays into the vessel's sides for a length of six cubits within and without, in the same way as the Corinthians had altered their prows before engaging the squadron at Naupactus. The Syracusans thought that they would thus have an advantage over the Athenian vessels, which were not constructed with equal strength, but were slight in the bows, from their being more used to sail round and charge the enemy's side than to meet him prow to prow, and that the battle being in the great harbor, with a great many ships in not much room, was also a fact in their favour. Charging prow to prow, they would stave in the enemy's bows, by striking with solid and stout beaks against hollow and weak ones; and secondly, the Athenians for want of room would be unable to use their favorite manoeuvre of breaking the line or of sailing round, as the Syracusans would do their best not to let them do the one, and want of room would prevent their doing the other. This charging prow to prow which had hitherto been thought want of skill in a helmsman, would be the Syracusans' chief manoeuvre, as being that which they should find most useful, since the Athenians, if repulsed, would not be able to back water in any direction except towards the shore, and that only for a little way, and in the little space in front of their own camp. The rest of the harbor would be commanded by the Syracusans; and the Athenians, if hard pressed, by crowding together in a small space and all to the same point, would run foul of one another and fall into disorder, which was, in fact, the thing that did the Athenians most harm in all the sea-fights, they not having, like the Syracusans, the whole harbor to retreat over. As to their sailing round into the open sea, this would be impossible, with the Syracusans in possession of the way out and in, especially as Plemmyrium would be hostile to them, and the mouth of the harbor was not large.

With these contrivances to suit their skill and ability, and now more confident after the previous sea-fight, the Syracusans attacked by land and sea at once. The town force Gylippus led out a little at first and brought them up to the wall of the Athenians, where it looked towards the city, while the force from the Olympieum, that is to say, the heavy infantry that were there with the horse and the light troops of the Syracusans, advanced against the wall from the opposite side; the ships of the Syracusans and allies sailing out immediately afterwards. The Athenians at first fancied that they were to be attacked by land only, and it was not without alarm that they saw the fleet suddenly approaching as well; and while some were forming upon the walls and in front of them against the advancing enemy, and some marching out in haste against the numbers of horse and darters coming from the Olympieum and from outside, others manned the ships or rushed down to the beach to oppose the enemy, and when the ships were manned put out with seventy-five sail against about eighty of the Syracusans.

After spending a great part of the day in advancing and retreating and skirmishing with each other, without either being able to gain any advantage worth speaking of, except that the Syracusans sank one or two of the

Athenian vessels, they parted, the land force at the same time retiring from the lines. The next day the Syracusans remained quiet, and gave no signs of what they were going to do; but Nicias, seeing that the battle had been a drawn one, and expecting that they would attack again, compelled the captains to refit any of the ships that had suffered, and moored merchant vessels before the stockade which they had driven into the sea in front of their ships, to serve instead of an enclosed harbor, at about two hundred feet from each other, in order that any ship that was hard pressed might be able to retreat in safety and sail out again at leisure. These preparations occupied the Athenians all day until nightfall.

The next day the Syracusans began operations at an earlier hour, but with the same plan of attack by land and sea. A great part of the day the rivals spent as before, confronting and skirmishing with each other; until at last Ariston, son of Pyrrhicus, a Corinthian, the ablest helmsman in the Syracusan service, persuaded their naval commanders to send to the officials in the city, and tell them to move the sale market as quickly as they could down to the sea, and oblige every one to bring whatever eatables he had and sell them there, thus enabling the commanders to land the crews and dine at once close to the ships, and shortly afterwards, the selfsame day, to attack the Athenians again when they were not expecting it.

In compliance with this advice a messenger was sent and the market got ready, upon which the Syracusans suddenly backed water and withdrew to the town, and at once landed and took their dinner upon the spot; while the Athenians, supposing that they had returned to the town because they felt they were beaten, disembarked at their leisure and set about getting their dinners and about their other occupations, under the idea that they had done with fighting for that day. Suddenly the Syracusans manned their ships and again sailed against them; and the Athenians, in great confusion and most of them fasting, got on board, and with great difficulty put out to meet them. For some time both parties remained on the defensive without engaging, until the Athenians at last resolved not to let themselves be worn out by waiting where they were, but to attack without delay, and giving a cheer, went into action. The Syracusans received them, and charging prow to prow as they had intended, stove in a great part of the Athenian foreships by the strength of their beaks; the darters on the decks also did great damage to the Athenians, but still greater damage was done by the Syracusans who went about in small boats, ran in upon the oars of the Athenian galleys, and sailed against their sides, and discharged from thence their darts upon the sailors.

At last, fighting hard in this fashion, the Syracusans gained the victory, and the Athenians turned and fled between the merchantmen to their own station. The Syracusan ships pursued them as far as the merchantmen, where they were stopped by the beams armed with dolphins suspended from those vessels over the passage. Two of the Syracusan vessels went too near in the excitement of victory and were destroyed, one of them being taken with its crew. After sinking seven of the Athenian vessels and disabling many, and taking most of the men prisoners and killing others, the Syracusans retired and set up trophies for both the engagements, being now confident of having a decided superiority by sea, and by no means despairing of equal success by land.

Source: Thucydides. *The Peloponnesian War*, Book 7.36–41. London: J. M. Dent; New York: E. P. Dutton, 1910.

9. Xenophon, Account of the Battle of Lechaion

The battle of Lechaion occurred in 390 BCE during the Corinthian War when Corinth, Thebes, and Athens, supplied with Persian wealth, allied against Sparta. Iphicrates and Callias were both Athenian commanders stationed at Corinth, but the *peltasts* were mercenaries paid for with Persian cash. The Spartan force had been making its way from Sicyon to Lechaion through Corinthian territory when it came under attack. Agesilaus II, king of Sparta, escorted the Spartan force home under cover of darkness to hide the shame of defeat. Despite Iphicrates' victory, this battle made little difference in the war. Iphicrates would be unable to duplicate his success later.

The battle is a good example of the ways in which Greek warfare changed significantly in the period after the fall of Athens in 404. This narrative highlights how the Spartans, who had only a few years previously won dominance in Greece, lost to *peltasts*. The Spartans lost in part because they faced an imaginative opponent in command of professional *peltasts*. In addition to demonstrating the value of *peltasts* and mercenaries, the incident also showed how important it was for hoplites of this period to be supported by light-armed troops or cavalry. This engagement was quite a change from the Persian Wars where the Greek hoplites repeatedly smashed Persian light infantry.

And he did not belie his words, but on the next day, after offering sacrifice, he led his army to the city. He did not throw down the trophy, but by cutting down and burning any fruit-tree that was still left, he showed that no one wanted to come out against him. When he had done this, he encamped near Lechaeum; as for the ambassadors of the Thebans, although he did not let them go into the city, yet he sent them home by sea to Creusis.[1] Now inasmuch as such a calamity had been unusual with the Lacedaemonians, there was great mourning throughout the Laconian army, except among those whose sons, fathers, or brothers had fallen where they stood; they, however, went about like victors, with shining countenances and full of exultation in their own misfortune.

Now it was in the following way that the disaster to the regiment happened. The Amyclaeans invariably go back home to the festival of the Hyacinthia for the paean to Apollo, whether they chance to be on a campaign or away from home for any other reason.[1] Accordingly Agesilaus had on this occasion left behind at Lechaeum all the Amyclaeans in the army. Now the polemarch in command of the garrison there detailed the garrison troops of the allies to guard the wall, and himself with the regiment of hoplites and the regiment of horsemen conducted the Amyclaeans along past the city of the Corinthians.

And when they were distant from Sicyon about twenty or thirty stadia, the polemarch with the hoplites, who were about six hundred in number, set out to return to Lechaeum, and ordered the commander of horse to follow after him with the regiment of horsemen after they had escorted the Amyclaeans as far as they themselves directed. Now they were by no means unaware that there were many peltasts and many hoplites in Corinth; but on account of their previous successes they contemptuously thought that no one would attack them.

But those in the city of the Corinthians, both Callias, the son of Hipponicus, commander of the Athenian hoplites, and Iphicrates, leader of the peltasts, when they descried the Lacedaemonians and saw that they were not only few in number, but also unaccompanied by either peltasts or cavalry, thought that it was safe to attack them with their force of peltasts. For if they should proceed along the road, they could be attacked with javelins on their unprotected side and destroyed; and if they should undertake to pursue, they with their peltasts, the nimblest of all troops, could easily escape the hoplites.

Having come to this conclusion, they led forth their troops. And Callias formed his hoplites in line of battle not far from the city, while Iphicrates with his peltasts attacked the Lacedaemonian regiment. Now when the Lacedaemonians were being attacked with javelins, and several men had been wounded and several others slain, they directed the shield-bearers to take up these wounded men and carry them back to Lechaeum; and these were the only men in the regiment who were really saved. Then the polemarch ordered the first ten year-classes to drive off their assailants.

But when they pursued, they caught no one, since they were hoplites pursuing peltasts at the distance of a javelin's cast; for Iphicrates had given orders to the peltasts to retire before the hoplites got near them; and further, when the Lacedaemonians were retiring from the pursuit, being scattered because each man had pursued as swiftly as he could, the troops of Iphicrates turned about, and not only did those in front again hurl javelins upon the Lacedaemonians, but also others on the flank, running along to reach their unprotected side. Indeed, at the very first pursuit the peltasts shot down nine or ten of them. And as soon as this happened, they began to press the attack much more boldly.

Then, as the Lacedaemonians continued to suffer losses, the polemarch again ordered the first fifteen year-classes to pursue. But when these fell back, even more of them were shot down than at the first retirement. And now that the best men had already been killed, the horsemen joined them, and with the horsemen they again undertook a pursuit. But when the peltasts turned to flight, at that moment the horsemen managed their attack badly; for they did not chase the enemy until they had killed some of them, but both in the pursuit and in the turning backward kept an[1] even front with the hoplites. And what with striving and suffering in this way again and again, the Lacedaemonians themselves kept continually becoming fewer and fainter of heart, while their enemies were becoming bolder, and those who attacked them continually more numerous.

Therefore in desperation they gathered together on a small hill, distant from the sea about two stadia, and from Lechaeum about sixteen or seventeen stadia. And the men in Lechaeum, upon perceiving them, embarked in small boats and coasted along until they came opposite the hill. Then the troops, being now desperate, because they were suffering and being slain, while unable to inflict any harm themselves, and, besides this, seeing the Athenian hoplites also coming against them, took to flight. And some of them plunged into the sea, and some few made their escape with the horsemen to Lechaeum. But in all the battles and in the flight about two hundred and fifty of them were killed. Thus it was that these events took place.

After this Agesilaus departed with the defeated regiment, and left another behind him in Lechaeum. And as he passed along homeward, he led his troops into the cities as late in the day as he could and set out again in the morning as early as he could. When he approached Mantinea, by leaving Orchomenus before dawn he passed by that city while it was still dark: so hard, he thought, would the soldiers find it to see the Mantineans rejoicing at their misfortune.

After this, Iphicrates was very successful in his other undertakings also. For although garrisons had been stationed in Sidus and Crommyon by Praxitas when he captured these strongholds, and in Oenoe by Agesilaus at the time when Piraeum was taken, Iphicrates captured all these places. In Lechaeum, however, the Lacedaemonians and their allies maintained their garrison. And the Corinthian exiles, no longer proceeding by land from Sicyon past Corinth, on account of the disaster to the regiment, but sailing along the coast to Lechaeum and sallying forth from there, caused annoyance to the people in the city even as they suffered annoyance themselves.

Source: Xenophon. *Xenophon in Seven Volumes,* 1 and 2, Book 4.5.10–19, translated by Carleton L. Brownson. Cambridge, MA: Harvard University Press; London: William Heinemann, Ltd. Vol. 1: 1918; Vol. 2: 1921.

10. Xenophon, Account of the Battle of Leuctra

The Spartans (Lacedaemonians) dominated Greek land warfare since well before the Persian Wars, but this dominance ended in 371 BCE when the king met Epameinondas at Leuctra in Boeotia. Cleombrotus had been ordered by Sparta to invade Boeotia from Phocis and chastise Thebes for ejecting a Spartan garrison several years earlier and for not allowing its neighbors to be autonomous as called for in the King's Peace. Epameinondas had been training the Theban Army and testing some new tactics. He did not wait for the Spartans, but marched to meet them on favorable ground. Cleombrotus was under pressure to be aggressive because of his failure to fight the previous year. The Theban victory resulted in the end of the Spartan mirage and the collapse of Spartan power.

This battle is another example of how warfare continued to evolve. The Spartans had repeatedly shown themselves unwilling or unable to change methods. Epameinondas used innovative tactics coupled with a mixture of units not unlike what the Boeotians had employed in 424 at Delium. As such, this battle should be seen as a transitional step between the hoplite tactics of the late fifth century and the Macedonian tactics of Philip II who undoubtedly learned from Epameinondas. There is also an accusation in the passage that Cleombrotus had been drinking wine before the engagement and may not have been at his best. We are hard pressed to say whether that was truly the case or whether it was a way for the Spartans to make excuses that would forgive the defeat without recognizing Epameinondas' superior skill in battle.

The Lacedaemonian assembly, however, upon hearing these words, came to the conclusion that he was talking nonsense; for at this moment, as it seems, Fate was leading them on; and they sent orders to Cleombrotus not to disband his army, but to lead it at once against the Thebans if they did not leave the cities independent. When, therefore, he learned that, so far from leaving the cities independent, the Thebans were not even disbanding their army, in order that they might marshal themselves against him, under these circumstances he undertook to lead his troops into Boeotia.

After accomplishing this exploit and marching up from the sea-coast, he encamped at Leuctra, in the territory of Thespiae. And the Thebans encamped on the opposite hill not very far away, with no allies except the Boeotians. Then his friends went to Cleombrotus and said.

"Cleombrotus, if you let the Thebans escape without a battle, you will be in danger of suffering the uttermost penalty at the hands of your state. For they will remember against you not only the time when you reached Cynoscephalae and laid waste no part of the country of the Thebans, but also the time when, on your later expedition, you were beaten back from effecting your entrance, although Agesilaus always made his entrance by way of Cithaeron. Therefore if you really have a care for yourself or a desire to see your fatherland again, you must lead against these men." Such were the words of his friends; but his opponents said: "Now is the time when the man will make it clear whether he is in truth partial to the Thebans, as rumour has it."

Cleombrotus, then, as he heard these things was spurred on to join battle. The leaders of the Thebans, on the other hand, calculated that if they did not fight, the cities round about would revolt from them and they would themselves be besieged; further, that if the people of Thebes were thus cut off from provisions, the city itself would be in danger of turning against them. And since many of them had been in exile before, they estimated that it was better to die fighting than to be exiled again.

Besides this, they were also somewhat encouraged by the oracle which was reported—that the Lacedaemonians were destined to be defeated at the spot where stood the monument of the virgins, who are said to have killed themselves because they had been violated by certain Lacedaemonians. The Thebans accordingly decorated this monument before the battle. Furthermore, reports were brought to them from the city that all the temples were opening of themselves, and that the priestesses said that the gods revealed victory. And the messengers reported that from the Heracleium the arms also had disappeared, indicating that Heracles had gone forth to the battle. Some, to be sure, say that all these things were but devices of the leaders.

But in the battle, at any rate, everything turned out adversely for the Lacedaemonians, while for the other side everything went prosperously, even to the gifts of fortune. For it was after the morning meal that Cleombrotus held his last council over the battle, and drinking a little, as they did, at the middle of the day, it was said that the wine helped somewhat to excite them.

Again, when both sides were arming themselves and it was already evident that there would be a battle, in the first place, after those who had provided the market and some baggage-carriers and such as did not wish to fight had set out to withdraw from the Boeotian army, the Lacedaemonian mercenaries under Hieron, the peltasts of the Phocians, and, among the horsemen, the Heracleots and Phliasians made a circuit and fell upon these people as they were departing, and not only turned them about but chased them back to the camp of the Boeotians. Thereby they made the Boeotian army much larger and more densely massed than it had been before.

In the second place, since the space between the armies was a plain, the Lacedaemonians posted their horsemen in front of their phalanx, and the Thebans in like manner posted theirs over against them. Now the cavalry of the Thebans was in good training as a result of the war with the Orchomenians and the war with the Thespians, while the cavalry of the Lacedaemonians was exceedingly poor at that time.

For the richest men kept the horses, and it was only when the ban was called out that the appointed trooper presented himself; then he would get his horse and such arms as were given him, and take the field on the moment's notice. As for the men, on the other hand, it was those who were least strong of body and least ambitious who were mounted on the horses.

Such, then, was the cavalry on either side. Coming now to the infantry, it was said that the Lacedaemonians led each half-company three files abreast, and that this resulted in the phalanx being not more than twelve men deep. The Thebans, however, were massed not less than fifty shields deep, calculating that if they conquered that part of the army which was around the king, all the rest of it would be easy to overcome.

Now when Cleombrotus began to lead his army against the enemy, in the first place, before the troops under him so much as perceived that he was advancing, the horsemen had already joined battle and those of the Lacedaemonians had speedily been worsted; then in their flight they had fallen foul of their own hoplites, and, besides, the companies of the Thebans were now charging upon them. Nevertheless, the fact that Cleombrotus and his men were at first victorious in the battle may be known from this clear indication: they would not have been able to take him up and carry him off still living, had not those who were fighting in front of him been holding the advantage at that time.

But when Deinon, the polemarch, Sphodrias, one of the king's tent-companions, and Cleonymus, the son of Sphodrias, had been killed, then the royal bodyguard, the so-called aides of the polemarch, and the others fell back under the pressure of the Theban mass, while those who were on the left wing of the Lacedaemonians, when they saw that the right wing was being pushed back, gave way. Yet despite the fact that many had fallen and that they were defeated, after they had crossed the trench which chanced to be in front of their camp they grounded their arms at the spot from which they had set forth. The camp, to be sure, was not on ground which was altogether level, but rather on the slope of a hill. After the disaster some of the Lacedaemonians, thinking it unendurable, said that they ought to prevent the enemy from setting up their trophy and to try to recover the bodies of the dead, not by means of a truce, but by fighting.

The polemarchs, however, seeing that of the whole number of the Lacedaemonians almost a thousand had been killed; seeing, further, that among the Spartiatae themselves, of whom there were some seven hundred there, about four hundred had fallen; and perceiving that the allies were one and all without heart for fighting, while some of them were not even displeased at what had taken place, gathered together the most important personages and deliberated about what they should do. And as all thought it best to recover the bodies of the dead by a truce, they finally sent a herald to ask for a truce. After this, then, the Thebans set up a trophy and gave back the bodies under a truce.

Source: Xenophon. *Xenophon in Seven Volumes*, 1 and 2, Book 6.4.3–15, translated by Carleton L. Brownson. Cambridge, MA: Harvard University Press; London: William Heinemann, Ltd. Vol. 1: 1918; Vol. 2: 1921.

11. Xenophon, Account of the Second Battle of Mantinea

In a reversal of roles Epameinondas' career ended in 362 BCE when he met an alliance of Sparta, Athens, Corinth, and other states at Mantinea. After nearly a decade of Theban hegemony in Greece, Epameinondas marched into the Peloponnese to crush the Spartan alliance for good. He enjoyed a broad alliance and again employed innovative tactics to achieve what should have been a great victory. However, in the middle of the battle Epameinondas was wounded. His collapse caused the Theban force to falter. When he died of his wounds soon afterward the Theban hegemony quickly unraveled.

This battle is another good example of how warfare continued to change. The narrative illustrates new combinations of light-armed and cavalry units as well as continued use of the oblique line. The Spartan alliance did adjust its tactics to meet some of these approaches, but insufficiently. The battle also demonstrates the importance of the commander's role. More than any other of the battles selected here, this battle demonstrates the role of fortune in military history.

Now the fact that Epameinondas himself entertained such thoughts, seems to me to be in no wise remarkable,—for such thoughts are natural to ambitious men; but that he had brought his army to such a point that the troops flinched from no toil, whether by night or by day, and shrank from no peril, and although the provisions they had were scanty, were nevertheless willing to be obedient, this seems to me to be more remarkable.

For at the time when he gave them the last order to make ready, saying that there would be a battle, the horsemen eagerly whitened their helmets at his command, the hoplites of the Arcadians painted clubs upon their shields, as though they were Thebans, and all alike sharpened their spears and daggers and burnished their shields.

But when he had led them forth, thus made ready, it is worth while again to note what he did. In the first place, as was natural, he formed them in line of battle. And by doing this he seemed to make it clear that he was preparing for an engagement; but when his army had been drawn up as he wished it to be, he did not advance by the shortest route towards the enemy, but led the way towards the mountains which lie to the westward and over against Tegea, so that he gave the enemy the impression that he would not join battle on that day.

For as soon as he had arrived at the mountain, and when his battle line had been extended to its full length, he grounded arms at the foot of the heights, so that he seemed like one who was encamping. And by so doing he caused among most of the enemy a relaxation of their mental readiness for fighting, and likewise a relaxation of their readiness as regards their array for battle. It was not until he had moved along successive companies to the wing where he was stationed, and had wheeled them into line thus strengthening the mass formation of this wing, that he gave the order to take up arms and led the advance; and his troops followed. Now as soon as the enemy saw them unexpectedly approaching, no one among them was able to keep quiet, but some began running to their posts, others forming into line, others bridling horses, and others putting on breast-plates, while all were like men who were about to suffer, rather than to inflict, harm.

Meanwhile Epameinondas led forward his army prow on, like a trireme, believing that if he could strike and cut through anywhere, he would destroy the entire army of his adversaries. For he was preparing to make the contest with the strongest part of his force, and the weakest part he had stationed far back, knowing that if defeated it would cause discouragement to the troops who were with him and give courage to the enemy. Again, while the enemy had formed their horsemen like a phalanx of hoplites,— six deep and without intermingled foot soldiers,—Epameinondas on the other hand had made a strong column of his cavalry, also, and had mingled foot soldiers among them, believing that when he cut through the enemy's cavalry, he would have defeated the entire opposing army; for it is very hard to find men who will stand firm when they see any of their own side in flight. And in order to prevent the Athenians on the left wing from coming to the aid of those who were posted next to them, he stationed both horsemen and hoplites upon some hills over against them, desiring to create in them the fear that if they proceeded to give aid, these troops would fall upon them from behind. Thus, then, he made his attack, and he was not disappointed of his hope; for by gaining the mastery at the point where he struck, he caused the entire army of his adversaries to flee.

When, however, he had himself fallen, those who were left proved unable to take full advantage thereafter even of the victory; but although the opposing phalanx had fled before them, their hoplites did not kill a single man or advance beyond the spot where the collision had taken place; and although the cavalry also had fled before them, their cavalry in like manner did not pursue and kill either horsemen or hoplites, but slipped back timorously, like beaten men, through the lines of the flying enemy. Furthermore, while the intermingled footmen and the peltasts, who had shared in the victory of the cavalry, did make their way like victors to the region of the enemy's left wing, most of them were there slain by the Athenians.

When these things had taken place, the opposite of what all men believed would happen was brought to pass. For since well-nigh all the people of Greece had come together and formed themselves in opposing lines, there was no one who did not suppose that if a battle were fought, those who proved victorious would be the rulers and those who were defeated would be their subjects; but the deity so ordered it that both parties set up a trophy as though victorious and neither tried to hinder those who set them up, that both gave back the dead under a truce as though victorious, and both received back their dead under a truce as though defeated, and that while each party claimed to be victorious, neither was found to be any better off, as regards either additional territory, or city, or sway, than before the battle took place; but there was even more confusion and disorder in Greece after the battle than before.

Thus far be it written by me; the events after these will perhaps be the concern of another.

Source: Xenophon. *Xenophon in Seven Volumes,* 1 and 2, Book 7.5.19–27, translated by Carleton L. Brownson. Cambridge, MA: Harvard University Press; London: William Heinemann, Ltd. Vol. 1: 1918; Vol. 2: 1921.

12. Diodorus Siculus and Polyaenus, Accounts of the Battle of Chaeronea

The Battle of Chaeronea occurred in 338 BCE as a result of the Fourth Sacred War. Philip II of Macedon moved into central Greece at the request of the Delphic Amphictiony and Athens and Thebes united to oppose him. As leader of Thessaly and the Amphictionic League, Philip had many allies. By this time he had completed his reforms of the Macedonian phalanx so that it was at the height of its power under his leadership. This was the last battle Philip would fight, but his son Alexander commanded the companion cavalry in the engagement.

The battle is poorly attested, but the combination of these two accounts provides some useful details. As with some other engagements, the commander's role is critical to success. Philip arrayed his men carefully with light-armed infantry holding one flank and a river anchoring the other flank. Additionally, the account of Polyaenus describes the oblique line and feigned retreat. Philip's phalanx was sufficiently disciplined to use these tactics to pretend retreat and draw out his less disciplined opponents. He had trained his cavalry to exploit the gaps that formed in the enemy battle line, as Alexander illustrated in the first passage.

At once they [Athens] designated Chares and Lysicles as generals and sent forth their entire army under arms into Boeotia. All their youth reported eager for battle and advanced with forced marches as far as Chaeroneia in Boeotia. Impressed by the promptness of the Athenian arrival and themselves no less ready to act decisively, the Boeotians joined them with their weapons and, brigaded together, all awaited the approach of the enemy. Philip's first move was to send envoys to the Boeotian League, the most eminent of whom was Pytho. He was celebrated for his eloquence, but judged by the Boeotians in this contest for their allegiance against Demosthenes, he surpassed all the other speakers, to be sure, but was clearly inferior to him. And Demosthenes himself in his speeches parades his success against this orator as a great accomplishment, where he says: "I did not then give ground before Pytho in spite of his confidence and his torrent of words against you."

So Philip failed to get the support of the Boeotians, but nevertheless decided to fight both of the allies together. He waited for the last of his laggard confederates to arrive, and then marched into Boeotia. His forces came to more than thirty thousand infantry and no less than two thousand cavalry. Both sides were on the edge for the battle, high-spirited and eager, and were well matched in courage, but the king [Philip] had the advantage in numbers and in generalship. He had fought many battles of different sorts and had been victorious in most cases, so that he had a wide experience in military operations. On the Athenian side, the best of their generals were dead—Iphicrates, Chabrias, and Timotheüs too—and the best of those who were left, Chares, was no better than any average soldier in the energy and discretion required of a commander.

The armies deployed at dawn, and the king stationed his son Alexander, young in age but noted for his valour and swiftness of action, on one wing, placing beside him his most seasoned generals, while he himself at the head of picked men exercised the command over the other; individual units were stationed where the occasion required. On the other side, dividing the line according to nationality, the Athenians assigned one wing to the Boeotians and kept command of the other themselves. Once joined, the battle was hotly contested for a long time and many fell on both sides, so that for a while the struggle permitted hopes of victory to both.

Then Alexander, his heart set on showing his father his prowess and yielding to none in will to win, ably seconded by his men, first succeeded in rupturing the solid front of the enemy line and striking down many he bore heavily on the troops opposite him. As the same success was won by his companions, gaps in the front were constantly opened. Corpses piled up, until finally Alexander forced his way through the line and put his opponents to flight. Then the king also in person advanced, well in front and not conceding credit for the victory even to Alexander; he first forced back the troops stationed before him and then by compelling them to flee became the man responsible for the victory. More than a thousand Athenians fell in the battle and no less than two thousand were captured. Likewise, many of the Boeotians were killed and not a few taken prisoners. After the battle Philip raised a trophy of victory, yielded the dead for burial, gave sacrifices to the gods for victory, and rewarded according to their deserts those of his men who had distinguished themselves.

Source: Diodorus Siculus. *Library of History,* Book 16.85.2–86, Loeb Classical Library, Vol VIII, translated by C. Bradford Welles, 75–81. Cambridge, MA: Harvard University Press, 1963.

Engaging the Athenians at Chaeronea, Philip made a sham retreat: when Stratocles, the Athenian general, ordered his men to push forward, crying out, "We will pursue them to the heart of Macedon." Philip coolly observed, "The Athenians know not how to conquer:" and ordered his phalanx to keep close and firm, and to retreat slowly, covering themselves with their shields from the attacks of the enemy. As soon as he had by the manoeuvre drawn them from their advantageous ground, and gained an eminence, he halted; and encouraging his troops to a vigorous attack, made such an impression on the enemy, as soon determined a brilliant victory in his favour.

Source: Polyaenus. *Stratagems of War,* Book 4.2.2, translated by R. Shepherd. London: Ares Publishers, Inc., 1793.

13. Arrian, Account of the Battle of Granicus River

The Battle of the Granicus River in 334 BCE was the first battle of Alexander's campaign in Persia. Alexander had invaded Asia Minor and linked up with the advance force his father had sent out in 336. He then marched east directly to meet the satraps' army. The satraps arrayed their army on the east bank of the river in a position they expected would be difficult to assault. Alexander started the infantry across, but then attacked first with his cavalry, smiting the Persian flank and driving them off the battlefield. His victory in this battle opened access to western Anatolia.

The passage selected here focuses on how Alexander employed his companion cavalry. He arranged them on the right of his line and led from the front. His phalanx had some difficulty crossing the stream, but made it across and engaged the enemy. Alexander's charge broke the enemy cavalry and led to the Persian units fleeing. His heavy reliance on the cavalry was typical of his later battles. The translator uses the word "foreigners" for the Greek word *barbaroi* to convey the sense that Greeks called non-Greek speakers, regardless of their culture, barbarians.

The Persian cavalry were about 20,000 in number, and their infantry, consisting of Greek mercenaries, fell a little short of the same number. They had extended their horse along the bank of the river in a long phalanx, and had posted the infantry behind the cavalry, for the ground above the bank was steep and commanding. They also marshalled dense squadrons of cavalry upon that part of the bank where they observed Alexander himself advancing against their left wing; for he was conspicuous both by the brightness of his arms and by the respectful service of his attendants. Both armies stood a long time at the margin of the river, keeping quiet from dread of the result; and profound silence was observed on both sides. For the Persians were waiting till the Macedonians should step into the water, with the intention of attacking them as they emerged. Alexander leaped upon his steed, ordering those about him to follow, and exhorting them to show themselves valiant men. He then commanded Amyntas, son of Arrhabaeus, to make the first rush into the river at the head of the skirmishing cavalry, the Paeonians, and one regiment of infantry; and in front of these he had placed Ptolemy son of Philip, in command of the squadron of Socrates, which body of men indeed on that day happened to have the lead of all the cavalry force. He himself led the right wing with sounding of trumpets, and the men raising the war-cry to Bnyalius. He entered the ford, keeping his line always extended obliquely in the direction in which the stream flowed, in order that the Persians might not fall upon him on the flank as he was emerging from the water, but that he might, as far as practicable, encounter them with his phalanx.

The Persians began the contest by hurling missiles from above in the direction where the men of Amyntas and Socrates were the first to reach the bank; some of them casting javelins into the river from their commanding position on the bank, and others stepping down along the flatter parts of it to the very edge of the water. Then ensued a violent struggle on the part of the cavalry, on the one side to emerge from the river, and on the other to prevent the landing. From the Persians there was a terrible discharge of darts; but the Macedonians fought with spears. The Macedonians, being far inferior in number, suffered severely at the first onset, because they were obliged to defend themselves in the river, where their footing was unsteady, and where they were below the level of their assailants; whereas the Persians were fighting from the top of the bank, which gave them an advantage, especially as the best of the Persian horse had been posted there. Memnon himself, as well as his sons, were running every risk with these; and the Macedonians who first came into conflict with the Persians, though they showed great valour, were cut down, except those who retreated to Alexander, who was now approaching. For the king was already near, leading with him the right wing. He made his first assault upon the Persians at the place where the whole mass of their horse and the leaders themselves were posted; and around him a desperate conflict raged, during which one rank of the Macedonians after another easily kept on crossing the river. Though they fought on horseback, it seemed more like an infantry than a cavalry battle; for they struggled for the mastery, horses being jammed with horses and men with men, the Macedonians striving to drive the Persians entirely away from the bank and to force them into the plain, and the Persians striving to obstruct their landing and to push them back again into the river. At last Alexander's men began to gain the advantage, both through their superior strength and military discipline, and because they fought with spearshafts made of cornel-wood, whereas the Persians used only darts.

Then indeed, Alexander's spear being broken to shivers in the conflict, he asked Aretis, one of the royal guards, whose duty it was to assist the king to mount his horse, for another spear. But this man's spear had also been shivered whilst he was in the thickest of the struggle, and he was conspicuous fighting with the half of his broken spear. Showing this to Alexander, he bade him ask some one else for one. Then Demaratus, a man of Corinth, one of his personal Companions, gave him his own spear; which he had no sooner taken than seeing Mithridates, the son-in-law of Darius, riding far in front of the others, and leading with him a body of cavalry arranged like a wedge, he rode on in front of the others, and hitting at the face of Mithridates with his spear, struck him to the ground. But hereupon, Rhoesaces rode up to Alexander and hit him on the head with his scimitar, breaking off a piece of his helmet. But the helmet broke the force of the blow. This man also Alexander struck to the ground, hitting him in the chest through the breastplate with his lance. And now Spithridates from behind had already raised aloft his scimitar against the king, when Clitus, son of Dropidas, anticipated his blow, and hitting him on the arm, cut it off, scimitar and all. Meantime, the horsemen, as many as were able, kept on securing a landing all down the river, and were joining Alexander's forces.

The Persians themselves, as well as their horses, were now being struck on their faces with the lances from all sides, and were being repulsed by the cavalry. They also received much damage from the light-armed troops who were mingled with the cavalry. They first began to give way where Alexander himself was braving danger in the front. When their centre had given way, the horse on both wings were also naturally broken through, and took to speedy flight. Of the Persian cavalry only about 1,000 were killed; for Alexander did not pursue them far, but turned aside to attack the Greek mercenaries, the main body of whom was still remaining where it was posted at first. This they did rather from amazement at the unexpected result of the struggle than from any steady resolution. Leading the phalanx against these, and ordering the cavalry to fall upon them from all sides in the midst, he soon cut them up, so that none of them escaped except such as might have concealed themselves among the dead bodies. About 2,000 were taken prisoners. The following leaders of the Persians also fell, in the battle: Niphates, Petines, Spithridates, viceroy of Lydia, Mithrobuzanes, governor of Cappadocia, Mithridates, the son-in-law of Darius, Arbupales, son of Darius the son of Artaxerxes, Pharnaces, brother of the wife of Darius, and Onares, commander of the auxiliaries. Arsites fled from the battle into Phrygia, where he is reported to have committed suicide, because he was deemed by the Persians the cause of their defeat on that occasion.

Of the Macedonians, about twenty-five of the Companions were killed at the first onset; brazen statues of whom were erected at Dium, executed by Lysippus, at Alexander's order. The same statuary also executed a statue of Alexander himself, being chosen by him for the work in preference to all other artists. Of the other cavalry over sixty were slain, and of the infantry, about thirty. These were buried by Alexander the next day, together with their arms and other decorations. To their parents and children he granted exemption from imposts on agricultural produce, and he relieved them from all personal services and taxes upon property. He also exhibited great solicitude in regard to the wounded, for he himself visited each man, looked at their wounds, and inquired how and in the performance of what duty they had received them, allowing them both to speak and brag of their own deeds. He also buried the Persian commanders and the Greek mercenaries who were killed fighting on the side of the enemy. But as many of them as he took prisoners he bound in fetters and sent them away to Macedonia to till the soil, because, though they were Greeks, they were fighting against Greece on behalf of the foreigners in opposition to the decrees which the Greeks had made in their federal council. To Athens also he sent 300 suits of Persian armour to be hung up in the Acropolis as a votive offering to Athena, and ordered this inscription to be fixed over them: "Alexander, son of Philip, and all the Greeks except the Lacedaemonians, present this offering from the spoils taken from the foreigners, inhabiting Asia."

Source: Arrian. *The Anabasis of Alexander*, Book 1.14.4–16, translated by E. J. Chinnock, 44–49. London: Hodder and Stoughton, 1884.

14. Arrian, Account of the Naval Action during the Siege of Tyre

By the time Alexander launched his campaign against Persia in 334 BCE naval warfare had undergone some significant changes. Philip and Alexander had created a Macedonian fleet that included triremes and even large ships, quadriremes and quinquiremes, capable of carrying many soldiers. As Alexander campaigned through Asia Minor he maneuvered in such a way as to capture the coastline. After Issus he turned south into Phoenicia to secure the Phoenician ports and deny Darius any naval strategy. Despite winning all of northern Phoenicia and later Cyprus to his side, Alexander laid siege to the large island port city, Tyre. The campaign was difficult, but it was his naval forces that made the victory possible.

The episode described here is from late in the siege of Tyre. Carthaginian ships tried a final breakout from Tyre, but were beaten back by Alexander's fleet. Arrian's account demonstrates how much naval warfare had changed. Alexander employed his large ships both in traditional ship-to-ship fighting and as active siege platforms. The result was that he broke the wall and assaulted the city from land and sea approaches. After the capture of Tyre, Alexander dismissed the fleet.

He had now collected many engineers both from Cyprus and the whole of Phoenicia, and many engines of war had been constructed, some upon the mole, others upon vessels used for transporting horses, which he brought with him from Sidon, and others upon the triremes which were not fast sailors. When all the preparations had been completed they brought up the engines of war along the mole that had been made and also began to shoot from ships moored near various parts of the wall and making trial of its strength. The Tyrians erected wooden towers on their battlements opposite the mole; from which they might annoy the enemy; and if the engines of war were brought near any other part, they defended themselves with missiles and shot at the very ships with fire-bearing arrows, so that they deterred the Macedonians from approaching the wall. Their walls opposite the mole were about one hundred and fifty feet high, with a breadth in proportion, and constructed with large stones imbedded in gypsum. It was not easy for the horse-transports and the triremes of the Macedonians, which were conveying the engines of war up to the wall, to approach the city, because a great quantity of stones hurled forward into the sea prevented their near assault. These stones Alexander determined to drag out of the sea; but this was a work accomplished with great difficulty, since it was performed from ships and not from the firm earth; especially as the Tyrians, covering their ships with mail, brought them alongside the anchors of the triremes, and cutting the cables of the anchors underneath, made anchoring impossible for the enemy's ships. But Alexander covered many thirty-oared vessels with mail in the same way, and placed them athwart in front of the anchors, so that the assault of the ships was repelled by them. But, notwithstanding this, divers under the sea secretly cut their cables. The Macedonians then used chains to their anchors instead of cables, and let them down so that the divers could do no more harm. Then, fastening slipknots to the stones, they dragged them out of the sea from the mole; and having raised them aloft with cranes, they discharged them into deep water, where they were no longer likely to do injury by being hurled forward. The ships now easily approached the part of the wall where it had been made clear of the stones which had been hurled forward. The Tyrians being now reduced to great straits on all sides, resolved to make an attack on the Cyprian ships, which were moored opposite the harbour turned towards Sidon. For a long time they spread sails across the mouth of the harbour, in order that the filling of the triremes might not be discernible; and about the middle of the day, when the sailors were scattered in quest of necessaries, and when Alexander usually retired from the fleet to his tent on the other side of the city, they filled three quinqueremes, an equal number of quadriremes and seven triremes with the most expert complement of rowers possible, and with the best-armed men adapted for fighting from the decks, together with the men most daring in naval contests. At first they rowed out slowly and quietly in single file, moving forward the handles of their oars without any signal from the men who give the time to the rowers; but when they were already tacking against the Cyprians, and were near enough to be seen, then indeed with a loud shout and encouragement to each other, and at the same time with impetuous rowing, they commenced the attack.

It happened on that day that Alexander went away to his tent, but after a short time returned to his ships, not tarrying according to his usual custom. The Tyrians fell all of a sudden upon the ships lying at their moorings, finding some entirely empty and others being filled with difficulty from the men who happened to be present at the very time of the noise and attack. At the first onset they at once sank the quinquereme of the king Pnytagoras, that of Androcles the Amathusiau and that of Pasicrates the Curian; and they shattered the other ships by pushing them ashore. But when Alexander perceived the sailing out of the Tyrian triremes, he ordered most of the ships under his command to be manned and to take position at the mouth of the harbour, so that the rest of the Tyrian ships might not sail out. He then took the quinqueremes which he had and about five of the triremes, which were manned by him in haste before the rest were ready, and sailed round the city against the Tyrians who had sailed out of the harbour. The men on the wall, perceiving the enemy's attack and observing that Alexander himself was in the fleet, began to shout to those in their own ships, urging them to return; but as their shouts were not audible, on account of the noise of those who were engaged in the action, they exhorted them to retreat by various kinds of signals. At last after a long time, perceiving the impending attack of Alexander's fleet, they tacked about and began to flee into the harbour; and a few of their ships succeeded in escaping, but Alexander's vessels assaulted the greater number, and rendered some of them unfit for sailing; and a quinquereme and a quadrireme were captured at the very mouth of the harbour. But the slaughter of the marines was not great; for when they perceived that their ships were in possession of the enemy, they swam off without difficulty into the harbour. As the Tyrians could no longer derive any aid from their ships, the Macedonians now brought up their military engines to the wall itself. Those which were brought near the city along the mole, did no damage worth mentioning on account of the strength of the wall there. Others brought up some of the ships conveying military engines opposite the part of the city turned towards Sidon. But when even there they met with no success, Alexander passed round to the wall projecting towards the south wind and towards Egypt, and tested the strength of the works everywhere. Here first a large piece of the wall was thoroughly shaken, and a part of it was even broken and thrown down. Then indeed for a short time he tried to make an assault to the extent of throwing a bridge upon the part of the wall where a breach had been made. But the Tyrians without much difficulty beat the Macedonians back.

The third day after this, having waited for a calm sea, after encouraging the leaders of the regiments for the action, he led the ships containing the military engines up to the city. In the first place he shook down a large piece of the wall; and when the breach appeared to be sufficiently wide, he ordered the vessels conveying the military engines to retire, and brought up two others, which carried his bridges, which he intended to throw upon the breach in the wall. The shield-bearing guards occupied one of these vessels, which he had put under the command of Admetus; and the other was occupied by the regiment of Coenus, called the foot Companions. Alexander himself, with the shield-bearing guards, intended to scale the wall where it might be practicable. He ordered some of his triremes to sail against both of the harbours, to see if by any means they could force an entrance when the Tyrians had turned themselves to oppose him. He also ordered those of his triremes which contained the missiles to be hurled from engines, or which were carrying archers upon deck, to sail right round the wall and to put in where it was practicable, and to take up position within shooting range, until it became impossible to put in, so that the Tyrians, being shot at from all quarters, might become distracted, and not know whither to turn in their distress. When Alexander's ships drew close to the city and the bridges were thrown from them upon the wall, the shield-bearing guards mounted valiantly along these upon the wall; for their captain, Admetus, proved himself brave on that occasion, and Alexander accompanied them, both as a courageous participant in the action itself, and as a witness of brilliant and dangerous feats of valour performed by others.

Source: Arrian. *The Anabasis of Alexander*, Book 2.21–23.4, translated by E. J. Chinnock, 127–32. London: Hodder and Stoughton, 1884.

15. Arrian, Account of the Battle of Issus

This excerpt comes from a description of the Battle of Issus in 333 between Alexander III and Darius III. Alexander had marched as far as southeast Asia Minor capturing Persian territory before he met Darius in battle. Darius managed to maneuver behind Alexander so that the Macedonian army had to turn around and march swiftly back north. Once they were ready for battle Alexander attacked. When he charged into the Persian flank and toward the center of their line Darius fled and took the rest of the army with him. Alexander's victory in this battle ensured him control of half the empire.

The narrative of part of this engagement highlights several important features. Alexander led from the front of his cavalry in order to inspire them and terrify the enemy. His phalanx got into trouble while crossing the stream and came under attack by mercenary hoplites. Alexander's units posted next to the phalanx were disciplined enough and well led so that they maneuvered around the mercenaries and attacked them in the flank. As this passage demonstrates, Alexander's phalanx was not a perfect weapon despite its strength; it needed to be supported by other units.

Having thus marshalled his men, he caused them to rest for some time, and then led them forward, as he thought the enemy's approach was very slow. For Darius was no longer leading the foreigners against him, as he had arranged them at first, but he remained in his position, upon the bank of the river, which was in many parts steep and precipitous; and in certain places, where it seemed more easy to ascend, he extended a stockade along it. By this it was at once evident to Alexander's men that Darius had become cowed in spirit. But when the armies at length met in conflict, Alexander rode about in every direction to exhort his troops to show their valour, mentioning with befitting epithets the names, not only of the generals, but also those of the captains of cavalry and infantry, and of the Greek mercenaries as many as were more distinguished either by rank or any merit. From all sides arose a shout not to delay but to attack the enemy. At first he still led them on in close array with measured step, although he had the forces of Darius already in full view, lest by a more hasty march any part of the phalanx should fluctuate from the line and get separated from the rest. But when they came within range of darts, Alexander himself and those around him being posted on the right wing, advanced first into the river with a run, in order to alarm the Persians by the rapidity of their onset, and by coming sooner to close conflict to receive little damage from the archers. And it turned out just as Alexander had conjectured; for as soon as the battle became a hand-to-hand one, the part of the Persian army stationed on the left wing was put to rout; and here Alexander and his men won a brilliant victory. But the Greek mercenaries serving under Darius attacked the Macedonians at the point where they saw their phalanx especially disordered. For the Macedonian phalanx had been broken and had disjoined towards the right wing, because Alexander had charged into the river with eagerness, and engaging in a hand-to-hand conflict was already driving back the Persians posted there; but the Macedonians in the centre did not execute their task with equal speed; and finding many parts of the bank steep and precipitous, they were unable to preserve the front of the phalanx in the same line. Here then the struggle was desperate; the aim of the Greek mercenaries of Darius being to push the Macedonians back into the river, and regain the victory, though their own forces were already flying; the aim of the Macedonians being not to fall short of Alexander's good-fortune, which was already manifest, and not to tarnish the glory of the phalanx, which up to that time had been commonly asserted to be invincible. Moreover the feeling of rivalry which existed between the Greek and Macedonian races inspired each side in the conflict. Here fell Ptolemy, son of Seleucus, after proving himself a valiant man, besides about one hundred and twenty other Macedonians of no mean repute.

Hereupon the regiments on the right wing, perceiving that the Persians opposed to them had already been put to rout, wheeled round towards the Greek mercenaries of Darius and their own hard-pressed detachment. Having driven the Greeks away from the river, they extended their phalanx beyond the Persian army on the side which had been broken; and attacking the Greeks on the flank, were already beginning to cut them up. However the Persian cavalry which had been posted opposite the Thessalians did not remain on the other side of the river—during the struggle, but came through the water and made a vigorous attack upon the Thessalian squadrons. In this place a fierce cavalry battle ensued; for the Persians did not give way until they perceived that Darius had fled and the Greek mercenaries had been cut up by the phalanx and severed from them. Then at last the flight of all the Persians was plainly visible. Their horses suffered much injury in the retreat, because the riders were heavily armed; and the horsemen themselves, being so many in number and retreating in panic terror without any regard to order along narrow roads, were trampled on and injured no less by each other than by the pursuing enemy. The Thessalians also followed them up with vigour, so that no fewer of the cavalry than of the infantry were slaughtered in the flight.

But as soon as the left wing of Darius was terrified and routed by Alexander, and the Persian king perceived that this part of his army was severed from the rest, without any further delay he began to flee in his chariot along with the first, just as he was.

Source: Arrian. *The Anabasis of Alexander*, Book 2.10–11.4, translated by E. J. Chinnock, 99–102. London: Hodder and Stoughton, 1884.

16. Arrian, Account of the Battle of Gaugamela

The Battle of Gaugamela in 331 BCE was the last battle between Alexander and Darius III. The new Persian army that Darius had raised since his loss at Issus was enormous, outnumbering Alexander's force by two or three times and including elephants and scythed chariots as well as infantry and cavalry. Darius also had time to pick the site so he prepared it for his cavalry and chariots. Alexander arrayed his lines as usual with cavalry on each flank and infantry in the center. He charged with his cavalry into the Persian cavalry on Darius' flank while the Macedonian phalanx pinned down the Persian center. Alexander fought hard, but when he overrode the enemy line he nearly lost the battle as his opposite flank was under heavy pressure. Alexander won the battle and captured Babylon and Susa soon afterward.

As noted before, Alexander relied heavily on his cavalry. This excerpt again demonstrates his reliance on the cavalry. He placed them on his right flank under his own command to attack the Persian flank in an attempt to drive to the Persian center and take on Darius directly. His left flank cavalry under Parmenio was to hold the position against the Persians long enough for Alexander to win. Since the companion cavalry could not charge into the Persian infantry it swung outside to wheel left into the Persian cavalry. In addition to the cavalry Darius also employed scythed chariots, but to no effect. The infantry fought hard, but it was Alexander's reliance on the cavalry that won the battle so quickly.

When the armies drew near each other, Darius and the men around him were observed; viz. the apple-bearing Persians, the Indians, the Albanians, the Carians who had been forcibly transported into Central Asia, the Mardian archers ranged opposite Alexander himself and his royal squadron of cavalry. Alexander led his own army more towards the right, and the Persians marched along parallel with him, far outflanking him upon their left. Then the Scythian cavalry rode along the line, and came into conflict with the front men of Alexander's array; but he nevertheless still continued to march towards the right, and almost entirely got beyond the ground which had been cleared and levelled by the Persians. Then Darius, fearing that his chariots would become useless, if the Macedonians advanced into un-even ground, ordered the front ranks of his left wing to ride round the right wing of the Macedonians, where Alexander was commanding, to prevent him from marching his wing any further. This being done, Alexander ordered the cavalry of the Greek mercenaries under the command of Menidas to attack them. But the Scythian cavalry and the Bactrians, who had been drawn up with them sallied forth against them, and being much more numerous they put the small body of Greeks to rout. Alexander then ordered Aristo at the head of the Paeonians and Greek auxiliaries to attack the Scythians; and the barbarians gave way. But the rest of the Bactrians drawing near to the Paeonians and Greek auxiliaries, caused their own comrades who were already in flight to turn and renew the battle; and thus they brought about a general cavalry engagement, in which many of Alexander's men fell, not only being overwhelmed by the multitude of the barbarians, but also because the Scythians themselves and their horses were much more completely protected with armour for guarding their bodies. Notwithstanding this, the Macedonians sustained their assaults, and assailing them violently squadron by squadron, they succeeded in pushing them out of rank. Meantime the foreigners launched their scythe-bearing chariots against Alexander himself, for the purpose of throwing his phalanx into confusion; but in this they were grievously deceived. For as soon as some of them approached, the Agrianians and the javelin-men with Balacrus, who had been posted in front of the Companion cavalry, hurled their javelins at them; others they seized by the reins and pulled the drivers off, and standing round the horses killed them. Yet some rolled right through the ranks; for the men stood apart and opened their ranks, as they had been instructed, in the places where the chariots assaulted them. In this way it generally happened that the chariots passed through safely, and the men by whom they were driven were uninjured. But these also were afterwards overpowered by the grooms of Alexander's army and by the royal shield-bearing guards.

As soon as Darius began to set his whole phalanx in motion, Alexander ordered Aretes to attack those who were riding completely round his right wing; and up to that time he was himself leading his men in column. But when the Persians had made a break in the front line of their army, in consequence of the cavalry sallying forth to assist those who were surrounding the right wing, Alexander wheeled round towards the gap, and forming a wedge as it were of the Companion cavalry and of the part of the phalanx which was posted here, he led them with a quick charge and loud battle-cry straight towards Darius himself. For a short time there ensued a hand-to-hand fight; but when the Macedonian cavalry, commanded by Alexander himself, pressed on vigorously, thrusting themselves against the Persians and striking their faces with their spears, and when the Macedonian phalanx in dense array and bristling with long pikes had also made an attack upon them, all things at once appeared full of terror to Darius, who had already long been in a state of fear, so that he was the first to turn and flee. The Persians also who were riding round the wing were seized with alarm when Aretes made a vigorous attack upon them. In this quarter indeed the Persians took to speedy flight; and the Macedonians followed up the fugitives and slaughtered them. Simmias and his brigade were not yet able to start with Alexander in pursuit, but causing the phalanx to halt there, he took part in the struggle, because the left wing of the Macedonians was reported to be hard pressed. In this part of the field, their line being broken, some of the Indians and of the Persian cavalry burst through the gap towards the baggage of the Macedonians; and there the action became desperate. For the Persians fell boldly on the men, who were most of them unarmed, and never expected that any men would cut through the double phalanx and break through upon them. When the Persians made this attack, the foreign prisoners also assisted them by falling upon the Macedonians in the midst of the action. But the commanders of the men who had been posted as a reserve to the first phalanx, learning what was taking place, quickly moved from the position which they had been ordered to take, and coming upon the Persians in the rear, killed many of them there collected round the baggage. But the rest of them gave way and fled. The Persians on the right wing, who had not yet become aware of the flight of Darius, rode round Alexander's left wing and attacked Parmenio in flank.

Source: Arrian. *The Anabasis of Alexander*, Book 3.13–15.4, translated by E. J. Chinnock, 164–69. London: Hodder and Stoughton, 1884.

17. Arrian, Account of the Battle of the Hydaspes River

The Battle of Hydaspes in 326 BCE was the last major pitched battle fought by Alexander. In 327 Alexander entered India and began fighting his way across it and into the Punjab, reaching the Hydaspes River in 326. There he encountered the large force arrayed by the Indian king Porus on the opposite bank of the river. Alexander used a variety of diversions to distract Porus while sending out his own scouts for a way to cross. Finding a crossing upriver at a bend shielded by several islands, Alexander crossed with part of his force during a rainy night. After getting across they were attacked by Porus' advanced guard of cavalry and chariots; having smote the chariots, Alexander rode against the rest of Porus' army. Alexander once again used his cavalry and infantry to win a great victory. Afterward he accepted Porus' surrender and made him regional governor. This battle turned out to be Alexander's last major pitched battle although a great deal of fighting down the Indus remained.

As noted before, Alexander relied heavily on his cavalry, but where he excelled over many of his opponents was in his ability to coordinate effectively a mixture of units. Alexander's experienced army had, by the time it reached the Hydaspes, been augmented by Indian cavalry and horse-archers from the local allies. In this passage Arrian describes how Alexander used the great mixture of units and coordinated them in the middle of battle in support of each other to win a thorough victory. The infantry, both phalanx and light-armed, fought hard once the cavalry broke into Porus' flanks breaking the Indian lines.

When he had also crossed this piece of water, he selected the choice guard of cavalry, and the best men from the other cavalry regiments, and brought them up from column into line on the right wing. In front of all the cavalry he posted the horse-archers, and placed next to the cavalry in front of the other infantry the royal shield-bearing guards under the command of Seleucus.

Near these he placed the royal foot-guard, and next to these the other shield-bearing guards, as each happened at the time to have the right of precedence. On each side, at the extremities of the phalanx, his archers, Agrianians and javelin-throwers were posted. Having thus arranged his army, he ordered the infantry to follow at a slow pace and in regular order, numbering as it did not much under 6,000 men; and because he thought he was superior in cavalry, he took only his horse-soldiers, who were 5,000 in number, and led them forward with speed. He also instructed Tauron, the commander of the archers, to lead them on also with speed to back up the cavalry. He had come to the conclusion that if Porus should engage him with all his forces, he would easily be able to overcome him by attacking with his cavalry, or to stand on the defensive until his infantry arrived in the course of the action; but if the Indians should be alarmed at his extraordinary audacity in making the passage of the river and take to flight, he would be able to keep close to them in their flight, so that the slaughter of them in the retreat being greater, there would be only a slight work left for him.

. . .

Ptolemy also says that Alexander in the first place sent the horse-archers against these, and led the cavalry himself, thinking that Porus was approaching with all his forces, and that this body of cavalry was marching in front of the rest of his army, being drawn up by him as the vanguard. But as soon as he had ascertained with accuracy the number of the Indians, he immediately made a rapid charge upon them with the cavalry around him. When they perceived that Alexander himself and the body of cavalry around him had made the assault, not in line of battle regularly formed, but by squadrons, they gave way; and 400 of their cavalry, including the son of Porus, fell in the contest. The chariots also were captured, horses and all, being heavy and slow in the retreat, and useless in the action itself on account of the clayey ground. When the horsemen who had escaped from this rout brought news to Porus that Alexander himself had crossed the river with the strongest part of his army, and that his son had been slain in the battle, he nevertheless could not make up his mind what course to take, because the men who had been left behind under Craterus were seen to be attempting to cross the river from the great camp which was directly opposite his position. However, at last he preferred to march against Alexander himself with all his army, and to come into a decisive conflict with the strongest division of the Macedonians, commanded by the king in person. But nevertheless he left a few of the elephants together with a small army there at the camp to frighten the cavalry under Craterus from the bank of the river. He then took all his cavalry to the number of 4,000 men, all his chariots to the number of 300, with 200 of his elephants and 30,000 choice infantry, and marched against Alexander. When he found a place where he saw there was no clay, but that on account of the sand the ground was all level and hard, and thus fit for the advance and retreat, of horses, he there drew up his army. First he placed the elephants in the front, each animal being not less than a plethrumi apart, so that they might be extended in the front before the whole of the phalanx of infantry, and produce terror everywhere among Alexander's cavalry. Besides he thought that none of the enemy would have the audacity to push themselves into the spaces between the elephants, the cavalry being deterred by the fright of their horses; and still less would the infantry do so, it being likely they would be kept off in front by the heavy-armed soldiers falling upon them, and trampled down by the elephants wheeling round against them. Near these he had posted the infantry, not occupying a line on a level with the beasts, but in a second line behind them, only so far distant that the companies of foot might be pushed forward a short distance into the spaces between them. He had also bodies of infantry standing beyond the elephants on the wings; and on both sides of the infantry he had posted the cavalry, in front of which were placed the chariots on both wings of his army.

Such was the arrangement which Porus made of his forces. As soon as Alexander observed that the Indians were drawn up in order of battle, he stopped his cavalry from advancing farther, so that he might take up the infantry as it kept on arriving; and even when the phalanx in quick march had effected a junction with the cavalry, he did not at once draw it out and lead it to the attack, not wishing to hand over his men exhausted with fatigue and out of breath, to the barbarians who were fresh and un-tired. On the contrary, he caused his infantry to rest until their strength was recruited, riding along round the lines to inspect them. When he had sur-veyed the arrangement of the Indians, he resolved not to advance against the centre, in front of which the elephants had been posted, and in the gaps between them a dense phalanx of men; for he was alarmed at the very arrangements which Porus had made here with that express design. But as he was superior in the number of his cavalry, he took the greater part of that force, and marched along against the left wing of the enemy for the purpose of making an attack in this direction. Against the right wing he sent Ooenus with his own regiment of cavalry and that of Demetrius, with instructions to keep close behind the barbarians when they, seeing the dense mass of cavalry opposed to them, should ride out to fight them. Seleucus, Antigenes, and Tauron were ordered to lead the phalanx of in-fantry, but not to engage in the action until they observed the enemy's cav-alry and phalanx of infantry thrown into disorder by the cavalry under his own command. But when they came within range of missiles, he launched the horse-archers, 1000 in number, against the left wing of the Indians, in order to throw those of the enemy who were posted there into confusion by the incessant storm of arrows and by the charge of the horses. He himself with the Companion cavalry marched along rapidly against the left wing of the barbarians, being eager to attack them in flank while still in a state of disorder, before their cavalry could be deployed.

Meantime the Indians had collected their cavalry from all parts, and were riding along, advancing out of their position to meet Alexander's charge. Ooenus also appeared with his men in their rear, according to his instructions. The Indians, observing this, were compelled to make the line of their cavalry face both ways; the largest and best part against Alex-ander, while the rest wheeled round against Ooenus and his forces. This therefore at once threw the ranks as well as the decisions of the Indians into confusion. Alexander, seeing his opportunity, at the very moment the cavalry was wheeling round in the other direction, made an attack on those opposed to him with such vigour that the Indians could not sustain the charge of his cavalry, but were scattered and driven to the elephants, as to a friendly wall, for refuge. Upon this, the drivers of the elephants urged forward the beasts against the cavalry; but now the phalanx itself of the Macedonians was advancing against the elephants, the men casting darts at the riders and also striking the beasts themselves, standing round them on all sides. The action was unlike any of the previous contests; for wherever the beasts could wheel round, they rushed forth against the ranks of infantry and demolished the phalanx of the Macedonians, dense as it was. The Indian cavalry also, seeing that the infantry were engaged in the action, rallied again and advanced against the Macedonian cavalry. But when Alexander's men, who far excelled both in strength and military discipline, got the mastery over them the second time, they were again repulsed towards the elephants and cooped up among them. By this time the whole of Alexander's cavalry had collected into one squadron, not by any command of his, but having settled into this arrangement by the mere effect of the struggle itself; and wherever it fell upon the ranks of the Indians they were broken up with great slaughter. The beasts being now cooped up into a narrow space, their friends were no less injured by them than their foes, being trampled down in their wheeling and pushing about. Accordingly there ensued a great slaughter of the cavalry, cooped up as it was in a narrow space around the elephants. Most of the keepers of the elephants had been killed by the javelins, and some of the elephants themselves had been wounded, while others no longer kept apart in the battle on account of their sufferings or from being destitute of keepers. But, as if frantic with pain, rushing forward at friends and foes alike, they pushed about, trampled down and killed them in every kind of way. However, the Macedonians retired whenever they were assailed, for they rushed at the beasts in a more open space, and in accordance with their own plan; and when they wheeled round to return, they followed them closely and hurled javelins at them; whereas the Indians retreating among them were now receiving greater injury from them. But when the beasts were tired out, and they were no longer able to charge with any vigour, they began to retire, facing the foe like ships backing water, merely uttering a shrill piping sound. Alexander himself surrounded the whole line with his cavalry, and gave the signal that the infantry should link their shields together so as to form a very densely closed body, and thus advance in phalanx. By this means the Indian cavalry, with the exception of a few men, was quite cut up in the action; as was also the infantry, since the Macedonians were now pressing upon them from all sides. Upon this, all who could do so turned to flight through the spaces which intervened between the parts of Alexander's cavalry.

At the same time Craterus and the other officers of Alexander's army who had been left behind on the bank of the Hydaspes crossed the river, when they perceived that Alexander was winning a brilliant victory. These men, being fresh, followed up the pursuit instead of Alexander's exhausted troops, and made no less a slaughter of the Indians in their retreat.

Source: Arrian. *The Anabasis of Alexander*, Book 5.13.4–14.2, 15–18.1, translated by E. J. Chinnock, 286–87 and 288–93. London: Hodder and Stoughton, 1884.

Chronology

510 BCE	Sparta assists Athens in ousting the tyrant Hippias. In return, Athens is forced to join Sparta's Peloponnesian League.
506 BCE	King Cleomenes of Sparta organizes a full-scale invasion by Peloponnesian League forces against Athens. Corinth, however, withdraws its support, and the plan collapses.
506 BCE	Athens defeats both the Boeotians and the Chalcidians.
500 BCE	The city-state of Athens establishes the office of *strategia* (generalship). Each of the 10 tribes elects its own *strategos*, and these men then form a council of war that has overall direction of military campaigns.
500 BCE	The Carthaginians oust the Greeks from Malta.
500–490 BCE	King Darius I of Persia is angered by the aid extended by some Greek city-states, including Athens, to a revolt of Greek city-states in Asia Minor against Persia. Darius demands earth and water, symbols of submission from the Greeks. While some Greek city-states, including Aegina, submit, both Athens and Sparta refuse, and the Greco-Persian Wars of 499–448 begin.
499–494 BCE	General revolt by the Ionian Greeks against Persian rule. The revolt, supported by several

	city-states of mainland Greece, ends with the fall of Miletus.
498 BCE	The Ionian Greeks capture the Persian satrapal city of Sardis in western Anatolia, burning the city entirely.
496 BCE	A force of Thracians and Scythians drives out the tyrant Miltiades the Younger from the Chersonese peninsula.
496 BCE	The island of Cyprus revolts against Persia, as does Caria on the coast of Asia Minor. A Persian army transported by the Phoenicians reconquers Cyprus, while a Phoenician fleet suppresses Caria.
494 BCE	Persia crushes the Ionian Revolt. An Ionian fleet is crushed by the Persians in a sea battle off Lade in the gulf opposite Miletus. The Persians then take and sack the city of Miletus, destroying much of the city, killing most of the men, and enslaving the women and children. The Persians capture all Ionian cities on the eastern shore of the Hellespont (Dardanelles) as well as Byzantium and Chalcedon on the western side. They also take and sack the islands of Chios, Lesbos, and Tenedos. The Ionian revolt is over.
494 BCE	Sparta defeats Argos in the Battle of Sepeia.
492 BCE	To punish the mainland Greek city-states for supporting the Ionian Revolt, Darius I of Persia sends Mardonius across the Hellespont (Dardanelles) at the head of a large fleet and army. The Persians subdue Thrace but suffer a check on the Macedonian border from a Thracian tribe. Meanwhile, the Persian fleet encounters a storm while rounding Mount Athos, and many of its ships are driven ashore and wrecked. Mardonius wisely returns to Persia, where Darius relieves him of command.
491 BCE	As his shipyards turn out new vessels, Darius I of Persia tests the morale of the Greek city-states by

sending out envoys demanding earth and water as symbols of vassalage. A number of the mainland cities, including most of those in northern Greece, submit but not Athens or Sparta.

490 BCE

The Greeks win a decisive victory at the Battle of Marathon. The victory, while decisive, is not conclusive, but it does hold the Persians at bay for a decade. Marathon also allows the Greeks to imagine that they might triumph a second time.

489 BCE

Athens sends Miltiades and 70 ships against islands that had assisted the Persians. Miltiades attacks the Cycladic island of Pardos but, following a month-long siege, is forced to withdraw. This brings his political ruin and imprisonment and the ascendancy of Themistocles, which has wide repercussions for the second Persian invasion.

486–485 BCE

New Persian preparations are made to invade Greece. Following the defeat of his forces in Greece, Darius I immediately begins raising a new and larger force. To pay for it, he raises taxes. This leads to a revolt in Persian-controlled Egypt in the winter of 486–485 that disrupts grain deliveries and diverts military resources to restore order in that important province. Darius dies in late 486. His son and successor, Xerxes, is temporarily distracted by the Egyptian revolt, but once that is crushed, he returns to the plans to invade Greece. In an effort to meet the Persian threat, Athenian leader Themistocles secures approval to increase the size of the Athenian Navy from 50 to 200 triremes.

481–480 BCE

When he at last sets out on his planned expedition to Greece in 481, Xerxes I commands an enormous invasion force. Athens and Sparta and their allies form the Hellenic Alliance. Athens provides the principal naval force, while Sparta furnishes the main contingent of land forces sent north against the Persians. The land force is commanded by King Leonidas of Sparta. The Greek plan is for the land forces to hold the Persians just long enough for the Greek fleet to be victorious and force a Persian withdrawal.

August 480 BCE — Themistocles leads the Athenian fleet. Joined by other Greek vessels, it sails north to meet the Persian naval force. A storm reduces the Persian naval forces to around 500 serviceable warships, but this is still a comfortable advantage in numbers over those of the Greeks. The Greek fleet attacks the Persian ships off the northern coast of Euboea at Artemisium. The Battles of Artemisium are inconclusive, although the Greeks manage to capture some 30 Persian vessels.

August 480 BCE — Battle of Thermopylae, fought between Persian and allied Greek forces. On the night of the second day of battle, when he learns from Ionian Greek deserters from Xerxes' army that the Greek defenders are going to be cut off, King Leonidas of Sparta permits the allied Greeks to withdraw. Seven hundred Thespians and 300 Thebans refuse and remain with the Spartans. All of the defenders are wiped out. The Battle of Thermopylae has far greater psychological than military importance. While some Greeks see it as an excuse to ally with the Persians, others admire the Spartan example and redouble their efforts to resist the invaders.

September 480 BCE — The Battle of Salamis results in a Greek victory. The battle means the end of the year's campaign. Xerxes leaves two-thirds of his forces in garrison in central and northern Greece and marches the remainder back to Sardis.

479 BCE — Battles of Plataea and Mycale. These two battles end the first phase of the Greco-Persian Wars. Greek control of the sea enables them to sweep Persian forces out of Greece.

478 BCE	The Delian League is founded against Persia under Athenian leadership. Athens is refortified.
477–467 BCE	Naval campaign by the Delian League, led by Cimon of Athens (son of Miltiades the Younger), culminating in the Battle of Eurymedon.
467 BCE	The Delian League sends out a trireme fleet commanded by Cimon of Athens to do battle with Persian naval forces. A Persian fleet, almost all of it Phoenician, are awaiting others when Cimon arrives at their location off Pamphylia at the mouth of the Eurymedon River. The Persians seek to avoid battle so that their reinforcements might come up, but Cimon attacks and wins. He is then able to land crews and also defeat the Persians ashore. Cimon then sets out for Cyprus to locate the remaining 80 Persian triremes. He encounters them the same day and destroys them all. These two naval battles effectively end the Persian threat.
465 BCE	Revolt of Thasos against the Delian League.
ca. 465 BCE	Earthquake at Sparta and revolt of Spartan helots.
460 BCE	The First Peloponnesian War begins when Megara, a small city-state strategically located near Corinth, withdraws from the Peloponnesian League.
458 BCE	Athens begins construction of the Long Walls, running from the city to the port of Piraeus. A Spartan-led army defeats the Athenians in the Battle of Tanagra near Thebes. Athens conquers Boeotia.
451 BCE	Athens and Sparta agree on a five-year truce.
449 BCE	The Peace of Callias ends hostilities between Athens and Persia.
447 BCE	Battle of Coronea and loss of Athenian control in Boeotia.
446 BCE	Revolt of Euboea.
445 BCE	Thirty Years' Peace between Athens and Sparta.
440 BCE	Samos revolts against the Athenian Empire.

435 BCE	War breaks out between Corinth and Corcyra over Epidamnus.
433 BCE	Athens allies with Corcyra. Sparta is allied with Corinth.
432 BCE	Potidaea revolts against Athens.
431–404 BCE	Second or Great Peloponnesian War. Triggered by Theban surprise attack on Plataea.
430 BCE	Plague at Athens.
429 BCE	Death of Athenian leader Pericles.
428 BCE	Revolt of Mytilene against Athens.
428–427 BCE	The Siege of Plataea ends in Spartan victory.
427 BCE	Athens captures Mytilene.
427 BCE	First Athenian expedition to Sicily.
425 BCE	Pylos is fortified, and Athens captures Sphacteria.
424 BCE	Boeotia defeats Athens in the Battle of Delium. Brasidas campaigns in northern Greece and captures Amphipolis.
423 BCE	Athens and Sparta conclude a one-year armistice.
422 BCE	Battle of Amphipolis. Cleon of Athens dies in battle and Brasidas of Sparta dies of his wounds.
421 BCE	Athens and Sparta agree to the Peace of Nicias.
418 BCE	Sparta defeats the Athenian-Argive coalition in the Battle of Mantinea. Following the battle, Sparta and Argos agree to a 30-year peace.
416 BCE	Athens attacks Melos, enslaving its inhabitants.
415–413 BCE	Athenian expedition against Syracuse.
413 BCE	Sparta renews the war with Athens and establishes a permanent fort in Attica at Decelea.
412 BCE	Athens' allies revolt. Persia enters the war by providing Sparta with wealth.
411 BCE	The Athenians under Alcibiades defeat the Peloponnesian fleet in the Battle of Abydos in the Hellespont (Dardanelles).
410 BCE	The Athenians defeat the Peloponnesian fleet at sea and the Persian Army ashore in the Battle

of Cyzicus. Sparta offers to make peace, but Athens, under the demagogue Clerophon, who has recently seized power, rejects it, and the war continues.

408 BCE	Alcibiades recaptures Byzantium, and Athens regains control of the Bosporus.
408–407 BCE	Sparta and Persia resume their cooperation in an effort to humble a resurgent Athens.
406 BCE	Spartan admiral Lysander defeats an Athenian fleet in the Battle of Notium. In the Battle of Arginusae, however, an Athenian fleet commanded by eight generals defeats a Spartan fleet under Callicratidas.
405 BCE	Battle of Aegospotami and siege of Athens.
404 BCE	Athens surrenders, and the Second Peloponnesian War ends.
404 BCE	Dionysius I, tyrant of Syracuse during 405–367, ends his war with Carthage.
403–400 BCE	Dionysius of Syracuse expands Syracusan control in Sicily.
401 BCE	Cyrus the Younger and 10,000 Greek mercenaries mount an expedition against Cyrus' older brother, King Artaxerxes II of Persia. Cyrus is killed in the Battle of Cunaxa, and the Greeks are forced to carry out an extraordinary retreat, the subject of Xenophon's *Anabasis.*
400–371 BCE	Following its victory in the Peloponnesian War, Sparta enjoys three decades of hegemony in Greece.
397 BCE	Dionysius I, tyrant of Syracuse develops artillery that he successfully employs in the siege of Motya in Sicily.
396–394 BCE	King Agesilaus II of Sparta carries out successful operations to free the Greeks in Ionia from Persian control.
395–387 BCE	Corinthian War. Angered by Spartan arrogance and seeking to take advantage of the presence of significant Spartan forces in Asia Minor, Corinth,

	Thebes, Argos, and Athens, all supported by Persia, wage war against Sparta.
395–393 BCE	Athens rebuilds the city's Long Walls.
395 BCE	Spartan admiral Lysander is killed during an unsuccessful Spartan attack on Haliartus.
394 BCE	Battle of Coronea. Agesilaus II returns to Greece from Asia Minor and engages an allied force chiefly drawn from Thebes, Argos, and Boeotia. The battle is inconclusive because the allies continue to resist the Spartans.
394 BCE	Battle of Cnidus. Near the island of Rhodes an Athenian-Persian fleet commanded by Athenian admiral Conon destroys a Spartan fleet commanded by Piesander, Lysander's brother-in-law. The Battle of Cnidus effectively ends the brief period of Spartan naval power.
394 BCE	Agesilaus II besieges Corinth.
392 BCE	The second war between Carthage and Dionysius I of Syracuse occurs. Carthage is again unsuccessful against Syracuse. The war ends with Dionysius taking most of Sicily. Carthaginian holdings are reduced to a few small enclaves in the western part of the island.
390–379 BCE	Dionysius I extends his control over much of southern Italy. Indeed, Dionysius makes Syracuse the dominant power in the entire central Mediterranean.
390 BCE	An Athenian army commanded by Iphicrates relieves the Spartan siege of Corinth. Alarmed by Athenian successes, Persia extends secret aid to its supposed enemy, Sparta, against its ally, Athens.
387 BCE	The Peace of Antalcidas (King's Peace) brings an end to the Corinthian War. In a compromise arrangement, Sparta acknowledges some Athenian gains while its own hegemony continues. The Greek city-states also agree to accept nominal Persian guarantee of the Common Peace.

387–379 BCE	Spartan hegemony in Greece continues, with Sparta maintaining garrisons in a number of Greek city-states and defeating several challenges to its rule, including that of Thebes.
385–376 BCE	The third war between Dionysius I of Syracuse and Carthage occurs. This time the Carthaginians enjoy success and considerably expand their holdings in western and central Sicily.
382 BCE	Spartan troops take the citadel of Thebes.
379–371 BCE	Successful revolt of Thebes against Sparta.
378 BCE	Athens and Thebes create an alliance, beginning the Second Athenian Confederacy. Although they are not able to decisively defeat the Spartans, the allies succeed in forcing them from central Greece.
376 BCE	Battle of Naxos. Athenian admiral Chabrias wins a major naval victory over Sparta off the Greek islands of Naxos.
375–372 BCE	Sparta takes advantage of disunity among the Second Athenian Confederacy allies to recover some lost territory.
371 BCE	Persia assists in bringing the parties in the war together for a peace settlement. However, Sparta rejects the notion of Thebes acting for other members of the Boeotian League, causing Theban leader Epameinondas to leave the negotiations. Spartan king Cleombrotus then invades southern Boeotia.
July 371 BCE	Battle of Leuctra. Not only does the battle lead to changes in tactics, but it marks the end of Spartan military invincibility and the beginning of a period of Theban hegemony in Greece. Thebes now raises up Messana as an independent state after centuries of helotage, an action that deprives Sparta of the economic means to maintain its traditional state structure on which its military supremacy rests. Sparta sinks to second-class status.

369 BCE	To the surprise of many, Athens and Sparta ally to try to thwart the supremacy of Thebes. Theban leader Epameinondas, however, proves more than a match for them on land and on sea.
368–367 BCE	The fourth and final war between Carthage and Dionysius of Syracuse occurs. The fighting is inconclusive and closes with the death of Dionysius.
365 BCE	Athens colonizes the island of Samos.
364 BCE	Theban general Pelopidas fights Alexander of Pherae, the ruler of Thessaly, in the Battle of Cynoscephalae. The battle is a draw, but Pelopidas is killed.
363 BCE	Epameinondas of Thebes defeats Alexander of Pherae.
362 BCE	Thebes and its allies invade the Peloponnesus. Epameinondas leads Thebes and its allies in the Arcadian League of the Peloponnesus (established in 370 to offset Sparta) in an invasion of the Peloponnesus against Sparta, Athens, and a few dissident members of the Arcadian League. Epameinondas is able to surprise his enemies and defeat them in the Battle of Mantinea. In the battle, Epameinondas utilizes the oblique attack similar to that employed in the earlier Battle of Leuctra. Epameinondas dies in the battle, however, and his successors prove incapable of exercising similarly strong leadership, with the result that Greece falls into even greater chaos.
359 BCE	Philip II becomes king of Macedon, inaugurating a new period in Greek history. Influenced in part by the example of Epameinondas, with whom he became acquainted while a hostage in Thebes, Philip organizes Macedonia for war and turns its army into a formidable military force.
358–353 BCE	As a result of agitation by Mausolus of Caria, the Social War erupts between Athens and its

own allies and colonies, resulting in the serious weakening of Athenian power just as Philip of Macedon was increasing his own influence in the north. Philip expands Macedonian territory in Illyria and toward the Danube.

357 BCE	War between Athens and Philip of Macedon. Philip captures the Athenian possession of Amphipolis in Thrace.
356 BCE	Phocis seizes Delphi with its sacred temple, provoking the Third Sacred War.
355–352 BCE	Third Sacred War. The Amphictionic Council of Delphi declares war against Phocis and its allies of Sparta, Athens, and Pherae (in Thessaly). Philip II eventually intervenes on the side of the Amphictionic Council and enters central Greece against them.
353 BCE	Following a two-year struggle, Philip II is named leader of Thessaly by the league of cities. This is confirmed in his victory over the Phocians in the Battle of Volo, where the Phocian general Onomarchus is among the dead.
352–346 BCE	Blocked by allied forces at the pass of Thermopylae, Philip returns north and conquers all Athenian territory in Thrace and Chalcidice.
348 BCE	Philip II seizes Olynthus.
346 BCE	Athens sues for peace from Macedon, and Philip II grants it generous terms. Philip then turns against Phocis, defeating it in a brief campaign and securing election as chairman of the Amphictionic Council.
345–339 BCE	Philip II consolidates his northern conquests, ending opposition to his rule in Epirus, Thessaly, and southern Illyria. He next secures the territory adjacent to the Danube River and then moves to take territory to the east in Thrace as far as the Black Sea. He is thwarted in his efforts to capture the fortified seaports of Perinthus and Byzantium, however, thanks to Athenian assistance.

344–339 BCE	Corinth sends Timoleon to drive Dionysius II out of Syracuse. He succeeds, but precipitates war between Carthage and Syracuse. Carthage again invades Sicily and besieges Syracuse, this time taking the city except for its citadel. Dissension and plague among the invaders assist Timoleon, who is then able to drive the Carthaginians from the city and decisively defeat them in the Battle of the Crimissus (ca. 341), forcing the Carthaginians to conclude peace.
341 BCE	Timoleon defeats the Carthaginians at Crimissus in Sicily.
339–338 BCE	Fourth Sacred War. Thanks in part to *The Philippics,* the speeches of Athenian orator Demosthenes, Athens and Thebes again go to war against Philip of Macedon and the Amphictionic Council.
338 BCE	The Battle of Chaeronea is fought between the forces of Philip II, king of Macedon, and those of Athens, Thebes, and other allied Greeks and mercenaries occurs in Boeotia in central Greece. The battle demonstrates the superiority of the Macedonian army over the Greek hoplites. One of the most decisive battles in Greek history, it extinguishes the independence of the city-states and makes Philip master of all Greece. He establishes permanent garrisons at Corinth, Ambracia, and Chalcis to control movement in Greece. He then begins to form a league based at Corinth that unites the many city-states and ends the intercity struggles.
337–336 BCE	Philip II calls a meeting of all the Greek city-states at Corinth. Representatives of all except Sparta attend. The conference establishes the so-called League of Corinth, a Hellenic League of all the Greek states in perpetual alliance with Macedonia. Philip is named its leader and general. This is the prerequisite to Philip's planned invasion of Persia. Numerous Greek

leaders had considered such a step as a means of uniting the Greek city-states.

336 BCE   Philip II sends his trusted general Parmenio to Asia Minor with an advance force. Philip is preparing to follow with the main invasion force when he is assassinated. Philip is succeeded by his son Alexander.

336–323 BCE   Reign of Alexander III of Macedon, known as Alexander the Great.

336 BCE   Alexander quickly marches to Corinth, where he secures election as leader and general of the Hellenic League, the same position held by his father.

335 BCE   Alexander III moves against the areas under Macedonian control to the north, which also have become restive, crushing a revolt in southern Illyria. There he learns that Athens and Thebes have risen against him. Alexander immediately marches south into Greece. Moving quickly, he surprises and takes Thebes, sacking and razing it. This action subdues the rest of Greece. Athens surrenders and is treated generously. Opposition to Alexander's rule ends.

334 BCE   Alexander III crosses from Europe by the Hellespont (Dardanelles) and invades the Persian Empire at the head of an army of some 30,000 infantry and 5,000 cavalry, including soldiers from the Greek states. He leaves behind his trusted general Antipater and an army of 10,000 men to hold Macedon and Greece in his absence. Over the next decade Alexander not only conquers Persia but also campaigns in Egypt and central Asia, Afghanistan, and the Punjab. Everywhere victorious, his conquests create what becomes known as the Hellenistic world.

May 334 BCE   Alexander III meets a Persian force of some 40,000 men in the Battle of the Granicus River in western Asia Minor. Alexander leads an assault

	across the river and is victorious in a short, decisive battle.
334 BCE	Alexander III liberates the Greek coastal cities of Asia Minor. His only real opposition comes at Miletus, which he takes following a brief siege. The only difficult operation is at Halicarnassus, which he takes following a siege.
334–333 BCE	Alexander III now controls all of Asia Minor, but the Persian fleet dominates the eastern Mediterranean and is thus in position to cut off his lines of communication back to Macedonia and Greece. Alexander plans to defeat the Persian fleet from land by taking its bases along the eastern Mediterranean coast.
November 333 BCE	Battle of Issus. Learning that Alexander III has moved south into Syria, Persian king Darius III moves in behind Alexander to cut off his line of communications. Darius' army outnumbers Alexander's army. Alexander turns to meet this threat, resulting in the Battle of Issus in November. Commanding the Macedonian heavy cavalry on his right flank, Alexander attacks the Persian archers and lightly armed infantry opposite him, who immediately break and run. Darius then panics and flees the field followed by the rest of the Persian Army. Persian losses may have been heavy. Among the captives are Darius' wife, mother, and children.
332 BCE	Siege of Tyre and Gaza. These successful sieges thoroughly demonstrate Alexander's mastery of this type of warfare and greatly add to his mystique of invincibility.
332 BCE	Darius III of Persia extends a peace offer to Alexander III of Macedon of 10,000 talents in gold, the territory of the empire west of the Euphrates River, and his daughter in marriage. Alexander rejects this overture, replying that he intends to conquer all Persia.

Autumn of 332 BCE	At the same time that he is laying siege to Tyre, Alexander III sends troops to take Syria and Palestine. Gaza alone resists, and Alexander goes there to mount a siege operation lasting two months, after which the city is stormed and sacked, its inhabitants sold into slavery.
332–331 BCE	Without significant opposition, Alexander III occupies Egypt. While there he founds Alexandria, only one of many cities to bear his name. While in Egypt, Alexander travels 200 miles into the desert to visit the Temple of Zeus Ammon and there receives confirmation of his divinity as the son of Zeus.
332–331 BCE	Revolt against Macedon. Taking advantage of Alexander's absence and with funds supplied by Persia, King Agis III of Sparta leads a revolt against Macedonian rule. Most of the southern Greek states join the revolt, besieging Megalopolis. Antipater immediately marches south with his army and defeats the rebels outside Megalopolis. Following the victory, Antipater sends Alexander reinforcements, who join him in Egypt. Alexander marches toward Babylon.
October 1, 331 BCE	Battle of Gaugamela. While Alexander was in Egypt, Darius III raised a new, large army and then prepared to meet Alexander at Gaugamela near the town of Arbela. Alexander defeats Darius' army that may have outnumbered his own by 3:1.
331 BCE	Babylon surrenders to Alexander.
330 BCE	Alexander loots Persepolis and then burns it. He declares the Greek war of revenge on Persia to be officially over and releases the League of Corinth soldiers. He reenrolls the Greek troops as mercenary volunteers if they wish to remain with the campaign. Darius is murdered by his own nobles.

329 BCE	Alexander III, pursuing the generals who had murdered Darius III, campaigns in Parthia and Bactria, then turns north across the Oxus River into Sogdiana.
328–327 BCE	Alexander III subdues Sogdiana and Bactria, and marries Roxane to stop the insurgency. He leaves 10,000 men behind to secure the region and then fights his way through the mountain passes north of the Kabul Valley and across the Indus River into India.
May 326 BCE	Alexander III campaigns in India. After crossing the Indus River with his army, he triumphs over King Porus of the Punjab in the Battle of the Hydaspes River. For the battle, Alexander deploys a force of only 11,000 men; Porus deploys perhaps 35,000 men and 100 war elephants. In the battle, Porus is wounded and taken prisoner. Alexander then conquers the Punjab and sails down the Indus River to the Indian Ocean.
July 326 BCE	Alexander III plans to continue campaigning in north-central India and to proceed to the Ganges River. He reaches only the Hyphasis (Beas) River when his men express discontent at going farther east. Reluctantly, Alexander agrees to halt.
326–324 BCE	Alexander III leads his army south down the Indus and is seriously wounded in battle. Recovering, he moves to the mouth of the Indus and there constructs a fleet. He sends part of his force under Nearchus across the Arabian Sea to the Persian Gulf. Another part of the army he sends back to Persepolis by way of the Bolan Pass and Kandahar. The remainder of the army, with Alexander, marches through Baluchistan, his men suffering great hardship in the desert. Twice the army links up with Nearchus' ships.
324–323 BCE	Returning to Persia and then Mesopotamia, Alexander III concentrates on restoring order in

his vast empire and attempting to combine the best of Greek and Persian cultures. He does not have the time necessary to make this work but dies at age 32 of a fever, possibly malaria, after a drinking bout. As he is dying, he is asked to whom he leaves his vast empire, and reportedly he replies "to the strongest." Following Alexander's death, first Perdiccas and then Antigonus the One-Eyed endeavor to maintain the unity of the empire. Soon, however, a dozen of Alexander's leading generals (the Diadochi, or successors) are fighting for control of the state. By 176 the three major power centers of the Hellenistic World are Macedon, Egypt, and the Seleucid Empire.

Spencer C. Tucker

Glossary

Acropolis—The fortified defensive highpoint in every city-state. In Athens it is still called the acropolis, but in Corinth it was Acrocorinth while in Thebes it was the Cadmeia.

Archon—term for a leader or magistrate in many Greek cities. In Athens the archons were originally elected magistrates, but by the time of Xerxes' invasion they were selected by lot. The leader of the Thessalian league was also called archon.

aspis—the shield carried by Greek hoplites. It was approximately 3 meters in diameter and hollowed out in a bowl shape so that it could be rested on the shoulder. Soldiers put a left arm through the arm grip and held it with the left hand. It was usually rimmed with bronze and had a center boss of bronze. Decoration varied widely.

cleruchy—a colony used by Athens to occupy territory and provide a garrison. Cleruchs were poor Athenian citizens and the colony remained Athenian territory even in allies.

coins—those Greek cities that adopted minting coins, minted in silver. The standard coin in each city was usually called the stater. Common smaller denominations included the drachma and obol. Every city determined the weights and value of their coins. Some cities minted coins more pure than others, making their coins more desirable outside their city. The connection between the adoption of coins and the need for cities to build fleets or hire armies remains a topic of debate.

Cuirass—bronze chest plate worn by elite soldiers and some cavalry. Those who could not afford it wore lighter chest protection including leather or stacked linen.

Delphic Amphictiony—the governing council for the sacred site of Delphi. They managed the oracle and the Pythian games, and could make rulings on issues that affected the sacred site. Membership on the council was distributed by tribe, primarily among the Phocians, Boeotians, Dorians, Ionians, and Thessalians. Philip II of Macedon acquired membership when he became leader of Thessaly.

diekplous—A naval tactic used by triremes in which the attacking line of ships sailed through the enemy line—"crossing the T" and then turned quickly to ram the opponent in the side or stern. Athens considered this tactic most effective, but it was difficult for inexperienced crews to use.

drachma/drachm—the common basic denominational coin in most Greek city states that minted silver coins. In Athens one drachm equaled six obols. Four drachms equal a stater, 25 staters equal a mina, and 60 minas equal one talent. A drachm was a day's pay for a rower in the fifth-century Athenian fleet.

greaves—bronze shin guards worn to protect a soldier's lower leg from debilitating injury in battle.

helot—state-owned slaves most common and important in Sparta where they were enslaved Messenians. They were tied to Spartan citizens' land and worked it to provide income and food for citizens. Their work made it possible for the Spartans to have a professional military.

hypaspists—the elite unit of the Macedonian army that included the royal *agema*. Armed more lightly than the Macedonian phalanx, they may have carried the *aspis* and thrusting spear of hoplites.

ile/ilia—A sub-unit of a hoplite phalanx. Its officers were often called *illiarchs* in many cities.

immortals—The Persian elite guard of the Achaemenid kings. The name came from Herodotus' *History* supposedly because the unit was always 10,000 strong.

kuklos—the circle, was a defensive naval formation in which the ships all turn so their sterns are in the center of the circle and their prows face out. The Athenians used this tactic successfully at Artemisium.

metics—registered foreign citizens in Athens and other cities. They were expected to participate in warfare. The trireme crews in many Greek cities, especially Athens, including many metics.

neodamodeis—these were former Spartan helots who had earned freedom through military activity authorized by the city. Brasidas had used many of these fighters on his Amphipolis campaign in 424.

panoply—the full set of armor worn by a hoplite. An *aspis*, helmet, greaves, and chest protection were the most common pieces.

periplous—a popular naval tactic in which the enemy tried to sail around the enemy and ram it in the rear or side.

quadrireme/quinquireme—ships larger than the trireme and probably invented by Phoenicians in the fourth century BCE. It remains unclear how the oars and men were arranged, but the ships were larger permitting more marines and cargo.

sarissa—a spear employed by Philip II of Macedon in his reformed phalanx. The spear was originally 15 feet long, extended to 18 later. Although some scholars see its origins in Iphicrates' peltasts, the ancient sources for that story are untrustworthy so it should be credited to Philip.

slaves—slavery was a regular part of Greek culture including warfare. Prisoners of war usually ended up as slaves of the captors or sold elsewhere. Greek soldiers often had slaves to carry material or tend horses and supply animals. Spartans reportedly marched with three slaves each. In emergencies slaves could be provided weapons to fight alongside masters in exchange for freedom as occurred probably at Thermopylae in 480 and with Brasidas' campaign in 425. Philip II of Macedon tightened discipline by banning soldiers from using slaves. During the Sicilian expedition some of the Athenian rowers were slaves.

symmachia—an alliance between city-states or kings. There were various types including the defensive alliance (e.g., Hellenic Alliance, Peloponnesian League) in which cities band together for common defense, but may pursue independent foreign policy so long as it did not hurt another member of the alliance. There were also alliances where members surrendered more autonomy (e.g., Delian League).

talent—a weight of precious metal. In Athens of fifth century a talent was the cost of equipping and maintaining a trireme for a month.

thetes—the poorest male citizens of Athens, they rowed the fleet since they could not afford the panoply and weapons. They probably fought as light troops or assisted in camp tasks when the fleet was beached on campaign.

Bibliography

Anderson, J. K. *Military Theory and Practice in the Age of Xenophon.* Berkeley, CA: University of California Press, 1970.

Asheri, David. "Carthaginians and Greeks." In *Cambridge Ancient History*, vol. 4, 2nd edition, ed. D. M. Lewis et al., 147–70. Cambridge: Cambridge University Press, 1988.

Asheri, David. "Sicily, 478–431." In *Cambridge Ancient History*, vol. 5, 2nd edition, ed. D. M. Lewis et al., 739–80. Cambridge: Cambridge University Press, 1988.

Baynam, E. J. "Antipater, Manager of Kings." In *Ventures in Greek History*, ed. I. Worthington, 331–56. Oxford: Clarendon Press, 1994.

Best, Jan G. P. *Thracian Peltasts and their Influence on Greek Warfare.* Groningen: Wolters-Noordhoff, 1969.

Billows, Richard A. *Marathon: How a Battle Changed Western Civilization.* New York: Overlook Duckworth, 2010.

Bloedow, Edmund F. "Alexander the Great at the Hydaspes River in 326 BC." *Athenaeum* 92 (2) (2008): 499–534.

Bloedow, Edmund F. "The Siege of Tyre, 332 BC: Alexander at the Crossroads in his Career." *La Parola del Passato* 301 (1998): 255–93.

Bloedow, Edmund F. "Why did Philip and Alexander Launch a War against the Persian Empire?" *L'Antiquite Classique* 72 (2003): 261–74.

Bosworth, A. B. *Alexander and the East: The Tragedy of Triumph.* Oxford: Oxford University Press, 1996.

Bosworth, A. B. *Conquest and Empire: The Reign of Alexander the Great.* Cambridge: Cambridge University Press, 1988.

Bosworth, A. B. *The Legacy of Alexander: Politics, Warfare, and Propaganda under the Successors.* Oxford: University of Oxford Press, 2002.

Briant, Pierre. *From Cyrus to Alexander: A History of the Persian Empire.* Winona Lake, IN: Indiana University Press, 2005.

Brice, Lee L. "The Athenian Expedition to Sicily." In *The Oxford Handbook of Classical Military History*, ed. Lawrence A. Tritle and Brian Campbell. Oxford: Oxford University Press, 2012.

Brice, Lee L. "Philip II, Alexander the Great, and the Question of a Macedonian Revolution in Military Affairs (RMA)." *Ancient World* 42 (2) (2011): 137–47.

Brice, Lee L. "Seleucus and Military Unrest in the Army of Alexander the Great." In *Seleucid Studies Presented to Getzel M. Cohen on the Occasion of his 70th Birthday*, eds. Roland Oetjen and Frank Ryan. Berlin: Steiner Verlag, forthcoming, 2012.

Brice, Lee L. and Jennifer Roberts, eds. *Recent Directions in the Military History of the Ancient World.* Claremont, CA: Regina, 2011.

Buckler, John. *Aegean Greece in the Fourth Century* BC. Leiden: Brill, 2003.

Buckler, John. *Philip II and the Sacred War.* Leiden: Brill, 1989.

Buckler, John. *The Theban Hegemony.* Cambridge, MA: Harvard University Press, 1980.

Burn, A. R. *Persia and the Greeks: The Defence of the West.* Stanford, CA: Stanford University Press, 1984.

Carney, Elizabeth. "Macedonians and Mutiny: Discipline and Indiscipline in the Army of Philip and Alexander." *Classical Philology* 91 (1) (1996): 19–44.

Cartledge, Paul. *Thermopylae: The Battle that Changed the World.* New York: Overlook Press, 2006.

Caven, Brian. *Dionysius I: Warlord of Sicily.* New Haven, CT: Yale University Press, 1990.

Cawkwell, George. *The Greek Wars: The Failure of Persia.* Oxford: Oxford University Press, 2005.

Conwell, David H. *Connecting a City to the Sea: The History of the Athenian Long Walls.* Leiden: Brill, 2008.

de Souza, Philip. *Piracy in the Graeco-Roman World.* Cambridge: Cambridge University Press, 2002.

Devine, A. M. "The Battle of Gaugamela: A Tactical and Source Critical Study." *Ancient World* 13 (1986): 87–116.

Devine, A. M. "Demythologizing the Battle of the Granicus." *Phoenix* 40 (1986): 265–78.

Ellis, Walter M. *Alcibiades.* New York: Routledge, 1989.

Erskine, Andrew, ed. *A Companion to the Hellenistic World*. Malden, MA: Wiley-Blackwell, 2005.

Fleiss, Peter. *Thucydides and the Politics of Bipolarity*. Baton Rouge, LA: Louisiana State University Press, 1966.

Forde, Steven. *The Ambition to Rule: Alcibiades and the Politics of Imperialism in Thucydides*. Ithaca, NY: Cornell University Press, 1989.

Foster, Edith. *Thucydides, Pericles, and Periclean Imperialism*. Cambridge: Cambridge University Press, 2010.

Foster, Edith and Donald Lateiner, eds. *Thucydides and Herodotus*. Oxford: Oxford University Press, 2012.

Fox, Robin Lane, ed. *Brill's Companion to Ancient Macedon*. Leiden: Brill, 2011.

Frost, Frank J. *Plutarch's Themistocles: A Historical Commentary*. Princeton, NJ: Princeton University Press, 1980.

Garland, Robert. *The Piraeus*. Ithaca, NY: Cornell University Press, 1988.

Hale, John. *Lords of the Sea: The Epic Story of the Athenian Navy and the Birth of Democracy*. New York: Viking Press, 2009.

Hamilton, Charles D. *Aegesilaus and the Failure of Spartan Hegemony*. Ithaca, NY: Cornell University Press, 1991.

Hammond, Nicholas G. L. "Alexander's Charge at the Battle of Issus in 333 BC." *Historia* 41 (4) (1992): 395–406.

Hammond, Nicholas G. L. *Alexander the Great: King, Commander, and Statesman*. London: Duckworth, 1981.

Hammond, Nicholas G. L. *The Genius of Alexander the Great*. Chapel Hill, NC: The University of North Carolina Press, 1997.

Hammond, Nicholas G. L. *The Macedonian State*. Oxford: Clarendon Press, 1989.

Hammond, Nicholas G. L. *Philip of Macedon*. London: Duckworth, 1994.

Hanson, Victor D., ed. *Hoplites: The Ancient Greek Battle Experience*. London: Routledge, 1991.

Hanson, Victor D., ed. *Makers of Ancient Strategy, from the Persian Wars to the Fall of Rome*. Princeton, NJ: Princeton University Press, 2010.

Hanson, Victor D. *Western Way of War: Infantry Battle in Classical Greece*, 3rd edition. Berkeley, CA: University of California Press, 2009.

Harrison, Thomas. "The Greek World, 478–432." In *A Companion to the Classical Greek World*, ed. Konrad Kinzl, 509–525. Malden, MA: Wiley-Blackwell, 2006.

Heckel, Waldemar. *The Conquests of Alexander the Great*. Cambridge: Cambridge University Press, 2008.

Heckel, Waldemar. *The Marshals of Alexander's Empire*. New York: Routledge, 1992.

Heckel, Waldemar and Lawrence A. Tritle, eds. *Alexander the Great: A New History*. Malden, MA: Wiley-Blackwell, 2009.

Hodkinson, Stephen and Anton Powell, eds. *Sparta and War*. Swansea: Classical Press of Wales, 2006.

Holt, Frank L. *Into the Land of Bones: Alexander the Great in Afghanistan*. Berkeley, CA: University of California Press, 2005.

Holt, Frank L. *Thundering Zeus: The Making of Hellenistic Bactria*. Berkeley, CA: University of California Press, 1999.

Hornblower, Simon. *A Commentary on Thucydides*, 3 vols. Oxford: Oxford University Press, 1991, 1996, and 2010.

Kagan, Donald. *The Fall of the Athenian Empire*. Ithaca, NY: Cornell University Press, 1987.

Kagan, Donald. *The Peace of Nicias and the Sicilian Expedition*. Ithaca, NY: Cornell University Press, 1981.

Kagan, Donald. *The Peloponnesian War*. New York: Penguin, 2003.

Kagan, Donald. *Thucydides: The Reinvention of History*. New York: Viking Press, 2009.

Keegan, John. *Face of Battle*. New York: Penguin, 1976.

Kennel, Nigel M. *Spartans: A New History*. Malden, MA: Wiley-Blackwell, 2010.

Keyser, Paul T. "Use of Artillery by Philip II and Alexander the Great." *Ancient World* 25 (1994): 27–59.

Kinzl, Konrad, ed. *A Companion to the Classical Greek World*. Malden, MA: Wiley-Blackwell, 2006.

Krentz, Peter. *The Battle of Marathon*. New Haven, CT: Yale University Press, 2010.

Kuhrt, Amélie. *The Ancient Near East*, 2 vols. New York: Routledge, 1995.

Laforse, Bruce. "The Greek World 371–336." In *A Companion to the Classical Greek World*, ed. Konrad Kinzl, 544–59. Malden, MA: Wiley-Blackwell, 2006.

Lazenby, J. F. *The Defense of Greece, 490–479 BC*. Warminster: Aris and Phillips, 1993.

Lazenby, J. F. *The Peloponnesian War: A Military Study*. New York: Routledge, 2004.

Lee, John W. I. *A Greek Army on the March: Soldiers and Survival in Xenophon's Anabasis*. Cambridge: Cambridge University Press, 2007.

Lendon, J. E. *Soldiers and Ghosts: A History of Battle in Classical Antiquity*. New Haven, CT: Yale University Press, 2006.

Marincola, John, ed. *A Companion to Greek and Roman Historiography*. Malden, MA: Wiley-Blackwell, 2007.

Marsden, Eric W. *The Campaign of Gaugamela*. Liverpool: Liverpool University Press, 1964.

Marsden, Eric W. *Greek and Roman Artillery: Historical Development*. Oxford: Clarendon Press, 1969.

Meckler, Michael. *Classical Antiquity and the Politics of America*. Waco, TX: Baylor University Press, 2006.

Morrison, J. S., J. F. Coates, and N. B. Rankov. *The Athenian Trireme*, 2nd edition. Cambridge: Cambridge University Press, 2000.

Munn, Mark. *The School of History: Athens in the Age of Socrates*. Berkeley, CA: University of California Press, 2000.

Murray, William. *The Age of Titans: The Rise and Fall of Great Hellenistic Navies*. Oxford: Oxford University Press, 2012.

Osborne, Robin. *Greece in the Making, 1200–479 BC*, 2nd edition. Routledge: New York, 2006.

Pritchett, W. Kendrick. *The Greek State at War*, 5 vols. Berkeley, CA: University of California Press, 1971–1991.

Raaflaub, Kurt A., ed. *War and Peace in the Ancient World*. Malden, MA: Blackwell, 2006.

Rawson, Elizabeth. *The Spartan Tradition in European Thought*. Oxford: Oxford University Press, 1991.

Rhodes, P. J. *Alcibiades*. Barnsley: Pen and Sword Military, 2011.

Rhodes, P. J. *A History of the Classical Greek World, 478–323 BC*, 2nd edition. Malden, MA: Wiley-Blackwell, 2010.

Roberts, Jennifer T. *Herodotus: A Very Short Introduction*. Oxford: Oxford University Press, 2011.

Roisman, Joseph and Ian Worthington, eds. *A Companion to Ancient Macedonia*. Malden, MA: Wiley-Blackwell, 2010.

Romane, Patrick. "Alexander's Siege of Gaza, 332 BC." *Ancient World* 18 (1988) 21–30.

Romm, James, ed. *The Landmark Arrian: The Campaigns of Alexander*. New York: Pantheon, 2010.

Rood, Tim. *American Anabasis: Xenophon and the Idea of America from the Mexican War to Iraq*. New York: Overlook, 2011.

Sabine, Philip, Hans Van Wees, and Michael Whitby, eds. *The Cambridge History of Greek and Roman Warfare*, vol. 1. Cambridge: Cambridge University Press, 2007.

Sanders, Lionel J. *Dionysius I of Syracuse and Greek Tyranny*. London: Croom Helm, 1987.

Sekunda, Nick V. "The Macedonian Army." In *A Companion to Ancient Macedonia*, eds. Joseph Roisman and Ian Worthington, 446–71. Malden, MA: Wiley-Blackwell, 2010.

Sidky, H. *The Greek Kingdom of Bactria: From Alexander to Eurcratides the Great*. Philadelphia, PA: University Press of America, 2000.

Strassler, Robert B., ed. *The Landmark Herodotus: The Histories*. New York: Anchor Books, 2009.

Strassler, Robert B., ed. *The Landmark Thucydides: A Comprehensive Guide to the Peloponnesian War*. New York: Free Press, 1998.

Strassler, Robert B., ed. *The Landmark Xenophon's Hellenika*. New York: Pantheon Books, 2009.

Strauss, Barry. *The Battle of Salamis: The Naval Encounter that Saved Greece—and Western Civilization*. New York: Simon and Schuster, 2004.

Strauss, Barry. *Masters of Command: Alexander, Hannibal, Caesar and the Genius of Command*. New York: Simon and Schuster, 2012.

Talbert, Richard J. A. "The Greeks in Sicily and south Italy." In *The Greek World in the Fourth Century from the Fall of the Athenian Empire to the Successors of Alexander*, ed. Lawrence A. Tritle, 137–65. New York: Routledge, 1997.

Talbert, Richard J. A. *Timoleon and the Revival of Greek Sicily 344–317 BC*. Cambridge: Cambridge University Press, 1974.

Tritle, Lawrence A. *Melos to My Lai: War and Survival*. New York: Routledge, 2000.

Tritle, Lawrence A. *A New History of the Peloponnesian War*. Malden, MA: Wiley-Blackwell, 2010.

Tritle, Lawrence A. and Brian Campbell, ed. *The Oxford Handbook of Classical Military History*. Oxford: Oxford University Press, 2012.

Trundle, Matthew. *Greek Mercenaries: From the Late Archaic Period to Alexander*. New York: Routledge, 2004.

Tuplin, Christopher. "All the King's Horse: In Search of Achaemenid Persian Cavalry." In *New Perspectives on Ancient Warfare*, eds. Garrett Fagan and Matthew Trundle, 101–82. Leiden: Brill, 2010.

van Wees, Hans. *Greek Warfare: Myths and Realities*. London: Duckworth, 2004.

van Wees, Hans, ed. *War and Violence in Ancient Greece*. Swansea: Classical Press of Wales, 2009.

Welwei, Karl-Wilhelm. "The Peloponnesian War and its Aftermath." In *A Companion to the Classical Greek World*, ed. Konrad Kinzl, 526–543. Malden, MA: Wiley-Blackwell, 2006.

Wheeler, Everett. "Greece: Mad Hatters and March Hares." In *Recent Directions in the Military History of the Ancient World*, eds. Lee L. Brice and Jennifer Roberts, 53–104. Claremont, CA: Regina, 2011.

Worthington, Ian. *Philip II of Macedonia*. New Haven, CT: Yale University Press, 2008.

Editor and Contributors

Editor

Dr. Lee L. Brice
Professor of Ancient History
Western Illinois University

Contributors

Dr. Lee L. Brice
Professor of Ancient History
Western Illinois University

Ryan Hackney
Independent scholar

Dr. Kevin Marsh
Department of History
Idaho State University

Roger Matuz
Independent scholar

Dr. George E. Pesely
Associate Professor of History
Austin Peay State University

Dr. Nancy Stockdale
Assistant Professor, Middle
Eastern history
University of North Texas

Dr. Spencer C. Tucker
Senior Fellow
Military History, ABC-CLIO,
LLC

Ken Tuite
Independent scholar

Tim Watts
Content Development Librarian
Kansas State University

Categorical Index

Index

Note: Page numbers in **bold** indicate main entries in the text.

About the Editor

Lee L. Brice, PhD, is professor of history at Western Illinois University, Macomb, where he has been teaching for eight years since he completed his doctorate at The University of North Carolina at Chapel Hill. He is coeditor of *Recent Directions in the Military History of the Ancient World* and author of articles on Philip II and Alexander the Great of Macedon, Octavian Caesar of Rome, the coins of Greek Corinth, and the Roman army in film. Brice is currently working on a study of mutinies in the ancient world.